D0207828

Multinational Management Accounting

Multinational Management Accounting

AHMED BELKAOUI

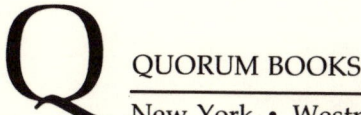

QUORUM BOOKS

New York • Westport, Connecticut • London

Library of Congress Cataloging-in-Publication Data

Belkaoui, Ahmed, 1943–
    Multinational management accounting / Ahmed Belkaoui.
      p.   cm.
    Includes bibliographical references and index.
    ISBN 0–89930–529–6 (alk. paper)
    1. International business enterprises—Accounting.   I. Title.
    HF5686.I56B445   1991
    657′.96—dc20   90–8896

British Library Cataloguing in Publication Data is available.

Library of Congress Catalog Card Number: 90–8896
ISBN: 0–89930–529–6

First published in 1991

Quorum Books, 88 Post Road West, Westport, CT 06881
An imprint of Greenwood Publishing Group, Inc.

Printed in the United States of America

The paper used in this book complies with the
Permanent Paper Standard issued by the National
Information Standards Organization (Z39.48–1984).

10 9 8 7 6 5 4 3 2 1

To Hedi and Janice,
two active members of the
global economy

Contents

Exhibits

Preface

Multinational firms have to function in a global economy where operating and managerial accounting decisions are made in a complex environment characterized by fluctuating exchange rates, innovative and flexible organizational structures, and a dynamic and diverse control strategy. As a result, managerial accounting techniques have to adapt to this new environment by devising new ways to solve decision problems that take into account the salient feature of this multinational context. Therefore, the objective of this volume is to elaborate on the specific environment of multinational management accounting and the unique managerial accounting techniques to be used for an efficient conduct of multinational operations. Specific new contexts described include (a) the new international business environment (Chapter 1); (b) the management of foreign exchange risk, including the determination and efficiency of the exchange rate (Chapter 2), the management of economic exposure (Chapter 3), and the management of transaction exposure (Chapter 4); (c) the organization and control of multinational operations, including the examination of the organizational structures of multinational operations (Chapter 5) and the performance evaluation techniques of multinational operations (Chapter 6); and (d) the techniques needed to solve management accounting issues, including international financial analysis, (Chapter 7), international capital budgeting (Chapter 8), pricing strategies for multinational operations (Chapter 9), analysis of the lease-or-buy decision (Chapter 10), and advanced capital budgeting (Chapter 11).

No book can be written without the help of numerous individuals and organizations that provide generous feedback and permission to reprint their material.

A special note of appreciation is extended to my teaching and research assistants, Kelly Karabatsos, Liz Kamilis, and Jyh-Herng Hsieh, for their cheerful and intelligent assistance. Finally, to Hedi and Janice, thanks for making every moment a treasure.

I

Introduction: The International Environment

1

The International
Business Environment

The international business environment is best characterized by the global linkages that tie the global economy together and by the growth of multinational enterprises, increasing international trade, and foreign direct investment. This chapter describes these crucial components of the new international business environments as they affect the conduct of international finance and multinational management accounting. An appreciation of the growth of multinationals, the international trade theories, and the theories of foreign direct investment enable managers of multinational enterprises faced with the realities of the global economy to create the overall framework for a global strategy.

GLOBAL ECONOMY

What is emerging is a multinational corporate world in which national borders are losing their importance. Partnerships are forming between companies of different nationalities, willing to forget their rivalries, in order to share in the profit opportunities of a world market, to share the material costs and risks associated with the development of products ranging from semiconductors to aircraft, to reduce the impact of fluctuating currencies around the world, and to get protectionism and government imposed obstacles such as tariffs, import limits, and regulations. The best example of such global strategy is the decision of General Dynamics Corporation, an American aerospace giant, to collaborate with Japanese companies or the development of the advanced FSX jet fighters. Other examples include the partnership of Whirlpool Corporation and the appliance division of the Dutch giant N.V. Philips and the partnership of Komatsu Ltd., the largest Japanese construction company, with Dresser Industries, Inc., of Dallas. The strategy amounts to the desire to be present in the three major markets—Japan, United States, and Europe—a strategy labeled "triad power," consisting of allocating manufacturing, marketing, financing, and administrative operations among the three markets.[1]

Another good example of the global economy is illustrated by how U.S. corporate giants try to achieve stronger trade ties in the Soviet Union. In dealing with Aeroflot, the world's largest airline, FMC Corporation, producer of machinery and agriculture, and Marriott Corporation used different strategies. FMC Corporation opted for countertrade, whereby it provides facilities and expertise, in this case processing equipment to make apple juice, in exchange for access to the end product, in this case the selling of the apple juice by FMC. This is not to be confused with barter trade, which involves the straight swap of one product for another. In the countertrade example, the profit on the sales of apple juice will be shared between Aeroflot and FMC Corporation. Marriott, on the other hand, preferred a joint-venture strategy with Aeroflot through the creation of a new company, Aeromar, with 45 percent owned by Marriott and 51 percent by Aeroflot. The new company will operate the Aeroflot food service.

A third example of the globalization movement is the more than 300 joint relationships formed by approximately twenty-five major car and truck manufacturers, making the world auto industry one great partnership.[2] Who makes a vehicle is a very difficult question to answer. As an example, Pontiac LeMans was engineered by Opel (GM's West German subsidiary) and is built by Daewoo in South Korea. In addition to undertaking these joint ventures, the companies are buying interests in each other.

The fact that natural boundaries are ignored in this global economy is not without its benefits to U.S. corporations and others. Manufacturing, financing, and marketing opportunities that exceed local opportunities are created through the existence of a global market and a world economy for the companies to function within.

There are, however, several issues to consider. One issue arising from the global economy is the potential loss of sovereignty since governments lose much of their power to control monetary and economic policies, especially if the policies enacted are made in a national rather than global context. A few years ago, what may have seemed to be fictional scenarios are now part of everyday reality. Japanese and other foreign investors, for example, are holding billions of dollars of U.S. government bonds, hence allowing the U.S. government to fund its continuous federal budget deficit. If these Japanese investors, anxious about a domestic or international development, should decide to stop buying these bonds, the Federal Reserve Board will find itself in the position of having to increase interest rates to make the same bonds more attractive. The rise in the interest rates may slow the economy as Americans reduce their buying of expensive items because of higher borrowing costs and as firms reduce their production, investments, and payrolls. What may follow is a recessionary trend in the economy followed by a reduction in the value of the stocks of American companies, and if the trend is not reversed, a market collapse may ensue. This scenario may well explain what happened on Wall Street on October 19, 1987. To avert these issues, policies need to be made in a global context, taking into account major developments in the global economy such as those described below.

Currency markets are now playing a vital role in the global economy as $50 trillion worth of various currencies are traded each year compared with a mere $2 trillion of trade in goods. The activity of the currency markets has been made possible by the use of (a) sophisticated data-processing capacity and high-capability communications and (b) a powerful information technology to move currency information across space and globally. Major currency trading centers include Chicago, New York, London, and Tokyo. Secondary centers include Paris, Frankfurt, Hong Kong, Singapore, and Sydney.

The power and role of the trading in currency markets are major factors that limit the ability of governments to control their economies. Cooperation among governments rather than the enactment of policies in a national context can alleviate some of the impact of the currency markets. Economic summits among leaders of the seven major industrial nations as well as cooperation and consultation among central bankers on policies affecting currency exchange rates and interest rates constitute a first step toward a global strategy and a trend toward making international economic policy a central function of government. Another example of the need for a global strategy is best illustrated by the situation after the October 19 crash when Japanese and American stock exchange officials, as well as the U.S. Securities and Exchange Commission chairman and Japanese Securities Bureau director, agreed to set up an around-the-clock telephone link to exchange information on future and spot markets. The idea is to reduce the chances that a Black Monday in one market will pull the others down.

Stocks and commodity markets are also edging toward international integration in the form of a global market. According to B. Balassa, "viewed as a state-of-affairs [integration] can be represented by the absence of various forms of discrimination between national economies."[3] Applied to the markets for real or financial assets, the definition leads to the law of one price or the law of one price change. Although the evidence is mixed on both laws, there are also some obstacles to the globalization of the stocks and commodities markets since countries have persisted in keeping different rules on the regulation of stocks, voting rights, corporate control, antitrust legislation, and accounting policies, to name only a few. A major obstacle to the globalization of commodities markets besides outright protectionist policies is the rising popularity of managed trade, or mercantilism, which is the use of government policies to maximize a nation's exports and minimize imports.[4] Another obstacle to the globalization of commodity markets is the presence in Japan of business networks, known as *Keiretsu*, that give them distinct advantages in the global economy. These networks are used as a structure through which giant Japanese companies share the same financial institutions, insurance companies, and trading companies and adopt the same industrial strategy. To get an idea of their importance, note that the main Japanese corporate groups, Mitsubishi, Dai-Ichi, Kangyo, Sumitomo, Mitsui, Fuyo, and Sanwa, in 1989 comprised 193 percent and subsidiary firms employed up to 5 percent of Japan's work force and accounted for up to 15 percent of annual sales.[5]

As more harmony occurs among nations, the globalization of the stocks and commodities will increase. Evidence of this increasing globalization includes the following examples.

The first example relates to the increasing number of stock markets, totaling four dozen in 1989, almost two per time zone. They are not comparable given the slight activity in some of them. A good example is the ninety minutes a day of stock trading in the Jordanian market. The three most important markets, known as the "golden triangle," include the New York Stock Exchange (NYSE), the London Stock Exchange (LSE), and the Tokyo Stock Exchange (TSE). These markets open at different times enabling the great trading houses—Merrill Lynch and Solomon in America, Nomura Securities International in Japan, and Barclays Bank PLC in the United Kingdom—to trade stocks, bonds, and currencies around the clock and around the world. This global trading in U.S. stocks, for example, may start with the trading at Tokyo and other Asian markets until closure, followed by the trading at the London and European markets until one o'clock London time, at which point the New York market will take over as will the other South American and North American markets. Profit opportunities abound. Consider the Istanbul stock exchange. The average return on most stocks in 1989 was 511 percent, with one stock's value soaring from 373 to more than 3,000. To get a piece of the action, a U.S. investor could choose from one of two options: (1) buy shares in the Turkey Fund, a closed end fund, trading on the New York Stock Exchange; or (2) wait for the Turkish stocks to be available in the U.S. through American deposit receipts.[6]

The second example relates to the increase in direct foreign investment since foreign ownership of national businesses are increasing despite the emotional backlash it seems to create in all countries affected. In 1987, for example, Europeans spent $37.1 billion acquiring U.S. companies, whereas U.S. companies spent $2.4 billion in Europe. It is far from being the American challenge (*Le Défi American*) but rather the European challenge. Typical American companies such as J. Walter Thompson, Brooks Brothers, Firestone, Doubleday, A&P, General Electric, Hilton International, and Marshall Field are foreign owned. In 1987 the amount of money that investors all over the world had put into stock outside their own countries amounted to $1.2 trillion, double the 1986 amount.

The third example relates to the increase in commodity trades and especially the creation of big trading blocks. The world seems to be edging toward at least five major trading blocks: (1) a North American block centered in the United States and best illustrated by the free-trade treaty between the United States and Canada, (2) the European block centered in the Common Market, (3) an Asian market centered in Japan, (4) a Communist trading block centered in the USSR, and (5) an Arab trading block centered in the member nations of the Arab League. Concerning these blocks, the most remarkable result is the 1992 creation of a European internal market to make trade among the twelve members of the European Common Market and their 320 million people as free as the trade among the fifty states of the U.S. and its 230 million people.

The fourth example relates to trading among units of multinational corporations encompassing up to 50 percent of the world's trade.[7]

NEW CHALLENGES IN THE GLOBAL ECONOMY

Various new challenges are characterizing the global economy. First, the global economy will take on an extraordinary new dimension when a unified Germany will again dominate Europe. It is certain that the slogan "Wir Sind Wieder Wer" (We Are Somebody Again) will become a reality, giving rise to a new superpower Germany with (a) exports, based on 1988 data, of $354.1 billion compared with $321.6 billion for the United States, $264.9 billion for Japan, and $110.6 billion for the Soviet Union; (b) a surplus balance of trade of $73.9 billion compared with $77.5 billion for Japan, $3.3 billion for the Soviet Union, and a deficit of $138.0 billion for the United States; and (c) a gross national product (GNP) per capita of $13,987 compared with $19,770 for the United States, $14,340 for Japan, and $8,850 for the Soviet Union.[8] The question still remains whether reunification, a boost to the German economy, will lead to another *Wirtschaftswunder* (economic miracle). German strength will undoubtedly be exercised in the council of Europe and impact the vision of the European Common Market.

Second, the new global economy is best characterized by the emergence of new economic powers competing with the established North American and European powers. Their success cannot be explained by classical theories of competitive advantage focusing on the availability of natural resources or any other cost factors. The new paradigm is that competition itself motivates the success of nations. Such is the thesis of Michael Porter, who maintains that the ability of a nation to upgrade its existing advantages to the next level of technology and productivity is the key to international success.[9] Four factors called the "diamond" of national competitive advantage are presented as the key to the success of these new technology partners.

1. Factor conditions, or the nation's ability to turn factor endowment into a specialized advantage

2. Demand conditions, or the existence of demanding, sophisticated customers

3. Related and supporting industries that provide supplier clusters to firms

4. Company, strategy, structure, and rivalry, or the conditions governing how firms in a nation are created and nurtured in the middle of stiff competition

The impact of these four factors is best summarized as follows:

The fundamental lesson is that the quiet life is an enemy of competitive advantage. Industries thrive when they are forced to overcome high labor costs or a lack of natural resources, when their customers won't accept inferior or outmoded products, when their local competitors are many and murderous, and when government offers no protection from fair competition, although it sets technical and regulatory standards.[10]

In addition, Porter blamed the drift in American industry on the following:

In many ways, what the U.S. needs most is a philosophical shift. Defensiveness and loss of confidence have crept into American industry and government. A mind-set had developed that U.S. industry is helped by devaluation, feeble antitrust enforcement, tax regulation, cooperation among leading competitors, policies that create a monopoly in particular technologies, and "temporary" protection. As appealing as these policies may seem in the short run, they will only make further loss of competitive advantage more likely.[11]

Third, the Third World is not benefiting to the necessary extent from the global economy. It is still relegated to the role of provider of basic products. Exhibit 1.1 shows the ratio of exports of basic products to total exports in the 1980 decade for the African countries. What one may notice immediately is the heavy dependence of these countries as they have little control in the world prices of these resources.

Fourth, what is the worst nightmare for this global economy and for the global banking system and global security markets? Is it military warfare? Is it the potential of a President Quayle in the United States? Is it the Red Army tanks storming through Europe? It is not any of the above. Instead, a 1990 Governmental Accounting Office report sees it as the threat of sabotage on the computer systems that transfer trillions of dollars daily among banks and security exchanges around the globe. One computer hacker cracking the codes for the banking system or for the securities markets would create havoc by introducing a computer virus in the system. It would bring the trading of 53 trillion shares a day to a noisy and fatal halt. Are these computers adequately protected? I hope so.

Fifth, the impact of greater market internationalization suggests several new points for debate: (a) The desire for foreign equities will increase in spite of serious market plunges since they "provide diversification that reduces portfolio risk." (b) Most stock exchanges act independently and "respond to specific economic, cultural and regulatory environments in their countries—differences that keep the various equity markets from marching in lock step." (c) Globalization will eventually lessen the control that governments exercise over their economy. (d) As money flows across borders with greater ease, policymakers will no longer be able to assume "that their nation's capital is captive," and financial markets will have a greater role in determining economic policy. (e) "When a worldwide market panic sets in, globalization can take a bad situation in one market and create an international crisis." In the October 1987 plunge, for example, investors who wanted to "liquidate their positions at any price

Exhibit 1.1

Ratios of Exports of Basic Products to Total Exports in the 1980s for African Countries

Country	Ratio for Agricultural Products	Ratio for Natural Resources	Total Rate
Algeria	--	86%	86%
Angola	21%	43%	64%
Benin	52.2%	42%	94.2%
Botswana	--	20%	20%
Burkina Faso	--	23.3%	23.3%
Burundi	52.4%	1%	53.4%
Cameroon	23%	51%	74%
Central Africa	18%	--	18%
Congo	1.5%	67%	68.5%
Egypt	25.5%	23.5%	49%
Ethiopia	52.5%	3%	55.2%
Equatorial Guinea	79.4%	--	79.4%
Gabon	0.4%	63%	63.4%
Gambia	62.9%	1%	63.9%
Ghana	46.5%	37%	83.5%
Guinea-Bissau	43.3%	--	43.3%
Ivory Coast	52.8%	4%	56.8%
Kenya	48.7%	14%	62.7%
Lesotho	96%	--	96%
Liberia	23.7%	57%	80.7%
Libya	--	90%	90%
Madagascar	39%	11%	50%
Malawi	83.1%	--	83.1%

Exhibit 1.1 (continued)

Country	Ratio for Agricultural Products	Ratio for Natural Resources	Total Rate
Mali	22.4%	--	22.4%
Morocco	--	40%	40%
Maurice	37.5%	--	37.5%
Mauritania	--	31%	31%
Mozambique	11.5%	--	11.7%
Niger	0.6%	86%	86.6%
Nigeria	2.8%	91%	93.8%
Rwanda	78.4%	9%	87.4%
Senegal	10.8%	17%	27.8%
Sierra Leone	29.2%	22%	51.9%
Somalia	13.6%	1%	14.6%
Sudan	50.9%	14%	64.9%
Swaziland	--	36.6%	36.6%
Tanzania	56.1%	7%	63.1%
Chad	54.6%	--	54.6%
Togo	29.4%	66%	95.4%
Tunisia	1%	46%	47%
Zaire	11.6%	63%	74.6%
Zambia	2.5%	93%	95.5%
Zimbabwe	31.3%	17%	48.3%

circled the globe." (f) Investors are less secure now since there is no longer any one "lender of last resort." Although nervous American markets were previously assured ample liquidity from the Federal Reserve, and although such assurances are still significant, "globalization lessens their impact." This is true because "central banks all have different national interests and cannot be expected to act as a united front during a crisis."[12]

Sixth, although the world's prosperity depends on a fluid and unfettered financial system, the lack of control has created a shadow economy of money laundering serving customers from cocaine cartels to tax-dodging companies, leading the Internal Revenue Service (IRS) in 1989 to claim that the tax cheats skim as much as $50 billion a year from legitimate cash-generating businesses to be laundered to avoid detection. Various laundering schemes are used. My favorite one concerns a banker in Willemstad, Netherlands Antilles, and an

American visitor who is expecting a six-figure cash windfall that he wants to bring ''quietly'' into the United States. After the banker is assured that the money isn't ''tainted,'' the banker states that he can set up a so-called ''Dutch sandwich.''

The Paris bank would set up a corporation for the customer in Rotterdam, where he would deposit his cash in the bank's local branch. The American would control the newly created Dutch Corporation through an Antilles trust company, but his identity as the owner would be protected by the island group's impenetrable secrecy laws. The Caribbean branch would then ''lend'' the American his own money held in Rotterdam.

If the American were questioned . . . he could point to his loan from a respected international bank.[13]

Seventh, a clear obstacle to an efficiently working global economy is the emerging racism, prejudice, and subjugation of ethnic minorities in the world. Examples include the following: (a) *Kokusaika*, meaning internationalization, is on Japanese lips nowadays, but the truth is that the country is a hotbed of the most flagrant racial and cultural discrimination against all types of foreigners and against their own Burakumin—Japanese racial outcasts who are descendants of families employed as tanners, butchers, executioners, and crematorium workers in preindustrial Japan. It is not *Kokusaika* that predominates but *Sakoku* (closed country) when it comes to racial and cultural tolerance. (b) Various ultraright movements are finding a sympathetic clientele in Western Europe. The most despicable is the ''Lepenism'' movement in France aimed at a systematic harassment of the 4.5 million hardworking North Africans. (c) A growing new ''underclass'' is forming in both the United States and Great Britain, deepening the class divisions. These are only some of the examples of an emerging intolerant world.

Eighth, another characteristic of the global economy is ''let's make a deal'' and ''let's not worry too much about money.'' Creativity is the name of the game, combining both money and barter to pay for the exchanges. In 1989, for example, to clinch a multibillion-dollar sale of F–16s to Turkey, General Dynamics agreed to purchase scores of Turkish products, invest in Hilton hotels, set up a joint venture to coproduce the F–16, and build housing, a school, and a mosque for 4,000 local workers. Exotic countertasks are the norm rather than the exception. In 1990, Pepsi entered into a $3 billion deal with the Soviet Union to barter Pepsicola for ten ships and shipments of Stolichnaya vodka. It is not without creating some worries. A 1989 survey of fifty top U.S. defense firms by the Office of Management and Budget found that between 1980 and 1987, $19.9 billion in offset commitments was made against sales worth $34.8 billion, which is equivalent to 57 percent of total revenues.

INTERNATIONAL BUSINESS: GROWTH AND OBSTACLES

Peace and absence of obstructions are necessary for international business to prosper. One is reminded of Pax Romana, or Roman peace, and the 1930s'

Smoot Hawley Act as clear examples. The first allowed international trade to prosper, and the second, by raising import duties, led the major U.S. trading partners to retaliate.

International business involves business transactions between two or more countries. The motivations are to expand sales, acquire resources, or diversify sources of sales and supplies. The operational means are varied including (a) merchandise exports and imports; (b) service exports and imports; (c) travel, tourism, and transportation; (d) performance of activities abroad (such as turnkey operations and management counteracts); (e) use of assets abroad (such as licensing agreements and franchising); (f) direct investment; and (g) portfolio investments.[14]

In spite of the benefits created by international business and international trade, governments all over the world engage in trade restrictions and marketing barriers aimed at the protection of local industries in general and meeting the following objectives in particular: (a) stopping money from leaving the country, (b) providing employment, (c) equalizing cost and price, (d) protecting national security, and (e) protecting infant industry.[15] An exhaustive list of the tariffs and nontariff barriers composing marketing barriers are shown in Exhibit 1.2. They point to the incredible array of obstacles that can be created to stop the growth of international business and trade.

INTERNATIONAL TRADE THEORY

Why do firms feel the need to expand internationally? Similarly, why do nations need to trade? International trade theories attempt to answer these fundamental questions. These theories are examined below, and each of them explains some of the national trade patterns and offers different prescriptions for trade relationship.

Mercantilism

Mercantilism, as expanded during the period from 1500 to 1800, holds that a country needs to export more than it imports to acquire wealth, generally in the form of gold.[16] Government monopolies were primarily involved in the trade aided by policies enacted to restrict imports and subsidize exports in the country, preventing colonies from manufacturing. Colonies were placed in the position of exporting cheaply priced raw materials and importing higher priced manufactured goods, a situation still encountered by some developing countries and termed as "deteriorating terms of trade" or "unfavorable balance of trade." Mercantilism as a trade philosophy has not completely disappeared since a neo-mercantilism or managed trade has appeared in countries dedicated to a strong and positive trade surplus.[17]

Exhibit 1.2
Marketing Barriers

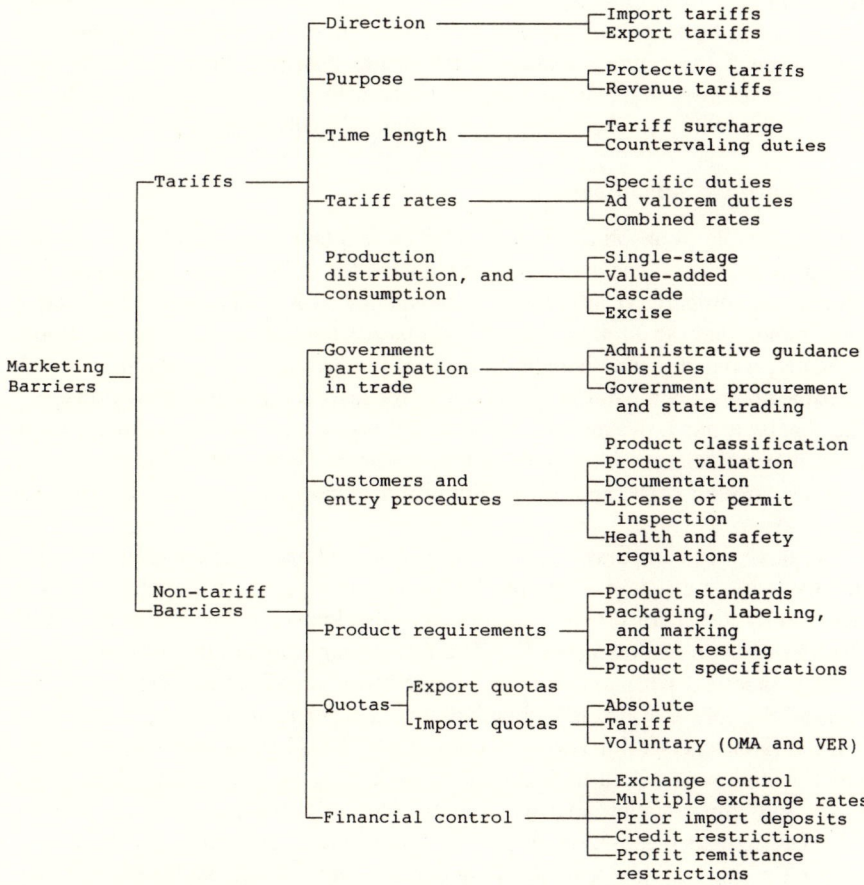

Source: Sak Onkvisit and John J. Shaw, "Marketing Barriers in International Trade," *Business Horizons*, May–June 1988, p. 66.

Absolute Advantage

The absolute advantage theory, or classical theory of trade, as introduced by Adam Smith and David Ricardo, argued that countries would benefit more if they produced those goods and services in which they had an advantage.

Adam Smith, in his 1776 book *The Wealth of Nations*, disagreed with the wealth accumulation thesis expressed by the mercantilists and maintained that the absolute advantage argument associated with free trade would lead to higher specialization and productivity in each country, followed by higher efficiency and profit that can be used by the country to increase its imports.[18]

David Ricardo extended the argument in his *Labor Theory of Value*.[19] He attributed the difference in price for the same goods in two countries to the difference in the productivity of labor in the two countries and hence the absolute advantage held by each country.

Absolute advantage also means either (a) natural advantage, whereby the country possesses natural conditions that insure it better efficiency in the production of more goods, or (b) acquired advantage, whereby the country has acquired the ability to excel in the production of a differentiated product.

Comparative Advantage

The principle of absolute advantage fails to explain what motivates a country to trade if the nation has an absolute advantage for all products considered. The principle of comparative advantage, as developed by Ricardo, holds that relative costs rather than absolute production costs are relevant as a basis for trade. Basically, a country may benefit more from producing those products in which it has the greatest comparative advantage or the least comparative disadvantage.[20] The theory rests, however, on the assumptions of (a) full employment; (b) a profit maximization objective; (c) a two countries, two commodities case; (d) no transportation costs; and (e) no mobility of goods and resources internationally.

The theory of comparative advantage did not address the question of why a country is more efficient in the production of some goods. An explanation was provided by the factor proportionate theory, also known as the Heckscher-Ohlin Theory of Factor Endowments.[21,22] The factor proportionate theory holds that a country endowed with a certain productive resource will specialize in the production of goods that use this abundant and cheaper resource.

If the Heckscher-Ohlin Theory is correct, we should expect the United States, which is endowed with a high capital to labor ratio, to export capital intensive goods and import labor intensive goods. The evidence provided by Wassily Leontieg, indicated, however, that U.S. exports were labor intensive relative to imports, a finding known as the Leontieg Paradox.[23] One explanation for the paradox is that U.S. labor is more productive than the labor of traded partners. The empirical evidence for this explanation, however, remains lacking.[24]

A sound explanation for the paradox is that U.S. labor can be characterized by better training and education, and that constitutes a form of capital invested in the labor force. Empirical evidence that includes an adjustment for the capital embodied in the U.S. labor force verified the Heckscher-Ohlin Theory and reversed the Leontieg Paradox.[25, 26] Basically, U.S. labor is effectively capital intensive.

The Product Life Cycle

Another international trade theory introduced by Raymond Vernon is the product life cycle theory.[27] This theory maintains that products go through a cycle comprising at least four stages: introduction, growth, maturity, and decline.

Exhibit 1.3

The IPLC Stages and Characteristics (for the initiating country)

Stage	Import/ Export	Target Market	Competitors	Production Cost
(0) local innovation	none	USA	few: local firms	initially high
(1) Overseas innovation	increasing export nations	USA & advanced	few: local firms	decline due to economies of scale
(2) maturity	stable export	advanced nations & LDCs	advanced nations	stable
(3) worldwide imitation	declining export	LDCs	advanced nations	increase due to lower economies of scale
(4) reversal	increasing import	USA	advanced nations & LDCs	increase due to comparative disadvantage

Source: Sak Onkvisit and John J. Shaw, "An Examination of the International Product Life Cycle and Its Application within Marketing," *Columbia Journal of World Business* 18 (Fall 1983): 74.

1. At the introduction stage, new products are introduced, produced, and mostly sold in the same country to satisfy domestic demand. At this stage the production may be labor intensive until the product is standardized and until the process technology is refined.

2. At the growth stage, competitors may enter the market, and the product may be produced and exported from foreign countries. Process technology reaches a higher level mainly due to economy of scale. The growth stage may also be termed the overseas innovation stage, whereas the introduction stage is a local innovation stage.

3. At the maturity stage, few of the producers lose to the increasing competition. The lower per unit cost may, however, increase the sales in the less developed countries (LDCs). There are net advantages even to moving production to the LDCs to capitalize on the supply of unskilled and inexpensive labor.

4. At the decline stage, worldwide imitation and new products may reduce the sales in both LDC and domestic markets and force the decision to produce exclusively in the LDCs. The decline stage represents a reversal stage in the product life cycle. The decline stage of the international product life cycle (IPLC) with the United States as the developer of the innovative product is shown in Exhibit 1.3. The life cycle curve for the same innovation including (a) the United States as the innovator, (b) other advanced countries, and (c) the LDCs is shown in Exhibit 1.4.

Various studies verified the explanatory power of the product life cycle theory, especially in the case of electronics, synthetic materials, and consumer durables.[28] The theory does not fare well for various types of products.[29] Those products for which the theory does not seem to be applicable include (a) products with a

Exhibit 1.4
The IPLC Curves

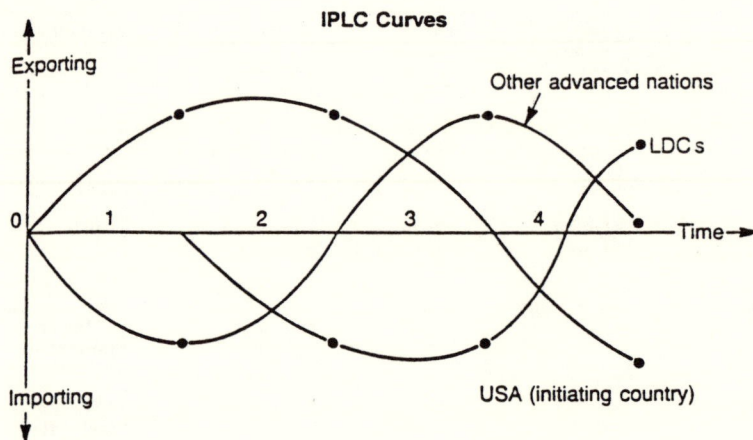

Source: Sak Onkvisit and John J. Shaw, ''An Examination of the International Product Life Cycle and Its Application within Marketing,'' *Columbia Journal of World Business* 18 (Fall 1983): 74.

short life cycle caused by rapid innovations, (b) luxury products for which the high prices do not phase the customers, (c) products plagued by high transportation costs that prohibit all types of exports, and (d) products that can be easily differentiated by the use of advertising and hence can have their life cycle extended.[30]

DIRECT FOREIGN INVESTMENT AND THE MULTINATIONAL CORPORATION

Direct foreign investment is on the increase in most countries. The motivations are numerous. First, firms may want to expand markets by producing and selling abroad:

a.   To reduce transportation costs

b.   Because of a lack of domestic capacity

c.   To achieve economics of scale in small-scale process technology

d.   To avoid trade or customer-imposed restrictions

e.   To follow customers and competitors

f.   To benefit from a different cost structure

g.   To achieve some vertical integration

h.   To rationalize production by taking advantage of varying costs of labor, capital, and raw materials

i.   To have access to production factors

j. To take advantage of government investment incentives
k. Because of political motives
l. To use a monopoly advantage over similar companies in the foreign countries
m. To have better profitability and stabler sales and earnings[31, 32]

The main result of the growth of foreign direct investment is a form of organization: the multinational enterprise (MNE). G. G. Mueller gave the following accurate characterization of this new form of business organization: "The international organization is emerging. This is a corporation which is internationally owned and controlled. It is a business organization with a truly international organization for all its business functions, including management, production, and finance."[33] More succinctly, an MNE is a company that owns and manages business operations in two or more countries.[34]

Direct foreign investment is playing a major role in economic development through the activities of the multinational corporations. The nature and the role of the multinational corporation are claimed to be either positive or negative depending on which side of the controversy one is on. Adolf Enthoven has successfully summarized the results, both positive and negative, claimed for multinational corporations by the spokespersons for developing countries as follows:

POSITIVE EFFECTS (*Benefits/Advantages*): 1. Transfer of capital; 2. transfer of know-how and management; 3. balance-of-payments benefits; 4. increase in competition and lower prices; 5. increase in entrepreneurial spirit; 6. help in training and education; 7. increase in employment; 8. help in infrastructure; 9. improvement of hiring conditions in developing countries; 10. identification, allocation, management, and efficient use of world material and human and financial resources; 11. greater international unity and interdependency; 12. ensuring a more equal distribution of income and wealth.
NEGATIVE EFFECTS (*Costs/Disadvantages*): 1. Hampering of balance of payments; exports of profits and interest beyond investment; 2. technology too advanced for country and too capital intensive; 3. limited trading and education; 4. input of foreign management to the neglect of local managers; 5. curbing of local enterprises; 6. enforcement of consumption functions (luxury items); 7. uneven distribution of income; 8. affecting employment; restricting transfer of know-how; 9. subordination of companies and countries to the multinational corporations, threatening the sovereignty of the nation state; 10. hampering of the endogenous socioeconomic development of a nation; 11. disruption of social, political, and cultural patterns in the host country; 12. resentment against foreign penetration, resulting in upsetting the social balance; 13. recession resulting from the inability of national industries to compete; 14. loss of national pride and nationalistic spirit.[35]

THEORIES OF FOREIGN DIRECT INVESTMENT

Foreign investment involves either portfolio investment, the purchase of foreign securities, or direct investment, the establishment of foreign operations.

Both require the transfer of productive resources, whereas foreign trade involves the transfer of goods and services. Certain theories explain foreign direct investment, which is the rationale behind the transfer of productive resources.[36]

One such theory is the classical theory of direct investment, which suggests that investments tend to be made where a high return can be secured.[37] The mobility of resources is taken for granted in the classical theory, leading capital rich countries to export capital goods and to invest abroad whereas labor rich countries export labor intensive goods and favor the migration of some of their labor force to the richer countries.

A second theory is embodied in the market disequilibrium hypotheses. Disequilibrium conditions lead foreign direct investment to flow in the affected countries until markets return to stability. The source of disequilibrium may be (a) differences in currency valuation, (b) differences in average rates of profit, (c) differences in labor costs, or (d) differences in rates of technical and technological innovation. Each of these situations creates opportunities for foreign direct investment to flow from one country to another until equilibrium is reestablished, at which point foreign direct investment will cease. Basically, it is beneficial to invest and hold assets in undervalued currencies, in areas where average rates of profit are higher, and in low-labor-cost countries, especially if the investing firm comes from a country experiencing a higher rate of technical and technological innovation.

A third theory, resulting, like the preceding one, from a form of market imperfections, is a disequilibrium hypothesis resulting from government imposed distortions. The difference from the previous theory is that no equilibrium force is selected to come to the situation unless all governments agree to adopt the same strategy. Some of the distortions that may trigger direct foreign investment include (a) trade barriers such as quotas and tariffs, (b) the levying of taxes, and (c) various forms of government regulations.[38]

A fourth theory is derived from the market structure imperfections brought up by monopolies and oligopolies. Both rely on a strategy that speculates on the opponents' reaction, favors barriers to entry, and infrequently favors direct expansion abroad. Product differentiation,[39,40,41] the stage in the product life cycle,[42] a strategy of "follow the leader,"[43] and a strategy of "imitate the other"[44] are a direct result of oligopolistic conditions and lead these firms to direct expansion abroad.

A fifth theory results from three types of market failures—external effects, public goods, and economics of scale—that force the duality between social efficiency and market performance to cease to exist.

A sixth theory, derived from attempts toward developing a global theory of the multinational firm, is the appropriability theory.[45,46] Multinational enterprises are very good at the production of "information" technology, the internalization of this information, and the approximation of the returns from this technology.

A seventh theory, also derived from attempts toward developing a global theory of the multinational firm, is the diversification theory. A firm may diversify internally and still be subject to fluctuations in the domestic economy. Alternatively, the firm will elect to diversify operations internationally and reduce the risk associated with operations.[47]

An eighth theory, also derived from attempts toward developing a global theory of the multinational enterprise, is the internalization theory. The MNE is formed as a result of the internalization of its markets across boundaries.[48] Alan Rugman provided the following rationale:

Briefly, internalization theory demonstrates that the MNE is an organization which uses its internal market to produce and distribute products in an efficient manner in situations where a regular market fails to operate. In particular, the MNE allocates intermediate products such as knowledge to desirable world markets. The internal market of the MNE is a device which permits the organization to assign property rights in knowledge to itself, such institutional control over this intermediate product being required since there is no regular (external) market for the pricing of knowledge, a public good. Yet the generation of knowledge involves the firm in private costs, in the form of expenditures on research and development. Therefore in most circumstances (in fact with the exception of public subsidies for research and development) it is necessary for the firm to overcome this appropriability problem of the creation of a monopolistic internal market where the knowledge advantage can be developed and explored in an optimal manner on a worldwide basis.[49]

International theory rests in fact on two options: (1) that the firms opt for the least cost location and (2) that the firms grow by internalizing markets up to the point where no additional benefits or costs can be secured.

A ninth theory, stemming from the failure of preceding theories to explain all the forces that create the multinational firm, has been termed the eclectic approach.[50] A. L. Calvet argued that the international involvement of firms is best accounted for by: "(1) location theory; (2) industrial organization theory; and (3) property rights theory."[51] As an example, he stated that "the higher the cost differentiates between countries, the higher the advantages to be gained from multiple locations in different countries; the more R & D or advertising expenditures, the stronger the patent protection or the monopolistic returns of firms, the more important the degree of multinationalism would be."[52] John Dunning, however, summarized his eclectic approach as follows:

A national firm supplying its own market has various avenues for growth: it can diversify horizontally or laterally into new product lines, or vertically into new activities, including the production of knowledge; it can acquire existing enterprises; or it can exploit foreign markets. When it makes good economic sense to choose the last route (which may also embrace one or more of the others), the enterprise becomes an international enterprise (defined as a firm which services foreign markets). However, for it to be able to produce alongside indigenous firms domiciled in these markets, it must possess additional *ownership* advantages sufficient to outweigh the costs of servicing an unfamiliar or distant environment.[53]

Exhibit 1.5

The Determinants of International Production

Types of International Production	Ownership Advantages	Location Advantages	Internalization Advantages	Illustration of types of activity which favor MNEs
1. Resource-based	Capital, technology, access to markets	Possession of resources	To ensure stability of supply at right price. Control of markets	Oil, copper, tin, zinc, bauxite, bananas, pineapples, cocoa, tea
2. Import substituting manufacturing	Capital, technology, management and organizational skills; surplus r & d & other capacity, economies of scale; Trade marks	Material & costs, markets, government policy (with respect to barrier to imports, investment incentives, etc.)	Wish to exploit technology advantages, High transaction or information costs Buyer uncertainty, etc.	Computers, pharmaceuticals, motor vehicles, cigarettes
3. Export platform manufacturing	As above, but also access to markets	Low labor costs Incentives to local production by host governments.	The economies of vertical integration	Consumer electronics, textiles & clothing, cameras, etc.
4. Trade & distribution	Products to distribute	Local markets. Need to be near customers. After-sales servicing, etc.	Need to ensure sales outlets & to protect company's name	A variety of goods-particularly those requiring close consumer contact
5. Ancillary services	Access to markets (in the case of other foreign investors)	Markets	Broadly as for 2/4	Insurance, banking & consultancy services
6. Miscellaneous	Variety-but include geographical diversification (airlines & hotels)	Markets	Various (see above)	Various kinds a) Portfolio investment-properties b) Where spatial linkages essential (airlines & hotels)

Source: John H. Dunning, "Toward an Eclectic Theory of International Production: Some Empirical Tests," *Journal of International Business Studies* 11, no. 1 (Spring/Summer 1980): 13. Reprinted with permission.

Dunning, in fact, referred to the presence of both firm- and country-specific factors accounting for foreign direct investment, which he termed "ownership-specific endowments," referring to the firm's internal factors, and "location-specific endowments," referring to the external factors.[54] To these two factors he also added internalization advantages or self-handling as the third determinant of international production and the third strand in his eclectic theory. He rationalized his third factor as follows:

> The basic incentive of a firm to internalize its ownership endowments is to avoid the disadvantages, or capitalize on the imperfections of one or the other of the two main external mechanisms of resource allocation—the market or price system and the public authority fiat. Market imperfections arise whenever negotiation or transaction costs are high, whenever the economies of interdependent activities cannot be fully captured, and whenever information about the product or service being marketed is not readily available or is costly to acquire. From a buyer's viewpoint, such imperfections include uncertainty over the availability and price of essential supplies and the inability to control their timing and delivery. From a seller's viewpoint, the preference for internalizing will be most pronounced where the market does not permit price discrimination, where the costs of enforcing property rights and controlling information flows are high, or where, in the case of forward integration, the seller wishes to protect his reputation by ensuring a control over product or service quality or after-sales maintenance.[55]

A matrix that relates the main types of activities in which multinational enterprises may be involved to the three main determinants of international involvement is shown in Exhibit 1.5.

CONCLUSION

The global economy requires that managers all over the world adopt a global strategy and be aware of the global linkages that tie together trade, investment, and growth. This chapter attempts to cover the various trade and foreign direct investment theories to identify better the parameters and variables that will characterize this global strategy and define the international finance and multinational management accounting techniques needed.

NOTES

1. Terry Atlas, "Global Markets Make Partners Out of Rivals," *Chicago Tribune*, April 25, 1989, Section 1, p. 18; Ohmae Kenishi, *Triad Power: The Coming Shape of Global Competition* (New York: The Free Press, 1985).

2. Frank Washington and David Pauly, "Driving Toward a World Car?" *Newsweek*, May 1, 1989, pp. 48–49.

3. B. Balassa, *The Theory of Economic Integration* (Homewood, Ill.: Irwin, 1961), p. 1.

4. Raymond Waldman, *Managed Trade: The Competition Between Nations* (Cambridge, Mass.: Ballinger, 1986). Another interesting factor is the intense bidding war

conducted by governments eager to attract companies and ready to use the government image of givebacks, grants, tax holidays, and subsidies as incentives. For a good presentation of the subject, see Robert Weigand, ''International Investment: Weighing the Incentives,'' *Harvard Business Review*, July/August 1983, pp. 146–152.

5. Ronald E. Yates, ''Wherever Japan's at, It's There for the Long Haul,'' *Chicago Tribune*, April 24, 1989, p. 1.

6. Stephen Franklin, ''Turks Bullish on Stock Market,'' *Chicago Tribune*, February 20, 1989, p. 17.

7. *CIA Handbook of Economic Statistics* (Washington, D.C.: Central Intelligence Agency, 1988), 1988 data.

8. Ibid., p. 15

9. Michael Porter, *The Competitive Advantage of Nations* (New York: The Free Press, 1989).

10. Ibid.

11. Ibid.

12. Leslie Wayne, ''The Realities of 'Friday the 13th,' '' *New York Times*, Sunday, October 22, 1989, pp. 2, 6.

13. Jonathan Beaty and Richard Hornik, ''A Torrent of Dirty Dollars,'' *Time*, December 18, 1989, p. 50.

14. R. C. Longworth, ''Vanishing Borders: Trade in the 1990's,'' *Chicago Tribune*, April 23, 1989, pp. 1, 97.

15. J. D. Daniels and L. H. Radebaugh, *International Business: Environments and Operations* (Reading, Mass.: Addison-Wesley, 1989).

16. Sak Onkvisit and John J. Shaw, *International Marketing: Analysis and Strategy* (Columbus, Ohio: Merrill, 1989), pp. 73–80.

17. Eli Heckscher, *Mercantilism* (London: George Allen & Unwin, 1935).

18. Adam Smith, *The Wealth of Nations* (New York: Northern Library, n.d.).

19. David Ricardo, *The Principles of Political Economy and Taxation* (Cambridge: Cambridge University Press, 1981).

20. Ibid.

21. Eli Heckscher, ''The Effects of Foreign Trade on the Distribution of Income,'' in *Readings in the Theory of International Trade*, ed. Howard S. Ellis and Lloyd A. Natzler (Homewood, Ill.: Irwin, 1949), pp. 20–35.

22. Bertil Ohlin, *Interregional and International Trade* (Cambridge, Mass.: Harvard University, 1933).

23. Wassily Leontieg, ''Domestic Production and Foreign Trade: The American Capital Position Reexamined,'' *Economia Internazionale* 7 (February 1954): 3–34.

24. Mordechai E. Kreinin, ''Comparative Labor Effectiveness and the Leontieg Scarce Factor Paradox,'' *American Economic Review* 55 (March 1965): 131–140.

25. Peter B. Kenen, ''Native of Capital and Trade,'' *Journal of Political Economy* 73 (October 1965): 437–460.

26. W. H. Branson and N. Monoyios, ''Factor Inputs in U.S. Trade,'' *Journal of International Economics* 7 (May 1977): 111–131.

27. Raymond Vernon, ''International Investment and International Trade in the Product Life Cycle,'' *Quarterly Journal of Economics*, May 1966, pp. 190–207.

28. James M. Lutz and Robert T. Green, ''The Product Life Cycle and the Export Position of the United States,'' *Journal of International Business Studies*, Winter 1983, pp. 77–93.

29. Ian Giddy, "The Demise of the Product Life Cycle in International Business Theory," *Columbia Journal of World Business*, Spring 1978, pp. 90–97.

30. Frances Stewart, "Recent Theories of International Trade: Some Implications for the South," in *Monopolistic Competition and International Trade,* ed. Henry Kienzowski (Oxford: Oxford University Press, 1984), pp. 11–33.

31. Daniels and Radebaugh, *International Business.*

32. J. C. Miller and B. Pras, "The Effects of Multinational and Export Diversification on the Profit Stability of U.S. Corporations," *Southern Economic Journal* 3 (1980): 78–79.

33. G. G. Mueller, "Ways and Hows of International Accounting," *The Accounting Review*, April 1965, p. 386.

34. N. H. Jacoby, "The Multinational Corporation," *The Center Magazine*, May 1970, p. 38.

35. Adolf J. H. Enthoven, *Social and Political Impact of Multinationals on Third World Countries (and Its Accounting Implications)* (Dallas: Center for International Accounting Development, The University of Texas at Dallas, 1976), p. 2.

36. Fisher Black, "The Ins and Outs of Foreign Investment," in *International Financial Management: Theory and Application*, ed. Donald R. Lessard (New York: Wiley, 1985), pp. 1–15.

37. For an excellent review of the theories covered in this section, see A. L. Calvet, "A Synthesis of Foreign Direct Investment Theories and Theories of the Multinational Firm," *Journal of International Business Studies*, Spring/Summer 1981, pp. 43–59.

38. T. O. Horst, "The Theory of the Multinational Firm: Optimal Behavior Under Different Tariffs and Tax Rates," *Journal of Political Economy*, September/October 1971, pp. 1059–1072.

39. Stephen H. Hymer, *The International Operations of National Firms: A Study of Direct Foreign Investment* (Cambridge, Mass.: MIT Press, 1976).

40. Charles P. Kindleberger, *The International Corporation: A Symposium* (Cambridge, Mass.: MIT Press, 1970).

41. R. E. Caves, "International Corporations: The Industrial Economics of Foreign Investment," *Economica*, February 1971, pp. 1–27.

42. F. T. Knickerbocker, *Oligopolistic Reaction and Multinational Enterprise* (Cambridge, Mass.: Harvard University Graduate School of Business, Division of Research, 1974).

43. E. M. Graham, "Oligopolistic Imitation and European Direct Investment in the United States" (Ph.D. diss., Harvard Business School, 1974).

44. P. Bohm, *Social Efficiency: A Concise Introduction to Welfare Economics* (New York: Wiley, 1973), p. 19.

45. S. P. Magee, "Technology and the Appropriability of the Theory of the Multinational Corporation," in *The New International Economic Order*, ed. Jagdish Bhajwati (Cambridge, Mass.: MIT Press, 1975), pp. 13–54.

46. S. P. Magee, "Multinational Corporations: The Industry Technology Cycle and Development," *Journal of World Trade Law*, July/August 1977, pp. 297–321.

47. John S. Hughes, Dennis Logue, and Richard Sweeney, "Corporate International Diversification and Market Assigned Measures of Risk and Diversification," *Journal of Financial and Quantitative Analysis*, November 1975, pp. 627–637; Tamir Agmon and Donald Lessard, "Investor Recognition of Corporate International Diversification," *Journal of Finance*, September 1977, pp. 1045–1055.

48. P. J. Buckley and M. C. Camon, *The Future of the Multinational Enterprise* (London: Macmillan, 1976).

49. Alan M. Rugman, "Internalization and Non-Equity Forms of International Involvement," in *New Theories of the Multinational Enterprise*, ed. Alan M. Rugman (New York: St. Martin's, 1982), p. 11.

50. J. G. Baumann, "Merger Theory, Property Rights, and the Pattern of U.S. Direct Investment in Canada," *Weltwirtschaftriches Archiv*. 7 (1975): 676–698.

51. A. L. Calvet, "A Synthesis of Foreign Direct Investment Theories and Theories of the Multinational Firm," *Journal of International Business Studies*, Spring/Summer 1981, p. 55.

52. Ibid.

53. John H. Dunning, "Toward an Eclectic Theory of International Production: Some Empirical Tests," *Journal of International Business Studies* 11, no. 1 (1980): 9.

54. Ibid., p. 10.

55. Ibid., p. 11.

REFERENCES

Agmon, Tamir, and Donald Lessard. "Investor Recognition of Corporate International Diversification." *Journal of Finance*, September 1977, pp. 1045–1055.

Atlas, Terry. "Global Markets Make Partners Out of Rivals." *Chicago Tribune*, April 25, 1989, sect. 1, p. 18.

Balassa, B. *The Theory of Economic Integration*. Homewood, Ill.: Irwin, 1961.

Baumann, J. G. "Merger Theory, Property Rights, and the Pattern of U.S. Direct Investment in Canada." *Weltwirtschaftriches Archiv*. 7 (1975): 676–698.

Beaty, Jonathan, and Richard Hornik. "A Torrent of Dirty Dollars." *Time*, December 18, 1989, p. 50.

Black, Fisher. "The Ins and Outs of Foreign Investment." In *International Financial Management: Theory and Application*. Edited by Donald R. Lessard. New York: Wiley, 1985, pp. 1–15.

Bohm, P. *Social Efficiency: A Concise Introduction to Welfare Economics*. New York: Wiley, 1973, p. 19.

Branson, W. H., and N. Monoyios. "Factor Inputs in U.S. Trade." *Journal of International Economics* 7 (May 1977): 111–131.

Buckley, P. J., and M. C. Camon. *The Future of the Multinational Enterprise*. London: Macmillan, 1976.

Calvet, A. L. "A Synthesis of Foreign Direct Investment Theories and Theories of the Multinational Firm." *Journal of International Business Studies*, Spring/Summer 1981, pp. 43–59.

Caves, R. E. "International Corporations: The Industrial Economics of Foreign Investment." *Economica*, February 1971, pp. 1–27.

CIA Handbook of Economic Statistics. Washington, D.C.: Central Intelligence Agency, 1988.

Daniels, J. D., and L. H. Radebaugh. *International Business: Environments and Operations*. Reading, Mass.: Addison-Wesley, 1989.

Dunning, John H. "Toward an Eclectic Theory of International Production: Some Empirical Tests." *Journal of International Business Studies* 11, no. 1 (Spring/Summer 1980).

Enthoven, Adolf J. H. *Social and Political Impact of Multinationals on Third World Countries (and Its Accounting Implications)*. Dallas: Center for International Accounting Development, The University of Texas at Dallas, 1976, p. 2.

Franklin, Stephen. "Turks Bullish on Stock Market." *Chicago Tribune*, February 20, 1989, p. 17.

Giddy, Ian. "The Demise of the Product Life Cycle in International Business Theory." *Columbia Journal of World Business*, Spring 1978, pp. 90–97.

Graham, E. M. "Oligopolistic Imitation and European Direct Investment in the United States." Ph.D. dissertation, Harvard Business School, 1974.

Heckscher, Eli. "The Effects of Foreign Trade on the Distribution of Income." In *Readings in the Theory of International Trade*. Edited by Howard S. Ellis and Lloyd A. Natzler. Homewood, Ill.: Irwin, 1949, pp. 20–35.

———. *Mercantilism*. London: George Allen & Unwin, 1935.

Horst, T. O. "The Theory of the Multinational Firm: Optimal Behavior Under Different Tariffs and Tax Rates." *Journal of Political Economy*, September/October 1971, pp. 1059–1072.

Hughes, John S., Dennis Logue, and Richard Sweeney. "Corporate International Diversification and Market Assigned Measures of Risk and Diversification." *Journal of Financial and Quantitative Analysis*, November 1975, pp. 627–637

Hymer, Stephen H. *The International Operations of National Firms: A Study of Direct Foreign Investment*. Cambridge, Mass.: MIT Press, 1976.

Jacoby, N. H. "The Multinational Corporation." *The Center Magazine*, May 1970, p. 38.

Kenen, Peter B. "Native of Capital and Trade." *Journal of Political Economy* 73 (October 1965): 437–460.

Kenishi, Ohmae. *Triad Power: The Coming Shape of Global Competition*. New York: The Free Press, 1985.

Kindleberger, Charles P. *The International Corporation: A Symposium*. Cambridge, Mass.: MIT Press, 1970.

Knickerbocker, F. T. *Oligopolistic Reaction and Multinational Enterprise*. Cambridge, Mass.: Harvard University, Graduate School of Business, Division of Research, 1974.

Kreinin, Mordechai E. "Comparative Labor Effectiveness and the Leontieg Scarce Factor Paradox." *American Economic Review* 55 (March 1965): 131–140.

Leontieg, Wassily. "Domestic Production and Foreign Trade: The American Capital Position Reexamined." *Economia Internazionale* 7 (February 1954): 3–34.

Longworth, R. C. "Vanishing Borders: Trade in the 1990's." *Chicago Tribune*, April 23, 1989, pp. 1, 97.

Lutz, James M., and Robert T. Green. "The Product Life Cycle and the Export Position of the United States." *Journal of International Business Studies*, Winter 1983, pp. 77–93

Magee, S. P. "Multinational Corporations: The Industry Technology Cycle and Development." *Journal of World Trade Law*, July/August 1977, pp. 297–321.

———. "Technology and the Appropriability of the Theory of the Multinational Corporation." In *The New International Economic Order*. Edited by Jagdish Bhajwati. Cambridge, Mass.: MIT Press, 1975, pp. 13–54.

Miller, J. C., and B. Pras. "The Effects of Multinational and Export Diversification on the Profit Stability of U.S. Corporations." *Southern Economic Journal* 3 (1980): 78–79.

Mueller, G. G. "Ways and Hows of International Accounting." *The Accounting Review*, April 1965, p. 386.

Ohlin, Bertil. *Interregional and International Trade*. Cambridge, Mass.: Harvard University, 1933.

Onkvisit, Sak, and John J. Shaw. *International Marketing: Analysis and Strategy*. Columbus, Ohio: Merrill, 1989, pp. 73–80.

Porter, Michael. *The Competitive Advantage of Nations*. New York: The Free Press, 1989.

Ricardo, David. *The Principles of Political Economy and Taxation*. Cambridge: Cambridge University Press, 1981.

Rugman, Alan M. "Internalization and Non-Equity Forms of International Involvement." In *New Theories of the Multinational Enterprise*. Edited by Alan M. Rugman. New York: St. Martin's, 1982, p. 11.

Smith, Adam. *The Wealth of Nations*. New York: Northern Library, n.d.

Stewart, Frances. "Recent Theories of International Trade: Some Implications for the South." In *Monopolistic Competition and International Trade*. Edited by Henry Kienzowski. Oxford: Oxford University Press, 1984, pp. 11–33.

Vernon, Raymond. "International Investment and International Trade in the Product Life Cycle." *Quarterly Journal of Economics*, May 1966, pp. 190–207.

Waldman, Raymond. *Managed Trade: The Competition Between Nations*. Cambridge, Mass.: Ballinger, 1986.

Washington, Frank, and David Pauly. "Driving Toward a World Car?" *Newsweek*, May 1, 1989, pp. 48–49.

Wayne, Leslie. "The Realities of 'Friday the 13th.' " *New York Times*, Sunday, October 22, 1989, pp. 2, 6.

Weigand, Robert. "International Investment: Weighing the Incentives." *Harvard Business Review*, July/August 1983, pp. 146–152.

Yates, Ronald E. "Wherever Japan's at, It's There for the Long Haul." *Chicago Tribune*, April 24, 1989, p. 1.

II

Managing Exchange Rate Risks

2

Exchange Rate Determination and Efficiency

Floating foreign exchange rates are at best characterized by high volatility. Evidence exists to suggest that the linear series representation of the natural logarithm of either spot or forward exchange rates are best described by a random walk process.[1,2,3] The time series suggests that a substantial amount of variation needs to be explained. Although this volatility implies efficiency of the foreign exchange markets since the time series would not contain any patterns or signals that could be used for a winning strategy, the multinational firms have to rely on some forecasting of the foreign exchange rate for various decisions including hedging, short-term financing, short-term investment, capital budgeting, long-term financing, and earning assessment decisions. What results is a plethora of exchange rate determination models competing for primacy in the prediction business. This chapter elaborates and evaluates these models with a view toward assessing the degree of efficiency of the foreign exchange market.

FORECASTING FOREIGN EXCHANGE RATES UNDER A FREELY FLOATING SYSTEM

The Traditional Approach

The traditional approach to exchange rate determination, as based on Keynesian economic theory, views the exchange rate as a price determined by supply and demand for goods and services entering international trade. It views the balance of payments (BOP) current account as a major determinant of exchange rate movements. *Ceteris paribus*, a surplus in the current account will lead to appreciation, whereas a deficit will lead to depreciation of the exchange rate.

This traditional approach, however, fails to link the short-term variations of the exchange rates to the BOP performance.[4]

The Monetary Theory

The monetary theory views the exchange rate as the relative price of two monies and best determined by stock equilibrium conditions in markets for national monies. Changes in the relative money stock growth rates and relative rates of return on financial amounts are assumed to affect the foreign exchange market and the foreign exchange rate. This effect is assumed to take place through several channels, to include nominal interest rates, relative prices, real income, and the demand for money.

The monetary approach to exchange rates with rational expectations is generally stated as:

$$S_t = (m_t - m_t^*) + \eta (y_t - y_t^*) + E[E_t(S_{t+1}) - S_t]$$

where m_t, y_t, and S_t are the logarithms of nominal money stock, real income, and spot exchange rates quoted in terms of home currency per unit of foreign currency. η is the elasticity of demand for money with respect to income, and E is the semielasticity of the demand for money with respect to nominal interest rates. The empirical expectations are as follows:

In empirical tests, we expect the coefficient of $(m - m^*)$ to be unity, confirming the neutrality of money. The elasticity coefficient should be positive and significant, should be in the neighborhood of 1.0 and E should approximate the interest rate elasticity of the demand for money, in the neighborhood of 0.04 for monthly data. Naturally, the coefficients should be stable, the model should explain a large fraction of exchange rate variation, and the error terms should satisfy classical properties.[5]

The Portfolio Balance Approach

The portfolio approach combines both the traditional and monetary approaches to the determination of exchange rates. Both monetary and real factors enter in the determination of the exchange rate since the exchange rate affects both the value of the money stock or the relative supplies of domestic foreign assets.[6] It follows that (a) a change in relative return and risk for a liquidity of a foreign financial asset not only affects their price but also the exchange rate, and (b) the changes in wealth affect the demand and supply of foreign assets and this in turn affects the exchange rate. The relationships defining the asset market equilibrium are as follows:

$$M = m(r, r') W$$
$$B = b(r, r') W$$

$$eF = f(r, r')\, W$$
$$W = B + M + eF$$

where M is the domestic money, B is the domestic bond earning an interest rate r and not internationally traded, F is the foreign issued bonds earning a fixed interest rate, e is the exchange rate, and W is the domestic financial wealth. Because of various methodologic problems, empirical evidence for the model is lacking.

The International Fisher Effect

The international Fisher Effect (also called Fisher Open) holds that the rate of change in the spot exchange rate is equal to the difference between the interest rates in the home country and the foreign country. In other words, any difference in the interest rates between two countries tends to be offset by an equal but opposite change in the spot exchange rate. Basically:

$$\frac{E(S) - S}{S} \times \frac{12}{\eta} \times 100 = i - i'$$

where

S   = the spot exchange rate (expressed in the number of home currency units for each unit of foreign currency)

E(S) = the expected future spot exchange rate months from now

i   = the nominal interest rate in the home country

i'   = the nominal interest rate in the foreign country

Therefore, the Canadian dollar will depreciate by 6 percent relative to the U.S. dollar if the interest rates are, respectively, 16 percent in Canada and 10 percent in the United States. The Canadian dollar will depreciate by 6 percent, to be consistent with a 6 percent higher interest rate. Evidence in the international Fisher Effect is mixed, especially in light of new evidence on the existence of a foreign exchange premium for most major currencies.[7,8]

The Fisher Effect

The Fisher Effect holds that the nominal interest rate in a country is equal to the required real interest rate plus the expected rate of inflation. For two countries, it would mean the following relationships:

Home interest rate: $i = r + M$ (a)

Foreign interest rate: $r' = r + M'$ (b)

Subtracting equation (b) from equation (a) gives

$$i - i' = (r - r') + (m - m') \qquad (c)$$

Given that investors can buy any interest-bearing securities in the world, the real rates of return should tend toward equality between two countries. The Fisher Effect holds, then, that nominal interest rates will vary by the difference in the expected rates of inflation, and

$$i - i' = m - m'$$

Therefore, if nominal interest rates in France and the United States on one-year maturities were, respectively, 16 and 10 percent, it would be consistent with the differences in inflation rates where these rates were, respectively, 13 percent in France and 7 percent in the United States. Empirical evidence of the Fisher Effect exists especially in the case of short-maturity government securities, such as Treasury bills and notes.

Purchasing Power Parity (PPP)

First popularized by Gustav Cassell in the 1920s,[9] the PPP doctrine holds that the rate of change in the spot exchange rate is equal to the difference between the inflation rates in the home country and the foreign country. In other words, any difference in percentage of inflation between two countries tends to be offset in the long run by an equal and opposite percentage change in the spot exchange rate. Basically:

$$S = (p - p^*)/(1 + p^*) \qquad (1)$$

where

S = rate of change in the spot exchange rate in percentage terms
p = domestic inflation rate in percentage terms
p^* = foreign inflation rate in percentage terms

Equation (2) is generally approximated as follows:

$$S = p - p^* \qquad (2)$$

Therefore, a 6 percent higher inflation rate in Canada will be offset by a 6 percent depreciation in the spot exchange rate of Canadian dollars for U.S. dollars. Statistical studies of PPP are mixed, showing that the theory may hold in the long run.[10]

Techniques used to test PPP include:

a. The regression analysis of the form

$$Ln \ S_t = a + b \ln (p/p^*)_t + U_t$$

for the absolute form or

$$\blacktriangle \ LnS_t = b1 \blacktriangle \ln (p/p^*)_t + V_t$$

for the relative form and where the test is that $a = 0$ and $b = 1$

b. The comparison of exchange rates that satisfies PPP ($S_{ppp,t+n}$) to the prevailing exchange rate S_{t+n}, where

$$S_{ppp, \ t+n} = S_t \frac{p^{t+1} / p^{*t+n}}{p_t / p_t^*}$$

c. The comparison of the movements of the dollar prices of foreign goods relative to their U.S. equivalent for specific goods[11]

Violations of the PPP in the short run led R. I. McKinnon to conclude that:

Until a more robust theory replaces it, I shall assume that the purchasing power parity among tradable goods tends to hold in the long run in the absence of overt impediments to trade among countries with convertible currencies. But . . . because commodity arbitrage is so imperfect in the short run, it cannot be relied on to contain nominal exchange rate movements within the predictable and narrow limits suggested by the law of one price.[12]

There are, however, several problems with the empirical tests of the PPP. These problems include (a) the use of the wholesale price index salaries considered a misleading index because of the inclusion of nontraded outputs in its construction, (b) the presence of restrictions on the movements of goods, (c) the failure to compare a similar basket of goods in each country with all of its trading partners, (d) the reliance on actual realized inflation rates rather than expected inflation rates, (e) the presence of various government interferences, and (f) the presence of other factors besides relative prices that influence the balance on current accounts.[13]

In addition, under suitable rigorous conditions, the PPP becomes a tautology. Witness the following comment: "If nothing changes in an economy except that all costs and prices double, the value of real assets and the quantity of financial assets doubles, the distribution of wealth is unchanged, and so on, then the equilibrium value of the currency used in that economy in terms of other currencies, will be halved."[14] But other factors do change.

Interest Rate Parity

The theory of interest rate parity holds that the difference in nominal interest rates between two countries should be equal but opposite in sign to the forward exchange rate discount or premium. Basically:

$$\text{Forward premium or discount as a percent per annum} = \frac{F - S}{S} \times \frac{12}{\eta} \times 100 = i - i^1$$

where

F = forward exchange rate for contracts due in η months
S = spot exchange rate
i = nominal interest rate in the home country
i^1 = nominal interest rate in the foreign country
η = number of months

Therefore, a 6 percent interest rate in Canada will be offset by a 6 percent discount in the Canadian dollar for delivery in one year.

The interest rate parity results from the use of interest arbitrage. It may be illustrated as follows:

An interest arbitrager may get an investment yield of either $1 + i$ from a deposit in home currency or $F/S (1 + i^1)$ from a deposition foreign currency because the arbitrager has to convert the home currency using the spot exchange rate S, receives a yield of $(1 + i')/S$, and has to stay covered by buying home currency at the forward rate F. Yet the return in the foreign units is high; more funds will move in, resulting in a reduction in i', an increase in S, and a decrease in F. Therefore, according to the interest rate parity hypothesis, the following relationship will hold:

$$(F (1 + i^*))/S = 1 + i$$

Dividing by $(1 + i')$ and subtracting i from each side yields:

$$\frac{F - S}{S} = \frac{i - i^*}{1 + i} = i - i^*$$

Bank traders use the interest rate parity to set forward rates as follows:[15]

$$F = S(1 + i)/(1 + i^*)$$

The consequences of arbitrage are as follows: "The trader *must* follow interest rate parity or else customers will exploit the cheaper techniques for establishing their forward positions. The implication is that arbitrage profit opportunities should never exist in a dispersed market which uses independent quotations on F, S, i and i*. Tests based on time-synchronomous data from independent sources have not been reported."[16]

The Forward Rate as an Unbiased Predictor of the Future Spot Rate

Assuming an efficient foreign exchange market, it may be advanced that the forward rate acts as an unbiased predictor of the future spot rate. In other words, a 6 percent one-year forward premium on the Canadian dollar acts as an unbiased predictor that the Canadian dollar will appreciate by 6 percent during the next year. This view is best expressed by Eugene Fama as follows:

When adjusted for variation through time in expected premiums, the forward rates of interest that are implicit in Treasury Bill prices contain assessments of expected future spot rates of interest that are about as good as those that can be obtained from the information on past spot rates. Moreover, in setting bill prices and forward rates, market reacts appropriately to the negative autocorrelation in monthly changes in the spot rate and to changes through time in the degree of its autocorrelation. This evidence is consistent with the market efficiency proposition that in setting bill prices, the market correctly uses the information in past spot rates.[17]

In fact, the foreign exchange market has not conclusively been proven to be efficient. For example, Richard Rogalski and Joseph Vinso,[18] Ian Giddy and Gunter Dufey,[19] and Steven Kohlhagen[20] provided evidence supporting the efficient market hypothesis for international money and foreign exchange markets. The so-called Jurgensen Report, written by the Working Group on Exchange Market Intervention, doubted the efficiency of the market.[21]

FORECASTING A FOREIGN EXCHANGE RATE UNDER A MANAGED OR FIXED EXCHANGE RATE SYSTEM

Besides considering the theories just presented, the forecasting process under a managed or fixed exchange rate system will need to examine the politics of devaluation and all economic and social indicators that may signal a change in the exchange rate. Ideally, a structural model of the economy may be specified when the spot rate is expressed as a function of lagged endogenous and exogenous variables. The estimated function may then be used for prediction purposes. Another approach generally used is to rely on indicators or indexes that indicate potential changes in the spot rate. These indicators may be devised from exchange determination models outlined earlier. In such a case the indicators or indexes will include the following:

1. Effective and real exchange rates
2. Current account balance of the balance of payments
3. Short-term interest rates
4. Inflation (consumer price indexes, wholesale price indexes)
5. Growth rate of the monetary aggregates
6. Capital account balance of the balance of payments
7. Economic and exchange rate policy and intervention
8. Forward exchange rates[22]

A Government Accounting Office (GAO) report suggested that the supply and demand for a nation's currency depends on differences between that nation and others in some or all of the following variables:

—Price levels and inflation rates
—Interest rates
—National money supplies
—National incomes
—Trade and investment flows
—Government and private debt
—Political risk, such as risk of government-directed economic changes or exchange controls[23]

D. K. Eiteman and A. I. Stonehill identified the following variables as possible indicators of pressure that could be placed on the exchange rate:

• The balance of payments deficit
• Future economic prospects (asset market approach)
• Differential national rates of inflation
• Growth in the money supply
• Lack of synchronization of national business cycles
• A decline in international monetary reserves
• Increased spread between official and "free" exchange rates
• Governmental policies that treat symptoms rather than causes
• Excessive government spending[24]

The problem remains to devise an appropriate procedure. L. L. Jacque developed a four-step procedure for forecasting pegged yet adjustable exchange rates.[25]

Step 1: To assess balance of payments outlook by using certain macroeconomic indicators as a warning system. The indicators include the rate of depletion or growth in international reserves, covering import spending by export earnings for the case of stabilized exchange rates, the consumer price index, the growth in the money supply, and the degree of diversification of exports.

Step 2: To measure the magnitude of required adjustments that may bring the balance of payments into equilibrium by measuring the pressures the market forces are exercising upon the prevailing exchange rates. This step may result in the determination of the magnitude of the possible devaluation or revaluation.

Step 3: To time the adjustment policies by an examination of the central bank's foreign exchange reserves.

Step 4: To predict the type of adjustment policies, either a parity change (devaluation or revaluation) or inflationary or deflationary policies, coupled with exchange controls and extensive international borrowing.

EFFICIENCY OF FOREIGN EXCHANGE MARKETS

It is generally assumed that the securities market is efficient. A perfectly efficient market is in continuous equilibrium so that the intrinsic values of securities vibrate randomly and market prices always equal underlying intrinsic values at every instance in time.[26] *Intrinsic value* is generally regarded as what the price ought to be and what the price would be given that other individuals possess the same information and competence as the person making the estimate. The most widely accepted definition, suggested by E. F. Fama, is that in an efficient market, prices "fully reflect the information available and, by implication, prices react instantaneously and without bias to new information."[27] A mathematical formulation of this definition, called the expected returns model or fair game model, is as follows:

$$Z_{j, t+1} = r_{j, t+1} - E(r_{j, t+1}/O_t)$$

and

$$E(Z_{j, t+1}/O_t) = 0$$

where

O_t = the information set assumed to be fully reflected in prices in period t
$Z_{j, t+1}$ = abnormal return on security j in period t + 1
$r_{j, t+1}$ = the realized return on security j in period t + 1
$E(r_{j, t+1})$ = the expected return on security j in period t + 1 conditional on O_t

In other words, the rate-of-return series ($r_{j, t+1}$) is "a fair game" relative to the information series (O_t). By defining the information set (O_t) in three ways, Fama distinguished three levels of market efficiency: the weak, the semistrong, and the strong forms.[28]

The weak form of the hypothesis states that the equilibrium expected returns (prices) "fully reflect" the sequence of past returns (prices). In other words, historical price and volume data for securities contain no information that may be used to earn a profit superior to a simple "buy-and-hold strategy."

The semistrong form of the hypothesis states that the equilibrium expected returns (prices) "fully reflect" all publicly available information. In other words, no trading rule based on available information may be used to earn an excess return.

The strong form of the hypothesis states that the equilibrium expected returns (prices) "fully reflect" all information (not just publicly available information). In other words, no trading rule based on any information, including inside information, may be used to earn an excess return.

The question of interest is whether the foreign exchange markets are efficient. Before attempting to answer the question it is important to remember that all tests of market efficiency are testing a joint hypothesis: on the one hand, the hypothesis that defines market equilibrium prices or expected returns as a function of the equilibrium prices or expected returns as a function of the information set O; and on the other hand, the hypothesis that economic agents can set actual prices to conform to their expected values. This is particularly crucial in the foreign exchange market since there are no general agreements on the appropriate model of equilibrium pricing comparable to that of capital markets. As stated by Richard Levich:

Simply put, it is difficult to test whether investors set the actual spot exchange rate equal to its equilibrium value unless there is some agreement in what the equilibrium value is. Similarly, it is difficult to test whether risk-bearing is efficiently rewarded if there is no agreement in the fundamental nature of foreign exchange risk, no adequate measure of it, and no model that determines the equilibrium fair return for bearing it.[29]

In spite of their difficulty in proving or disproving the efficiency hypothesis in the foreign exchange markets, vanishes tests are still possible. The results of these tests are as follows:

First, if profit can be made from (a) *spatial arbitrage* due to the dispersion of quotations on individual currencies among market makers as in the case of price differences between interbank forward rate quotations and futures contracts of similar maturity on Chicago's International Monetary Market; (b) *triangular arbitrage*, the process that keeps cross-exchange rates consistent in the direct exchange rates; and (c) *covered interest arbitrage*, the foreign exchange markets cannot be proven to be efficient. For example, departures from interest rate parity can be expressed as:

$$\Sigma = (i - i') - [(F - S)/S]*(1 + i')$$

where Σ is the interest disparity. Evidence of those parities exist.[30] They are generally attributed to less than infinite elasticities for foreign exchange and securities, transaction costs, noncomparable risk in securities, and exchange controls (political risks and taxes).[31] It is interesting to note, however, that the covered arbitrage opportunities between Eurocurrency assets (generally similar in terms of issues, credit risk, and maturity and in all other aspects except currency of denomination) are too small to disprove the efficiency hypothesis.[32,33,34]

Second, spot speculation involves borrowing domestic currency at interest rate i, buying foreign exchange in the spot market at the rate S_t, and investing in a foreign currency denominated asset at interest rate i*. One test of spot market efficiency is to show that the exchange rates follow a "random walk," a phenomena disproved by empirical tests.[35,36] A second test of spot market efficiency is to show the absence of profit opportunities in the use of technical trading rules or filter rules. Evidence supports the efficiency of these rules and therefore the inefficiency of the foreign exchange market.[37]

Third, forward speculation involves borrowing domestic currency at interest rate i, buying foreign exchange in the forward market at the rate F, and investing in a foreign currency denominated asset at i*. Tests of forward market efficiency have focused on the relationship between the current forward rate F, the expected future spot rate $E(S_{t+n})$, and the actual future spot rate S_{t+n}. If the forward rate is unbiased, it fully reflects all available information about the future spot rate. It is tested by the following regression.

$$S_t = a_o + a_1 F_{t-1} + a_2 X_t + e_t$$

where

S_t = spot rate at time t
F_{t-1} = forward rate at time $t-1$
e_t = error term
a_o = intercept
a_1 and a_2 = regression coefficients
X_t = other variables

If the forward rate is unbiased, it follows that $a_1 = o$, $a_2 = 1$, and $a_3 = 0$. In that case the forward rate will not overestimate or underestimate the spot rate. The evidence could not reject this simple efficiency hypothesis.[38]

EVALUATION OF EXCHANGE RATE FORECASTING TECHNIQUES

Various methods are used in practice for the forecasting of the exchange rate including (a) technical techniques, (b) fundamental techniques, (c) market based techniques, and (d) mixed techniques. The technical forecasting techniques rely on the historical exchange rate to predict future values. Basically, the technique used past observations and a time series of past observation to develop more rules about the future behavior of the exchange rate. Specter analysis, or Box Jenkins models, for example, may be used to uncover any systematic pattern in the historical exchange rate.

The fundamental techniques rely on the potential relationships existing between exchange rates and various economic variables. The exchange rate change as a dependent variable is regressed against economic variables assumed to have an impact on the exchange rates. In his review of formal economic models used by exchange rate forecasting services, Stephen Goodman listed the following independent variables: (a) interest rate differentials, (b) relative inflation rates, (c) balance of payments flows, (d) reserve asset positions, and (d) a measure of the sentiment of foreign exchange market participants as reflected in their portfolio asset composition.[39] The fundamental forecasting techniques suffer, however, from more serious limitations that include (1) the lack of knowledge of the precise timing of the impact of the independent variables, (2) the need for accurate forecasted values for some of the independent variables themselves, (3) the failure to include all of the diagnostic independent variables in the model, and (4) the sensitivity of the coefficients of the independent variables to a host of other factors.[40]

The market based forecasting techniques use market indicators to forecast either the spot rate or the forward rate. As seen earlier, for example, the forward rate is used as an unbiased predictor of the spot rate and vice versa. These market based forecasting techniques are used in spite of the empirical evidence showing the forward rate to be a poor predictor. Bedford Cornell, for example, showed that the best simple autoregressive models provided a more accurate indication of the spot rate than did the forward rate.[41] A second example is provided by Ian Giddy and Gunter Dufey's findings of the superiority over the forward rate of a number of sample models, with martingale and submartingale models generally doing the best.[42]

An evaluation of the forecasting accuracy of these techniques is accomplished by the computation of the absolute forecast error as a percentage of the realizable value as follows:

$$\begin{matrix} \text{Absolute forecast error} \\ \text{as a percentage of the} \\ \text{realizable value} \end{matrix} = \frac{\text{Forecasted value} - \text{Realized value}}{\text{realized value}}$$

Goodman, however, suggested an evaluation based on three measures: accuracy in predicting trend, accuracy of their point estimates, and speculative return on capital at risk.[43] They are defined as follows:

Accuracy in predicting trend is defined as the share of each month's forecasts for which the spot exchange rate moves in the predicted direction in the three-month period following the forecast (for the three-month forecast) or in the six-month period following the forecast (for the six-month forecast). Accuracy of the point estimate is defined as the share of each month's forecast for which the predicted rate is closer to the spot rate, three and six months later (for the three-month and six-month forecasts, respectively) than is the three-month and six-month forward rate at the time of the forecast.

Speculative return on capital at risk—the most important measure in assessing market efficiency—is defined as the return, at an annual percentage rate, on the total open position in a currency if a speculator each month blindly followed the services recommendations.[44]

The use of these techniques and the forecasting of the exchange rates is important to the firms in fulfilling necessary functions including (a) hedging decisions, (b) short-term financing decisions, (c) capital budgeting decisions, (d) long-term financing decisions, and (e) earnings assessments.[45] Given the importance of these functions, various exchange rate services have been formed to offer their services. The performance of those institutions is nationally of importance. Goodman examined the performance of these services.[46] Although the performance of the economics-oriented forecasting services was found to be poor, the performance of the technically oriented services suggested that speculative runs do occur in the exchange market and that the foreign exchange market might not be efficient. The market performance of the exchange services was also verified by Richard Levich.[47]

CONCLUSION

This summary of exchange rate determination models and efficiency of the foreign exchange market points to two main results:

1. The predictive ability of the existing foreign exchange rate determination models is at best mixed. Because of the extreme volatility of the floating exchange rate, better specified models are required.
2. The efficiency of the foreign exchange markets remain an issue difficult to prove or disapprove. Efficiency appears salient when judged by the randomness of exchange rates and the accuracy of the forward rate in predicting the spot rate. It is, however, less salient when judged by covered interest differentials, which may be due to risks, taxes, liquidity, and other factors.

NOTES

1. W. Poole, "Speculative Prices as Random Walks: An Analysis of Ten Time Series of Flexible Exchange Rates," *Southern Economic Journal* 33 (1967): 468–478.

2. R. Meese and K. Rogoff, "Empirical Exchange Rate Models of the Seventies: Do They Fit Out of Sample?" *Journal of International Economics* 14 (1983): 3–24.

3. R. Meese and K. Rogoff, "The Out-of-Sample Failure of Empirical Exchange Rate Models: Sampling Error or Misspecification?" In *Exchange Rates and International Macroeconomics*, ed. G. A. Frankel (Chicago: University of Chicago Press, 1983).

4. Ian H. Giddy and Gunter Dufey, "The Random Behavior of Flexible Exchange Rates: Implications for Forecasting," *Journal of International Business Studies*, Spring 1975, pp. 1–32; Andrew Crockett, "Determinants of Exchange Rate Movements: A Review," *Finance and Development*, March 1981, pp. 333–374.

5. Richard M. Levich, "Empirical Studies of Exchange Rates: Price Behavior, Rate Determination, and Market Efficiency," in *Handbook of International Economics*, vol. 2, ed. R. W. Jones and P. B. Kenen (Amsterdam: Elsevier, 1985), p. 1009.

6. R. Doenbush, "Exchange Rate Risk and the Macroeconomics of Exchange Rate Determination," in *Internationalization of Financial Markets and National Economic Policy,* ed. R. Hawkins, R. Levich, and C. Wihlborg (Greenwich, Conn.: JAI Press, 1982), pp. 23–42.

7. R. E. Cumby and M. Obstfeld, "A Note on Exchange-Rate Expectations and Nominal Interest Differentials: A Test of the Fisher Hypothesis," *Journal of Finance,* June 1981, pp. 697–703.

8. F. S. Mishkin, "Are Real Interest Rates Equal Across Countries: An Empirical Investigation of International Parity Conditions," *Journal of Finance,* December 1984, pp. 1345–1357.

9. Gustav Cassell, *Money and Foreign Exchange After 1914* (London: Macmillan, 1923).

10. Lawrence H. Officer, "The Purchasing-Power-Parity Theory of Exchange Rates: A Review Article," *IMF Staff Papers,* March 1976, pp. 1–60.

11. P. Isard, "How Far Can We Rush the Law of One Price?" *American Economic Review* 67 (1977): 942–948.

12. R. I. McKinnon, *Money in International Exchange* (New York: Oxford University Press, 1979), p. 136.

13. D. K. Eiteman and A. I. Stonehill, *Multinational Business Finance* (Reading, Mass.: Addison-Wesley, 1989), p. 74.

14. Crockett, "Determinants of Exchange Rate Movements: A Review," p. 336.

15. A. V. Deardorff, "One-way Arbitrage and Its Implications for the Foreign Exchange Markets," *Journal of Political Economy* 87 (1979): 351–364.

16. Levich, "Empirical Studies of Exchange Rates," p. 102.

17. Eugene F. Fama, "Forward Rates as Predictors of Future Spot Rates," *Journal of Financial Economics*, October 1976, pp. 361–377.

18. Richard J. Rogalski and Joseph D. Vinso, "Price Level Variations as Predictors of Flexible Exchange Rates," *Journal of International Business Studies*, Spring/Summer 1977, pp. 71–82.

19. Giddy and Dufey, "The Random Behavior of Flexible Exchange Rates," pp. 1–32.

20. Steven W. Kohlhagen, "The Performance of the Foreign Exchange Markets, 1971–1974," *Journal of International Business Studies,* Fall 1975, pp. 33–39.

21. Jurgensen Report, *Report of the Working Group on Exchange Market Intervention* (Washington, D.C.: U.S. Treasury, 1983).

22. Harvey A. Poniachek, "The Determination of Exchange Rates," in *International Finance Handbook,* ed. A. M. George and I. H. Giddy (New York: Wiley, 1983), p. 33.

23. Report by the U.S. General Accounting Office, *Floating Exchange Rates in an Interdependent World: No Simple Solutions to the Problems* (Washington, D.C.: U.S. General Accounting Office, 1989), p. 5.

24. Eiteman and Stonehill, *Multinational Business Finance*, p. 165.

25. L. L. Jacque, *Management of Foreign Exchange Risk* (Lexington, Mass.: Lexington Books; D. C. Heath, 1978), p. 99.

26. P. Samuelson, "Proof That Properly Discounted Present Values of Assets Vibrate Randomly," *Bell Journal of Economics and Management Science*, Autumn 1973, pp. 369–379.

27. Eugene F. Fama, "Efficient Capital Markets: A Review of Theory and Empirical Work," *Journal of Finance*, May 1970, pp. 383–417.

28. Ibid., p. 383.

29. Levich, "Empirical Studies of Exchange Rates," p. 1029.

30. L. H. Officer and T. D. Willet, "The Covered-Arbitrage Schedule: A Critical Survey of Recent Developments," *Journal of Money, Credit, and Banking* 2 (1973): 247–257.

31. Levich, "Empirical Studies of Exchange Rates," p. 1026.

32. E. Wayne Clendenning, *The Euro-dollar Market* (Oxford: Clarendon Press, 1970).

33. R. Z. Aliber, "The Interest Rate Parity Theorem: An Interpretation," *Journal of Political Economy* 81 (1973): 1451–1459.

34. J. A. Frenkel and R. M. Levich, "Covered Interest Arbitrage: Unexpected Profits?" *Journal of Political Economy* 83 (1975): 325–338.

35. Poole, "Speculative Prices as Random Walks," pp. 468–478.

36. John Burt, R. Karen, and G. Booth, "Foreign Exchange Market Efficiency Under Flexible Exchange Rates," *Journal of Finance* 32 (1977): 1325–1330.

37. M. P. Dooley and J. R. Shafer, "Analysis of Short-Run Exchange Rate Behavior: March 1973 to November 1981," in *Exchange Rate and Trade Instability*, ed. D. Bigman and T. Taya (Cambridge, Mass.: Ballinger, 1983), pp. 32–52.

38. A. C. Stockman, "Risk, Information, and Forward Exchange Rates," in *The Economics of Exchange Rates*, ed. J. Frenkel and H. Johnson (Reading, Mass.: Addison-Wesley, 1978), pp. 110–132.

39. Stephen H. Goodman, "Foreign Exchange Rate Forecasting Techniques: Implications for Business and Policy," *Journal of Finance*, May 1979, pp. 418–419.

40. Jeff Madura, *International Financial Management* (St. Paul, Minn.: West, 1989), pp. 212–213.

41. Bedford Cornell, "Spot Rates, Forward Rates, and Exchange Market Efficiency," *Journal of Financial Economics*, January 1977, pp. 55–65.

42. Giddy and Dufey, "The Random Behavior of Flexible Exchange Rates," pp. 1–32.

43. Goodman, "Foreign Exchange Rate Forecasting Techniques," p. 419.

44. Ibid.

45. Madura, *International Financial Management*, pp. 206–207.

46. Goodman, "Foreign Exchange Rate Forecasting Techniques," pp. 415–427.

47. Richard Levich, "Analyzing the Accuracy of Foreign Exchange Advisory Services: Theory and Evidence," in *Exchange Risk and Exposure: Current Developments in International Financial Management*, ed. Richard Levich and Clas Whilberg (Lexington, Mass.: D. C. Heath; Lexington Books, 1980), pp. 61–81.

REFERENCES

Aliber, R. Z. "The Interest Rate Parity Theorem: An Interpretation." *Journal of Political Economy* 81 (1973): 1451–1459.

Burt, John, R. Karen, and G. Booth. "Foreign Exchange Market Efficiency Under Flexible Exchange Rates." *Journal of Finance* 32 (1977): 1325–1330.

Cassell, Gustav. *Money and Foreign Exchange After 1914.* London: Macmillan, 1923.

Clendenning, E. Wayne. *The Euro-dollar Market.* Oxford: Clarendon Press, 1970.

Cornell, Bedford. "Spot Rates, Forward Rates, and Exchange Market Efficiency." *Journal of Financial Economics*, January 1977, pp. 55–65.

Crockett, Andrew. "Determinants of Exchange Rate Movements: A Review." *Finance and Development*, March 1981, pp. 333–374.

Cumby, R. E., and M. Obstfeld. "A Note on Exchange-Rate Expectations and Nominal Interest Differentials: A Test of the Fisher Hypothesis." *Journal of Finance*, June 1981, pp. 697–703.

Deardorff, A. V. "One-way Arbitrage and Its Implications for the Foreign Exchange Markets." *Journal of Political Economy* 87 (1979): 351–364.

Doenbush, R. "Exchange Rate Risk and the Macroeconomics of Exchange Rate Determination." In *Internationalization of Financial Markets and National Economic Policy*. Edited by R. Hawkins, R. Levich, and C. Wihlborg. Greenwich, Conn.: JAI Press, 1982, pp. 23–42.

Dooley, M. P., and J. R. Shafer. "Analysis of Short-Run Exchange Rate Behavior: March 1973 to November 1981." In *Exchange Rate and Trade Instability*. Edited by D. Bigman and T. Taya. Cambridge, Mass.: Ballinger, 1983, pp. 32–52.

Eiteman, D. K., and A. I. Stonehill. *Multinational Business Finance*. Reading, Mass.: Addison-Wesley, 1989.

Fama, Eugene F. "Efficient Capital Markets: A Review of Theory and Empirical Work." *Journal of Finance*, May 1970, pp. 383–417.

———. "Forward Rates as Predictors of Future Spot Rates." *Journal of Financial Economics*, October 1976, pp. 361–377.

Frenkel, J. A., and R. M. Levich. "Covered Interest Arbitrage: Unexpected Profits?" *Journal of Political Economy* 83 (1975): 325–338.

Giddy, Ian H., and Gunter Dufey. "The Random Behavior of Flexible Exchange Rates: Implications for Forecasting." *Journal of International Business Studies*, Spring 1975, pp. 1–32.

Goodman, Stephen H. "Foreign Exchange Rate Forecasting Techniques: Implications for Business and Policy." *Journal of Finance*, May 1979, pp. 415–427.

Isard, P. "How Far Can We Rush the Law of One Price?" *American Economic Review* 67 (1977): 942–948.

Jacque, L. L. *Management of Foreign Exchange Risk*. Lexington, Mass.: Lexington Books; D. C. Heath, 1978.

Jurgensen Report. *Report of the Working Group on Exchange Market Intervention*. Washington, D. C.: U.S. Treasury, 1983.

Kohlhagen, Steven W. "The Performance of the Foreign Exchange Markets, 1971–1974." *Journal of International Business Studies*, Fall 1975, pp. 33–39.

Levich, Richard. "Analyzing the Accuracy of Foreign Exchange Advisory Services: Theory and Evidence." In *Exchange Risk and Exposure: Current Developments in International Financial Management*. Edited by Richard Levich and Clas Whilberg. Lexington, Mass.: D. C. Heath; Lexington Books, 1980, pp. 61–81.

———. "Empirical Studies of Exchange Rates: Price Behavior, Rate Determination, and Market Efficiency." In *Handbook of International Economics*. Vol. 2. Edited by R. W. Jones and P. B. Kenen. Amsterdam: Elsevier, 1985.

Madura, Jeff. *International Financial Management*. St. Paul, Minn.: West, 1989.

McKinnon, R. I. *Money in International Exchange*. New York: Oxford University Press, 1979.

Meese, R., and K. Rogoff. "Empirical Exchange Rate Models of the Seventies: Do They Fit Out of Sample?" *Journal of International Economics* 14 (1983): 3–24.

———. "The Out-of-Sample Failure of Empirical Exchange Rate Models: Sampling

Error or Misspecification?'' In *Exchange Rates and International Macroeconomics*. Edited by G. A. Frankel. Chicago: University of Chicago Press, 1983.

Mishkin, F. S. ''Are Real Interest Rates Equal Across Countries: An Empirical Investigation of International Parity Conditions.'' *Journal of Finance*, December 1984, pp. 1345–1357.

Officer, Lawrence H. ''The Purchasing-Power-Parity Theory of Exchange Rates: A Review Article.'' *IMF Staff Papers*, March 1976, pp. 1–60.

Officer, L. H., and T. D. Willet. ''The Covered-Arbitrage Schedule: A Critical Survey of Recent Developments.'' *Journal of Money, Credit, and Banking* 2 (1973): 247–257.

Poniachek, Harvey A. ''The Determination of Exchange Rates.'' In *International Finance Handbook*. Edited by A. M. George and I. H. Giddy. New York: Wiley, 1983, p. 33.

Poole, W. ''Speculative Prices as Random Walks: An Analysis of Ten Time Series of Flexible Exchange Rates.'' *Southern Economic Journal* 33 (1967): 468–478.

Report by the U.S. General Accounting Office. *Floating Exchange Rates in an Interdependent World: No Simple Solutions to the Problems*. Washington, D.C.: U.S. General Accounting Office, 1989.

Rogalski, Richard J., and Joseph D. Vinso. ''Price Level Variations as Predictors of Flexible Exchange Rates.'' *Journal of International Business Studies*, Spring/Summer 1977, pp. 71–82.

Samuelson, P. ''Proof That Properly Discounted Present Values of Assets Vibrate Randomly.'' *Bell Journal of Economics and Management Science*, Autumn 1973, pp. 369–379.

Stockman, A. C. ''Risk, Information, and Forward Exchange Rates.'' In *The Economics of Exchange Rates*. Edited by J. Frenkel and H. Johnson. Reading, Mass.: Addison-Wesley, 1978, pp. 110–132.

Appendix 2.A

Forecasting Exchange Rates Under a Freely Floating Exchange Rate System

Assume the following situation between the United States and France.

a. Expected changes in the general price level for one year:

United States:	P_{US} = 9.20% or 0.092
France:	P_{FR} = 5.00% or 0.050

b. Risk-free nominal interest rate available today:

United States:	I_{US} = 13.36% or 0.1336
France:	I_{FR} = 9.00% or 0.090

c. Today's foreign exchange quotations:

Spot rate	S = FF 6.5026/$
One-year forward rate	F = FF 6.50/$

The analysis is as follows: Under the Fisher Effect, the nominal interest rate will vary by the differences in the expected inflation rates. Therefore,

$$\frac{1 + \text{inflation rate in US}}{1 + \text{inflation rate in FR}} - 1 = \frac{1 + \text{nominal interest rate in US}}{1 + \text{nominal interest rate in FR}}$$

$$\frac{1 + 0.092}{1 + 0.050} - 1 = \frac{1 + 0.1336}{1 + 0.0900} - 1$$

$$0.04 \text{ or } 4\% = 0.04 \text{ or } 4\%$$

Similarly, the real rate of interest is:

$$\text{Real rate of interest} = \frac{1 + \text{nominal interest rate}}{1 + \text{inflation rate}} - 1$$

In spite of this difficulty to prove or disprove the efficiency hypothesis in the foreign exchange markets, various tests are still possible with these results: If profit can be made from (a) *spatial arbitrage* due to the dispersion of quotations on individual currencies across market makers as in the case of price differences between interbank forward rate quotations; and futures contracts of similar maturity on Chicago's International Monetary Market; (b) *triangular* arbitrage, the process that keeps cross-exchange rates consistent with direct exchange rates; and (c) *covered interest arbitrage*, then the foreign exchange markets cannot be proven to be efficient. For example, departures from interest rate parity can be expressed as:

$$\Sigma = (i - i^1) - \left[\frac{(F - S)}{S} \right] \times (1 + i^1)$$

where Σ is the interest disparity. Evidence of those disparities exist.[1] They are generally attributed to less than infinite elasticities for foreign exchange and securities, transaction costs, noncomparable risk in securities, and exchange controls (political risks and taxes).[2]

NOTES

1. L. H. Officer and T. D. Willet, "The Covered-Arbitrage Schedule: A Critical Survey of Recent Developments," *Journal of Money, Credit, and Banking* 2 (1973): 247–257.

2. Richard M. Levich, "Empirical Studies of Exchange Rates: Price Behavior, Rate Determination, and Market Efficiency," in *Handbook of International Economics*, vol. 2, ed. R. W. Jones and P. B. Kenen (Amsterdam: Elsevier, 1985), p. 1026.

Appendix 2.B

Covered Interest Arbitrage

Make the following assumptions between the United States and France:

Spot exchange rate: FF6.4251/$

Three-month forward rate: FF6.48748/$

Three-month U.S. interest rate: 12% per annum or 3% per quarter

Three-month France interest rate: 16% per annum or 4% per quarter

Transaction size: $1,000,000

The American multinational company may elect to invest $1,000,000 for three months yielding $1,030,000. Or it may elect to purchase FF6,425,100 at today's spot rate (FF6.4251) and invest it in a three-month French security that will yield FF6,682,104 in three months. The same amount could at the same time be sold forward at the forward exchange rate of FF6.48748, which will yield $1,030,000 in three months, and that will eliminate the exchange risk. The situation described is typical of an equilibrium caused by an interest rate parity.

Assume, however, that the French interest has increased to 20 percent per annum or 5 percent per quarter. In such a case a profit can be generated through a covered interest arbitrage as follows: Today:

Step 1: Borrow $1,000,000 U.S. at 3% per quarter for three months.

Step 2: Acquire FF6,425,100 at the spot market after exchanging the $1,000,000.

Step 3: Invest the FF6,425,100 in France at 5% interest per quarter, which will yield in three months FF6,746,355.

Step 4: Assume the transaction costs to be $500.

Step 5: Sell the FF6,746,355 forward three months at FF6.48748.

Three months from now:

Step 6: Receive FF6,746,355 from the French bank for your investment.

Step 7: Complete the forward contract by delivering FF6,746,355 at FF6.48748 and receive $1,039,903.70.

Step 8: Deliver to the U.S. bank the amount of $1,030,000 for the three-month loan.

What results from these transactions is as follows:

Return from forward contract	$1,039,903.70
Minus reimbursed loan	1,030,000.00
Minus transaction cost	500.00
Net yield before tax	$9,403.70

3

Economic Exposure: Nature, Measurement, and Management

Multinational firms face exchange risk as a result of the impact of the changes of exchange rates on their operations. Various types of exposure are identified in the literature including economic exposure, transaction exposure, and translation exposure. This chapter elaborates on the nature, measurement, and management of economic exposure. The following two chapters deal with transaction and translation exposure, respectively.

IS FOREIGN EXCHANGE RISK RELEVANT?

The fluctuations in foreign exchange rates create one of the most complex uncertainties faced by multinational firms. These fluctuations create a risk to these firms known as foreign exchange risk—a risk that affects firms' cash flows as a result of currency fluctuations. It can also affect contractual cash flows arising from debt payables or receivables or noncontractual cash flows that are usually associated with expected revenues and expenses.

Is there a case for corporate management of foreign exchange risk? Six arguments may be used that oppose hedging at the level of the firm because either foreign exchange risk does not exist or, if it exists, it does not need to be hedged: the purchasing power parity, the capital asset pricing model, the Modigliami-Miller Theorem, the concept of self-insurance and the efficient market hypothesis, the hedging of consumption bundles, and the uncertainty of forward rates and spot rates. Each of these arguments may be used against corporate management of foreign exchange risk. The same arguments, however, may also be used to argue for corporate management of foreign exchange risk as summarized in Exhibit 3.1. Because real-world imperfections do exist, firms can be subject to exchange risk, and corporate management of foreign exchange may be sup-

Exhibit 3.1

Arguments against and for Corporate Management of Foreign Exchange Risk: Summary

Against	For
1. *Purchasing Power Parity Theorem:* PPP implies off-setting changes in price levels and exchange rates: hence, there is no exposure to exchange risk.	1. Deviations from PPP have been well documented: the shorter the time horizon, the greater the deviations. Even if PPP holds with respect to an index of tradeable goods, a particular firm may still be exposed to exchange risk, since the relative price of its inputs and outputs may change.
2. *Capital Asset Pricing Model (CAPM):* According to CAPM, what matters is only one systematic risk: it does not matter whether exchange risk is managed separately in foreign exchange markets, or passed along to the capital market.	2. When default risk is important, hedging can reduce default risk and add to the debt capacity of the firm.
3. *Modigliani-Miller (MM) Theorem:* According to MM, what the firm does, an investor can do: hence, there is no need for corporate management of exchange risk.	3. There are several obstacles to individuals in coping better with exchange risk. A firm is in a position to obtain a low-cost hedge: also information on the firm's exposure is not symmetrically distributed between shareholders and managers.
4. *The Concept of Self-Insurance:* The forward market is a fair bet and does not provide bargains. The foreign exchange gains and losses average out over a period.	4. This concept implies maximizing expected value without regard to variance, and thus assumes risk neutrality. However, economic agents are usually risk-averse.
The Efficient Market Hypothesis: Since the foreign exchange markets are efficient, forward contracts are priced properly and there are no excess returns from hedging.	The objective of hedging is not to earn excess returns, but to achieve a desired pattern of risk and return.
5. *Hedging of Consumption Bundle:* A firm's exchange-related gains and losses may be useful to hedge the consumption bundles of its shareholders.	5. As the consumption bundle is investor-specific, its management is better left to the shareholder. Firms should hedge exchange risk and shareholder should hedge consumption bundle risk.
6. *The Uncertainty of Forward Rates and Spot Rates:* Since future forward rates are as uncertain as future spot rates, hedging is of dubious value.	6. Hedging makes available exact information regarding anticipated cash flows: such information can be useful for activities for which the planning and action horizon is the same as the maturity of the forward contract.

Source: Gunter Dufey and S. L. Srinivasulu, "The Case of Corporate Management of Foreign Exchange Risk," *Financial Management* 12, no. 4 (1983): 55. Reprinted with permission.

ported. These market imperfections may include incomplete securities markets, positive transaction and information costs, the dead-weight cost of financial distress, and agency cost considerations.

Given this eventuality, firms need to reduce their exposure to the foreign exchange risk. Techniques for managing exposure are reviewed in this chapter as well as the next two chapters. The three types of exposure are defined next before a greater focus is placed on the nature, measurement, and management of economic exposure.

TYPES OF FOREIGN EXCHANGE EXPOSURE

Foreign exchange risk results from the changes in foreign exchange rates and the impact it has on the profitability, financial position, and transactions of a firm. As such, it results in three main types of foreign exchange exposure: economic, transaction, and translation.

A *transaction exposure* arises whenever a firm has a receivable, a payable, a revenue, an expense, or a forward contract denominated in other than its functional currency, which is usually the local currency or the currency in which the firm does most of its business. If a U.S. firm has a payable in the French franc, for example, and the French franc depreciates relative to the dollar, the number of dollars needed by the U.S. firm decreases, resulting in an exchange gain. If, instead, the French franc appreciates relative to the dollar, the number of dollars needed by the U.S. firm increases, resulting in an exchange loss. The transaction exposure is present whenever a cash flow in a specific transaction is affected by the changes in the foreign exchange rate.

A *translation exposure*, also called accounting exposure, results from the necessity of periodically consolidating or aggregating parent companies' and subsidiaries' financial statements. To do so, the subsidiaries' financial statements have to be translated into the parent company's currency before being consolidated with the parent company's financial statements. Translation exposure results from the possibility that a change in exchange rates will create an exchange gain or loss and therefore depends on the translation method and the exchange rate used for the translation of individual items in the balance sheet and income statement. The items to be translated at the historical exchange rate are unexposed while the items to be translated at the current exchange rate are considered exposed, and their translation results in translation losses or gains. These losses and gains do not involve any cash flows but result from the desire to disclose earnings valued in a single numeraire (reference currency).

An *economic exposure*, also called operating exposure or "residual foreign exchange exposure," results from the possibility that a firm's economic value will change as a result of change in the future operating cash flows following an unexpected change in the foreign exchange rate. The economic exposure results from the impact of a currency change or the cost of a firm's inputs and the price and volume of its output, which affects its competitive strength.

The classification of foreign exchange exposure into economic, transaction, and translation exposure rested in the nature of the foreign exchange risk as discriminatory factors. Other discriminatory factors result in other classification of foreign exchange risk. As Exhibit 3.2 shows, the classification may be in terms of

a. Before or after tax exposure when tax is the discriminating factor
b. Currency or country exposure and subsidiary or corporate exposure when organizational structure is the discriminating factor
c. Proforma or actual exposure when planning is used as the discriminating factor
d. Long-term, medium-term, or short-term exposure when the time frame is used as the discriminating factor
e. Diversifiable or undiversifiable exposure when diversifiability is the discriminating factor
f. Actual or contingent exposure when contingency is used as the discriminating factor
g. On-balance sheet exposure or off-balance sheet exposure when relation to the balance sheet is used as the discriminating factor

These classifications are not mutually exclusive.

NATURE OF ECONOMIC EXPOSURE

Economic exposure results from the impact of unexpected changes in exchange rates as a firm incorporates the expected changes in its investment, production, financing, and pricing decisions. Only unexpected changes are assumed to cause the market value of a firm to change as the expected changes are assumed under an efficient market hypothesis to be impounded in the market value. Translation exposure, unlike economic exposure, does not distinguish between expected and unexpected changes in the foreign exchange rate. Exhibit 3.3 contrasts the various differences between accounting and economic exposure concepts.

Economic exposure may be separated into two components: a competitive effect and a conversion effect. As stated by Eugene Flood and Donald Lessard:

The competitive effect is the sensitivity of the local currency cash flows to changes in the exchange rate, which is shown to depend on the competitive structure of the markets in which the firm sells its products and the sources of its inputs. The conversion effect is purely the one-for-one mapping of the resulting local currency cash flows into dollars. While dollar cash flows are, by definition, not subject to the conversion effect, they may be subject to a competitive effect.[1]

Although the economic exposure affects mainly firms involved in international business, it does have an effect on domestic firms as well. A domestic producer that sells only domestically, for example, may be affecting a change in the foreign exchange rate if a foreign competitor's price decreases as a result of a

Exhibit 3.2
Foreign Exchange Exposure: A Classification

Discriminating Factor	Types	Brief Definition
1. Nature	a. Translation exposure	Translation exposure is the extent of mismatch between "exposed assets and liabbilities where the translation method defines the items that are to be treated "exposed." In U.S., FASB No. 52 guidelines are to be used. This primarily arises during the consolidation of financial statements.
	b. Transaction exposure	Transaction exposure is the foreign-currency-denominated contracts such as account receivables/payables, and loans/investments with nominal rates of return. If the same transaction is on the books at more than one reporting period. It causes translation exposure also.
	c. Economic exposure	Economic exposure is the impact of currency realignments on future cash flows and hence the value of a firm.
2. Tax	a. Before-tax exposure	Exposure is calculated without considering taxes.
	b. After-tax exposure	Here, tax impact is taken into account.
3. Organizational Structure	a. Currency exposure	For a multinational firm with operations in many countries and many cross-border transactions and investments, these are different. Currency exposure will show the net assets (or liabilities) that are exposed, say, in £. Hence these assets will be affected if £ value changes. It is obtained by aggregating exposure in that currency by all units of the firm. Useful concept.
	b. Country exposure	Country exposure means the amount of assets exposed in a particular country (of all subsidiaries in that country). It will be in various currencies, e.g.: All subs in Britain have +50 DM, −200 yen, +100 S.Fr. etc. exposed.

Exhibit 3.2 (continued)

Discriminating Factor	Types	Brief Definition
4. Organizational Structure	a. Subsidiary exposure	Each sub calculates its exposure in various currencies.
	b. Corporate exposure	Exposure of all units is aggregated at corporate headquarters, currency-by-currency. Same as 3a.
5. Proforma vs. Actual	a. Proforma exposure	In any of the categories from 1 to 4, proforma exposure is what a firm budgets at the beginning of the planning period.
	b. Actual exposure	Actual amount exposed may differ from that planned because of variations in activity levels.
6. Time Frame		Lock-in effect of each decision is the main criteria for classifying exposure on this score: Example in each category follows.
	a. Long-term exposure	Long Term: Plant location, choice of technology, development of markets, long-term financing.
	b. Medium-term exposure	Medium Term: Development of sources, product mix, pricing policies.
	c. Short-term exposure	Short Term: Money management, leads/lags. This classification is firm-specific because different firms have different degrees of flexibility in changing prices, input mix, or product mix.
7. Diversifiability	a. Diversifiable	The exposure in a portfolio of currencies is less than the sum of exposures in individual currencies. For example, if a firm has a receivable in DM and an equivalent payable in yen and if both DM and yen move together, rising and falling by the same amount, the firm has no exposure at all. If DM moves down, dollar-equivalent of receivable goes down; but as DM moves down, yen also moves down and hence dollar-equivalent of payable also goes down; the firm has no exposure. This is illustrative of an extreme situation. Actual exposure in a portfolio depends on the covariance of exchange rate movements.
	b. Undiversifiable	

8. Contingency	a. Actual exposure	This classification is due to differences in the nature of underlying transactions that give rise to exposure. In an unconditional contract such as a foreign currency receivable, the extent and duration of exposure are certain. On the other hand, in a contingent contract such as a foreign-currency-denominated bid, exposure is contingent upon the bid being accepted.
	b. Contingent exposure	
9. Relation to Balance Sheet	a. On balance sheet exposure	Some contracts involving foreign exchange exposure are recorded on the balance sheet, while others are not. For example, foreign-currency-denominated receivables payables, loans, and investments are on the balance sheet. However, contracts such as foreign-currency-denominated leases, toward foreign exchange contracts, and agreements for the future sale of goods are all off the balance sheet.
	b. Off balance sheet exposure	

Source: S. L. Srinivasulu, "Classifying Foreign Exchange Exposure." Used by permission from *Financial Executive*, February 1983, copyright 1983 by Financial Executive Institute, pp. 38–39.

Exhibit 3.3
Comparison of Accounting and Economic Exposure Concepts

Accounting Exposure	Economic Exposure
1. Static concept: refers to a particular point in time, the date of financial statements.	1. Dynamic concept: refers to all relevant future.
2. Retrospective: measurement of events prior to and up to the date of preparation of financial statements.	2. Prospective: measurement of change in future cash flows as a result of change in exchange rates.
3. The extent of accounting exposure is determined by accounting conventions such as FASB No. 8 or FASB No. 52.	3. The extent of economic exposure is determined by a firm's position in its product and factor markets; effect is due to nature of operations (source of input, destination of output, debt policy).
4. Easy to compute the extent of exposure and the exact consequences of a given exchange rate change; an exchange rate change will result in immediate translation gains/losses.	4. Difficult to compute; effects of an exchange rate change will be reflected in successive future income statements.
5. Usual financial accounting can capture translation exposure and gains/losses thereof.	5. Good variance accounting is needed to isolate the effect of an exchange rate change on costs, prices, volume, and profits.
6. Usually, financial hedging is recommended to cope with it; tactical decisions; the extent of accounting exposure can be quickly changed; short-term perspective.	6. Operational hedging is the optimal alternative; strategic decisions; longer lock-in effects are involved; takes time to develop new technology, sources, products, or rationalize production on a global basis; long-term perspective.
7. Focus, here, is on current reported income; likely to be the center of management's current attention.	7. Focus is on future cash flows and their variability.
8. Avoidance may cause economic exposure.	8. Avoidance may cause translation exposure.
9. A purely paper loss is to be avoided at a real cost.	9. Economic and opportunity loss is to be avoided by proper operational changes.
10. The concept and measurement is based on total change in exchange rates.	10. Based on only the unexpected changes in exchange rates.

Exhibit 3.3 (continued)

Accounting Exposure	Economic Exposure
11. Based on the book value of assets and liabilities; book value, usually, does not correspond to market value.	11. Based on the true market value of assets and liabilities; market value, in turn, is based on the ability to generate (absorb) future cash flows.
12. Does not consider exposure of contracts not appearing on the balance sheet (e.g., leases, purchase/sale contracts for future delivery).	12. Considers all contracts, both on- and off-balance sheet, that will affect future cash flows.
13. Management of accounting exposure is largely a function of the treasury.	13. Management of economic exposure involves virtually all functions including marketing, production, logistics, sourcing, and the treasury.

Source: S. L. Srinivasulu, ''Classifying Foreign Exchange Exposure.'' Used by permission from *Financial Executive*, February 1983, copyright 1983 by Financial Executives Institute, pp. 38–39.

depreciation in the exchange rate of the foreign currency and customers abandon the local company to benefit from the lower prices of the foreign producers. As stated by S. L. Srinivasulu:

The primary reason given by any government for devaluing its currency is to make its exportables from that country competitive in international markets. A firm may lose a market because currency changes affect its ability to compete there. The essence of economic exposure is that currency changes alter the cost of a firm's inputs and the price of its output, thereby shifting the focus of a multinational corporation's relative competitive strength across its many product/market segments.[2]

The economic exposure can also be indirect. Consider, for example, the case of a U.S. importer of a good with payments denominated in U.S. dollars. If the foreign currency depreciates, the U.S. importer does not face a direct economic exposure. It is possible, however, for the foreign exporter to decide to charge a higher price to offset the devaluation in the foreign currency. In that case the U.S. importer will be facing an indirect economic exposure.

IMPACT OF ECONOMIC EXPOSURE

The impact of economic exposure varies depending on the types of activities of a multinational corporation. Examples of the contingent impact of economic exposure include the following:

1. An increasing strong U.S. dollar vis-à-vis other foreign currencies can result in a con of market share for U.S. exports as well as for local sales of foreign subsidiaries of U.S. multinationals. A foreign subsidiary's competitive position in the local markets can be such that increasing prices to offset an exchange rate depreciation can result in a loss of sales.

2. Credit policies can be such that the longer the credit term granted, the larger the risk for economic loss resulting from exchange depreciation. The more the exchange risk can be passed to or shared with a customer, the less economic risk will be absorbed by the corporation.

3. The more (or less) the corporation can pass increasing costs, due to inflation and foreign exchange, onto a customer, the less (or more) the economic risk will be.

4. The lower (or higher) the level of working capital, the lower (or higher) the less economic risk will be.

5. The more contractual prices can be adjusted for inflation and foreign exchange, the less economic risk will be.

6. The more local earnings are repatriated through dividend payments, the less economic risk will be.

7. The more volatile the foreign exchange and capital markets, the more uncertain the cost of financing will be as measured by the sum of interest expense and debt-related transaction-translation gain or loss.[3]

Various factors affect the impact of economic exposure: First, the impact of economic exposure depends on whether the foreign exchange rate has depreciated or appreciated. In the case of a local currency appreciation, for example, its local cash inflows are decreased by (a) a decrease in local sales as foreign substitutes become cheaper, (b) a decrease in its foreign exports denominated in local currency as a result of the increase in the price of its products in foreign countries, (c) a decrease in its foreign exports denominated in foreign currency as the value of its exports converted in local currency is lower, and (d) a decrease in any interest or dividends from foreign investments due to their reduced value when converted in local currency. Similarly, in the case of a local currency appreciation, its local cash outflows will be decreased by (a) a decrease in the value of the imported supplies denominated in foreign currency and (b) a decrease in any interest or dividends to pay to foreign investors due to the reduced value of these payments when converted into local currency. In the case of a local currency depreciation, the opposite may happen as its overall cash outflows and inflows may increase.[4]

Second, the impact of the economic exposure on a firm's expected cash flows depends on the time horizon used, resulting in a four-level impact: short run, medium run—equilibrium case, medium run—disequilibrium case, and long run.[5] In the short run little can be done about the change in the exchange rates resulting in a difference between realized cash flows and budgeted cash flows. In the medium run, as expressed in two- to five-year budgets and assuming an equilibrium condition among foreign exchange rates, national inflation rates, and national interest rates, the firm is in a position to adjust prices and costs to maintain the expected level of cash flows, with the result of a minimum to zero economic exposure. In the medium run and disequilibrium case, the firm is unable to adjust its prices and costs, resulting in a difference between the expected and realized cash flows. In the long run all firms are subject to economic exposure if the foreign exchange markets are not continuously in equilibrium.[6]

Economic Exposure Formulas

First Formula: One formula for the computation of economic exposure is based on the difference between the firm's net present value before and after the predicted change in the exchange rate. For example, the economic exposure in dollars to a firm operating in a foreign country with foreign currency FC is:

Economic exposure:

$$\sum_{i=1}^{n} \frac{\text{Original FC cash flow} \times ER_t}{(1 + r)^n} - \sum_{i=1}^{n} \frac{\text{Adjusted FC cash flow} \times ER_{at}}{(1 + r)^n}$$

where

ER_t = series of exchange rates expected before the change in the value of the exchange rate

ER_{at} = series of exchange rates expected after the change in the value of the exchange rate

The adjusted FC cash flows are those cash flows that do not adjust proportionally to the change in the exchange rate. In other words, a 100 percent adjustment in cash flow results in zero economic exposure. There is, however, a small exchange loss even when there is a 100 percent adjustment in the cash flows. Assume, for example, that the cash flow of a foreign subsidiary for one year is FC100 = $100.00 (a) If the devaluation of the FC currency is 10 percent, and the percentage adjustment in cash flows is 100 percent, the economic exposure is zero. However, the change in the FC cash flow is 10 percent, resulting in a new exchange rate of 0.90, a new FC cash flow of FC110 (FC110 × 1.10), and a new dollar cash flow of $99.00 (FC110 × 0.90). Therefore, the exchange loss is equal to $1.00 (original $100.00 − new dollar cash flow of $49.00). (b) If the devaluation of the FC is still 10 percent and the percentage adjustment is 60 percent, the economic exposure is 40 percent (100% − 60%). However, the change in FC is 6 percent (60% of 10%), the new exchange rate is 0.90 (10% of FC100), resulting in a new FC cash flow of $106.00 (FC100 × 1.06) and a new dollar cash flow of $95.40. Therefore the exchange loss is equal to $4.60 ($100.00 − $95.40).

Using the above analysis, R. M. Rodriguez and E. Eugene Carter deduced the following formula for economic exposure:[7]

FC economic exposure: [(Original FC cash flow) (1 − percentage adjustment in cash flows) + (expected change in FC cash flows) (expected percentage change in exchange rate)]

In other words, the economic exposure resulting from a devaluation of 10 percent and a percentage adjustment of cash flows of 60 percent is equal to:

$$
\begin{aligned}
\text{Economic exposure} &= [100\ (1 - 60\%) + 6\%]\ 10\% \\
&= 40 \times 10\% + 6\% \times 10\% \\
&= 4 + 0.60 \\
&= \$4.60
\end{aligned}
$$

The \$4.60 loss is due to a 10 percent loss in the economic exposure of FC40 plus the 10% loss on the increased cash flow of FC6. Similarly, the economic exposure resulting from a devaluation of 10 percent and a percentage adjustment of 100 percent is equal to:

$$
\begin{aligned}
\text{Economic exposure} &= [100\ (1 - 100\%) + 10\%]\ 10\% \\
&= 0 + 1 \\
&= \$1
\end{aligned}
$$

The \$1 loss is due to a 10 percent loss on the economic exposure of FCO plus the 10 percent loss on the increase cash flow of FC10.

Second Formula: Christine Heckman proposed a formula whereby the economic foreign exposure is determined by subtracting a natural hedge parameter m1 from the financial hedge parameter α as follows:[8]

Net exposure coefficient: $\alpha - \text{m1}$

which is equivalent to the difference between the proportion of value not hedged financially and the proportion of value naturally hedged.

To derive α, which measures financial exposure, that is, the proportion of nominal cash flows that remains unhedged, Heckman proposed the following formula:

$$
\alpha = \frac{C_\kappa - D_\kappa - C_\kappa^x}{C_\kappa}
$$

where

C_κ = the operating cash flows
D_κ = the cash payments to debt holders (after tax)
C_κ^x = the level of sales of forward foreign currency contracts

To derive m1, the proportion of value naturally hedged, Heckman suggested that it is equal to the product of the sensitivity of foreign returns to inflation and the sensitivity of foreign inflation to exchange rate changes. The sensitivity of foreign returns to inflation is computed as follows:

$$C_\kappa = 1\,P_\kappa$$

where

C_κ = the percentage change in the foreign currency cash flow forecasts
P_κ = the percentage change in expected foreign inflation
1 = the firm's average inflation sensitivity parameter

The sensitivity of foreign inflation to exchange rate changes is computed as follows:

$$P_\kappa = m(P_{\phi T} - S)$$

where

P_κ = the percentage change in expected foreign price levels
$P_{\phi T}$ = the percentage change in expected U.S. price levels
S = the percentage change in the expected foreign currency exchange rate

Therefore, the sensitivity of foreign currency returns to exchange rate changes is equal to the product of the parameters 1 and m, reflecting the degree to which the cash flows are naturally hedged.

Income Statement Sensitivity to Potential Exchange Rate Changes

Another method of measuring economic exposure consists of predicting the impact of the changes in exchange rates on each of the income statement items. This method requires, first, the use of the budgeted income statement of the firm and its foreign subsidiary. Consider the budgeted income statement of Lacrosse Companie, for example, a French based company and its Tunisian subsidiary, as shown in Exhibit 3.4. Second, the method requires different estimates to be made on the potential changes in the exchange rate. Assume here that the expected values of the Tunisian dinar are, respectively, FFO.90 and FFO.80. Third, it is also generally assumed that the sales in local currency will increase following an increase in the value of the foreign currency. The assumptions in this example are as follows:

Exhibit 3.4
Budgeted Income Statement: The Lacrosse Companie
(Millions, in France francs [FF] and Tunisian Dinars [TD])

	French Business	Tunisian Business
Sales	FF 250	TD 50
Cost of Goods Sold	- 50	- 20
Gross Profit	FF 200	TD 30
-Operating Expenses	- 50	- 10
Earnings before interest & taxes	FF 200	TD 20
-Interest expenses	- 60	- 5
Earnings before taxes	FF 140	TD 15

Expected Exchange Rate	Expected French Sales
FFO.90	300
FFO.80	200

The impact of the potential changes of the exchange rate in the earnings of the Lacrosse Companie is shown in Exhibit 3.5. The example shows that a stronger Tunisian dinar affects the financial performance of the Lacrosse Companie positively.

The analysis described for the Lacrosse Companie could be extended to more than one year if more than a one-year forecast of the income statement were available.

Regression analysis can be used to determine a model of the firm's economic exposure. Basically, the historical percentage changes when inflation-adjusted cash flows are regressed against an index reflecting the percentage change in the exchange rate of one currency or an index representing the percentage change in a composite of currencies where the weight assigned to each currency amounts to the proportion of total foreign cash flows attributable to that currency. Hence,

$$CCFP_v = a_0 + a_1 ERC_v + a_v \qquad (1)$$

where

$CCFP_v$ = percentage change in inflation-adjusted cash flows at time t
ERC_v = percentage change in the exchange rate of one currency at time t

Exhibit 3.5
Impact of Expected Exchange Rate on Financial Performance

	TD = FF .90	TD = FF .80
Sales		
1) French	FF 300	FF 200
1) Tunisian	TD 50 = FF 45	TD 50 = FF 40
	------	------
3) Total	FF 345	FF 240
Cost of Goods Sold		
1) French	FF 50	FF 50
2) Tunisian	TD 20 = FF 18	TD 20 = FF 16
	-----	-----
3) Total	FF 68	FF 66
	----------	----------
Gross Profit	FF 277	FF 174
Operating Expenses		
1) French	FF 50	FF 50
2) Tunisian	TD 10 = FF 9	TD 10 = FF 8
	-----	-----
3) Total	FF 59	FF 58
	----------	----------
Earnings before interest & taxes	FF 218	FF 116
Interest		
1) French	FF 60	FF 60
2) Tunisian	TD 5 = FF 4.5	TD 5 = FF 4
	------	------
3) Total	FF 64.5	FF 64
	------------	------
Earnings before taxes	FF 153.5	FF 52

a_0 = intercept
a_1 = regression coefficient
a_v = random variable

or

$$CCFP_v = a_0 + a_1 IERC_v + a_v \tag{2}$$

where

IERC = index of percentage change in several currencies

If the impact of the currency changes were lagged, the equation would become:

$$CCFP_v = a_0 + a_1 IERC_v + a_2 IERC_{v-1} + a_v \tag{3}$$

In each of equations 1, 2, and 3, a_1 and a_2 indicate the impact of changes in the values of currencies on the values of cash flows.

If the relationships described by these equations are judged stable, the equations may then be used to predict the future impact of changes in the values of currencies on the values of cash flows.

The above three equations used cash flows as a proxy for firm value. Another application of the regression approach to assessing a firm's economic exposure to currency movements consists of using the percentage change in stock prices as a proxy for a firm's value and dependent variable and regressing it against both percentage change in a marked index of stocks and percentage change in the value of a currency or an index of currencies. Hence,

$$PCS_v = a_0 + a_1 PCIS_v + a_2 PCVC_v + \alpha_v \tag{4}$$

where

PCS_v   = percentage change in the stock price of a company
PCIS   = percentage change in the market index of stocks
PCVC   = percentage change in the value of a currency or composite of currencies

As in the previous discussion, regression number 4 could be lagged. Hence,

$$PCS_v = a_0 + a_1PCIS_v + a_2PCVC_v + a_3PCVC_{v-1} + \alpha_v \qquad (5)$$

Equation 5 applies when the previous change in the exchange rate has an impact on the changes in cash flows.

The Regression Approach

The regression approach to the definition and measurement of economic exposure rests on the idea that the regression decomposes the probability distribution of a risky asset's domestic currency price of a future with two components: one that is correlated with the exchange rate(s) and therefore can be removed by hedging and another that is independent of the exchange rate(s), whose variance is minimal and remains after hedging. As stated by Michael Adler and Bernard Dumas:

Measuring an asset's exposure by its regression coefficient or coefficients essentially means splitting the random future dollar price into two components. One is the exposure. It is the equivalent of a foreign currency deposit (or a portfolio of foreign currency deposits if the regression is run over many exchange rates.) This component can be perfectly hedged. . . . The second component is not exposed to exchange risk, in the specific sense that its randomness is not correlated with any exchange rate. It may, of course, be exposed to other identifiable risks: but these cannot be hedged with forward currency transactions.[9]

MANAGING ECONOMIC EXPOSURE

Economic exposure is considerably more important to the multinational firm than translation or transaction exposure. It is more difficult to detect, given that it depends on the estimation procedures used to forecast cash flows. It does not result, however, from the idiosyncrasies of the accounting process but from an economic analysis and planning. As such, it requires from management an integrated planning process involving strategies in finance, marketing, production, and so forth. The planning has to start at the strategic rather than the management or operational level to be preventive rather than reactive. Gilles Puchon stated the case as follows: "A proper strategic planning framework that gives full recognition of the financial and operating implications of inflation and foreign exchange can provide senior management greater effectiveness in managing economic exposure in the long run. It might require the integration of operating and financial responsibilities from the policy-making level down to the implementation and performance evaluation levels."[10]

Reacting to economic exposure requires strategic planning in the functional areas of marketing, finance, and production. Marketing strategies may involve careful planning of pricing, product promotion, and distribution to be implemented in the event of exchange rate change. Production strategies may involve securing alternative sources and plants to be used for changes in production techniques and locations in the event of exchange rate changes. Similarly, financial strategies may involve securing alternative lines of credit in various countries to be used in the event of exchange rate changes. In short, the management of economic exposure rests on a proper and timely diversification by the firm of its operations and financing base.

First, a firm, by diversifying its operations intentionally, is in a position to detect disequilibrium when it occurs and to react to worldwide competitive changes by altering its production, sourcing, and sales policies. To the contrary, a purely domestic firm is not in a position to detect disequilibrium in a timely fashion and manage the economic exposure it suffers from international competitors from countries with undervalued currencies.

Second, a firm, by diversifying its financing sources, is in a position to take advantage of unexpected interest differentials, resulting from temporary deviations from the International Fisher Effect, and to reduce default risk by matching the mix of currencies it borrows to the mix of currencies to be realized through its operations.[11]

CONCLUSION

This chapter elaborated on the various problems identifiable with (a) the nature of economic exposure, (b) the impact of economic exposure, (c) the measurement of economic exposure, and (d) the management of economic exposure. It stressed the complexity and the importance of these issues for the profitability of multinational firms and suggested various solutions proposed in practice and in the literature.

NOTES

1. Eugene Flood, Jr., and Donald R. Lessard, "On the Measurement of Operating Exposure to Exchange Rates: A Conceptual Approach," *Financial Management*, Spring 1986, p. 26.

2. S. L. Srinivasulu, "Classifying Foreign Exchange Exposure," *Financial Executive*, February 1983, p. 38.

3. Gilles Puchon, "Defining and Measuring Currency Exposure," in *International Finance Handbook*, vol. 2., ed. Abraham M. George and Ian H. Giddy (New York: Wiley, 1983), pp. 7–8.

4. Jeff Madura, *International Financial Management* (St. Paul, Minn.: West, 1989), pp. 250–251.

5. Arthur I. Stonehill, Niels Ravn, and Kare Dullum, "Management of Foreign Exchange Economic Exposure," in *International Financial Management*, ed. Goran Bergendahl (Stockholm: Norstedts, 1982), pp. 128–148.

6. D. K. Eiteman and A. I. Stonehill, *Multinational Business Finance* (Reading, Mass.: Addison-Wesley, 1989), pp. 174–175.

7. Rita M. Rodriguez and E. Eugene Carter, *International Financial Management*, 3rd ed. (Englewood Cliffs, N.J.: Prentice-Hall, 1984), p. 310.

8. Christine R. Heckman, "Don't Blame Currency Values for Strategic Errors," *Midland Corporate Finance Journal*, Fall 1986, pp. 45–55.

9. Michael Adler and Bernard Dumas, "Exposure to Currency Risk: Definition and Measurement," *Financial Management*, Spring 1984, p. 47.

10. Puchon, "Defining and Measuring Currency Exposure," p. 7.

11. Eiteman and Stonehill, *Multinational Business Finance*, p. 184.

REFERENCES

Abuaf, Niso. "The Nature and Management of Foreign Exchange Risk." *Midland Corporate Finance Journal*, Fall 1986, pp. 30–44.

Adler, Michael, and Bernard Dumas. "Exposure to Currency Risk: Definition and Measurement" *Financial Management*, Spring 1984, pp. 41–50.

———. "International Portfolio Choice and Corporation Finance: A Synthesis." *Journal of Finance*, June 1983, pp. 925–984.

Aliber, Robert Z. *Exchange Risk and Corporate International Finance*. New York: Wiley; Halsted Press, 1978.

Ankrom, Robert K. "Top-Level Approach to the Foreign Exchange Problem." *Harvard Business Review*, July–August 1974, pp. 79–90.

Antl, Boris, and Richard Ensor, eds. *Management of Foreign Exchange Risk*. 2d ed. London: Euromoney Publications, 1982.

Barnett, John S. "Corporate Foreign Exposure Strategy Formulations." *Columbia Journal of World Business*, Winter 1976, pp. 87–97.

Boothe, Robert, and Jeff Madura. "Reducing Exposure to Exchange Rate Risk: A Case Study." *Long-Range Planning*, June 1985, pp. 98–101.

Calderon-Rossell, Jorge R. "Covering Foreign Exchange Risks of Single Transactions: A Framework for Analysis." *Financial Management*, Autumn 1979, pp. 78–85.

Carter, E. Eugene, and Rita M. Rodriguez. "Foreign Exchange Models: What 40 U.S. Multinationals Think." *Euromoney*, March 1978, pp. 95–111.

Christofides, N., R. D. Hewins, and G. R. Salkin. "Graph Theoretic Approaches to Foreign Exchange Operations." *Journal of Financial and Quantitative Analysis*, September 1979, pp. 481–500.

Dufey, Gunter. "Corporate Finance and Exchange Rate Variations." *Financial Management*, Summer 1972, pp. 51–57.

Eaker, Mark R., and Dwight Grant. "Optimal Hedging of Uncertain and Long-Term Foreign Exchange Exposure." *Journal of Banking and Finance*, June 1985, pp. 222–231.

Einzig, Paul. *A Textbook on Foreign Exchange*. London: Macmillan, 1966.

Eiteman, D. K., and A. I. Stonehill. *Multinational Business Finance*. Reading, Mass.: Addison-Wesley, 1989.

Enthoven, Adolf J. H. "International Management Accounting: A Challenge for Accountants." *Management Accounting*, September 1980, pp. 25–32.

Everett, Robert M., Abraham M. George, and Aryeh Blumberg. "Appraising Currency Strengths and Weaknesses: An Operational Model for Calculating Parity Exchange Rates." *Journal of International Business Studies*, Fall 1980, pp. 80–91.

Flood, Eugene, Jr., and Donald R. Lessard. "On the Measurement of Operating Exposure to Exchange Rates: A Conceptual Approach." *Financial Management*, Spring 1986, pp. 25–36.

Frankel, J. A. "The Diversifiability of Exchange Risk." *Journal of International Economics*, no. 9 (1979): 379–393.

Fredrikson, E. Bruce. "On the Measurement of Foreign Income." *Journal of Accounting Research*, Autumn 1968, pp. 208–221.

George, Abraham. "Cash Flow versus Accounting Exposures to Currency Risk." *California Management Review*, Summer 1978, pp. 50–54.

Giddy, Ian H. "Exchange Risk: Whose View?" *Financial Management*, Summer 1977, pp. 23–33.

Gray, S. J. "The Impact of International Accounting Differences from a Security-Analysis Perspective: Some European Evidence." *Journal of Accounting Research*, Spring 1980, pp. 69–76.

Gull, Don S. "Composite Foreign Exchange Risk." *The Columbia Journal of World Business*, Fall 1975, pp. 51–69.

Hagemann, Helmut. "Anticipate Your Long-Term Foreign Exchange Risks." *Harvard Business Review*, March/April 1977, pp. 81–88.

Heckerman, Donald. "The Exchange Risks of Foreign Operations." *Journal of Business*, January 1972, pp. 42–48.

Heckman, Christine R. "Don't Blame Currency Values for Strategic Errors." *Midland Corporate Finance Journal*, Fall 1986, pp. 45–55.

———. "Measuring Foreign Exchange Exposure: A Practical Theory and Its Application." *Financial Analysts Journal*, September–October 1983, pp. 59–65.

Heywood, John. *Foreign Exchange and the Corporate Treasurer*. London: A. & C. Black, 1979, p. 59.

Imai Yutaka. "Exchange Rate Risk Protection in International Business." *Journal of Financial and Quantitative Analysis*, September 1975, pp. 447–456.

Jacque, L. L. "Management of Foreign Exchange Risk." *Journal of International Business Studies*, Spring/Summer 1981, pp. 81–101.

Kaufold, Howard, and Michael Smirlock. "Managing Corporate Exchange and Interest Rate Exposure." *Financial Management*, Autumn 1986, pp. 64–72.

Koenig, Peter. "Using a Captive to Cope with Currency Exposure." *Institutional Investor*, November 1981, pp. 191–194.

Kohlhagen, Steven W. "A Model of Optimal Foreign Exchange Hedging without Exchange Rate Projections." *Journal of International Business Studies*, Fall 1978, pp. 9–19.

Kwok, Chuck C. Y. "Hedging Foreign Exchange Exposure: Independent vs. Integrative Approaches." *Journal of International Business Studies*, Summer 1987, pp. 33–52.

Lessard, Donald R., and S. B. Lightstone. "Volatile Exchange Rates Can Put Operations at Risk." *Harvard Business Review*, July–August 1986, pp. 107–114.

Levich, Richard M., and Clas G. Wihlborg, eds. *Exchange Risk and Exposure*. Lexington, Mass.: Lexington Books, 1980.

Logue, Dennis E., and George S. Oldfield. "Managing Foreign Assets When Foreign Exchange Markets Are Efficient." *Financial Management*, Summer 1977, pp. 16–22.

Madura, Jeff. *International Financial Management*. St. Paul, Minn.: West, 1989.

Madura, Jeff, and L. A. Soengen. "Asymmetric Risk Aversion and the Real Costs of Hedging in the Foreign Exchange Market." *European Journal of Accounting and Finance*, July–August 1985, pp. 304–309.

Madura, Jeff, and E. Theodore Veit. "Use of Currency Options for International Cash Management." *Journal of Cash Management*, January–February 1986, pp. 42–48.

Makin, John H. "The Portfolio Method of Managing Foreign Exchange Risk." *Euromoney*, August 1976, pp. 58–64.

Olstein, Robert A. "Devaluation and Multinational Reporting." *Financial Analysts Journal*, September–October 1973, pp. 65–73.

Pleak, R. E. "An Analysis of the FASB's Treatment of Foreign Currency Translation." *Management Accounting*, September 1977, pp. 29–32.

Puchon, Gilles. "Defining and Measuring Currency Exposure." In *International Finance Handbook*, vol. 2. Edited by Abraham M. George and Ian H. Giddy. New York: Wiley, 1983.

Prindl, Andreas R. *Foreign Exchange Risk*. New York: Wiley, 1976.

Reier, Sharon. "Socal's Great Currency Debate." *Institutional Investor*, January 1982, pp. 210–212.

Rodriguez, Rita M. "Corporate Exchange Risk Management: Theme and Aberrations." *Journal of Finance*, May 1981, pp. 427–439.

———. "FASB No. 8: What Has It Done for Us?" *Financial Analysts Journal*, March–April 1977, pp. 40–48.

Rodriguez, Rita M., and E. Eugene Carter. *International Financial Management*. 3rd ed. Englewood Cliffs, N.J.: Prentice-Hall, 1984.

Roll, Richard, and Bruno Solnik. "A Pure Foreign Exchange Asset Pricing Model." *Journal of International Economics*, May 1977, pp. 161–179.

"The Rush to Hedge Currency." *Business Week*, July 20, 1981, p. 147.

Schoenfeld, Hanns-Martin. "International Accounting: Development, Issues, and Future Directions." *Journal of International Business Studies*, Fall 1981, pp. 83–100.

Shank, John K., Jesse F. Dillard, and Richard J. Murdock. *Assessing the Economic Impact of FASB No. 8*. New York: Financial Executives Research Foundation, 1979.

Shapiro, Alan C., and David P. Ruttenberg. "Managing Exchange Risks in a Floating World." *Financial Management*, Summer 1976, pp. 48–58.

Shepherd, Sidney A. "Forwards, Futures, and Currency Options as Foreign Exchange Risk Protection." *Canadian Banker*, December 1983, pp. 22–25.

Smith, Alan F. "Temporal Method: Temporary Mode?" *Management Accounting*, February 1978, pp. 21–26.

Soenen, Luc A., and E. G. F. van Winkel. "The Real Costs of Hedging in the Forward Exchange Market." *Management International Review* 22, no. 1 (1982): 53–59.

Srinivasulu, S. L. "Classifying Foreign Exchange Exposure." *Financial Executive*, February 1983, p. 38.

———. "Currency Denomination of Debt: Lessons from Rolls-Royce and Laker Airways." *Business Horizons*, September–October 1983, pp. 19–23.

Stanley, Marjorie T., and Stanley B. Block. "Portfolio Diversification of Foreign Exchange Risk: An Empirical Study." *Management International Review*, no. 1 (1980): 83–92.

Stonehill, Arthur I., Niels Ravn, and Kare Dullum. "Management of Foreign Exchange Economic Exposure." In *International Financial Management*. Edited by Goran Bergendahl. Stockholm: Norstedts, 1982, pp. 128–148.

"Treasures of Multinationals Plan Ways to Handle Currency Swings." *The Wall Street Journal*, January 24, 1984, p. 35.

Westerfield, Janice M. "How U.S. Multinationals Manage Currency Risk." *Business Review*, March–April 1980, pp. 19–27.

Wihlborg, Clas. "Economics of Exposure Management of Foreign Subsidiaries of Multinational Corporations." *Journal of International Business Studies*, Winter 1980, pp. 9–18.

Yang, James G. S. "Managing Multinational Exchange Risks." *Management Accounting*, February 1986, pp. 45–52.

4

Managing Transaction Exposure

The previous chapter introduced the three types of exposure affecting a multi-national corporation and focused on the management of economic exposure. This chapter continues with the management of exposure paradigm by focusing particularly on the management of transaction exposure. As a result of the focus on the management of transaction exposure, currency trading has reached the phenomenal figure of \$128.9 billion a day;[1] 64 percent of the trades are in the spot market, consisting of traders' communication via telephones and computers. The rest of the market includes the forward market, the currency options and futures market, and the swap market. Hence, this chapter elaborates on techniques used to manage the transaction exposure in order to avoid serious economic losses. These techniques include contractual hedges, operating strategies, and swap agreements.

NATURE OF TRANSACTION EXPOSURE

Transaction exposure arises whenever the future transaction of a firm is affected by potential exchange rate fluctuations. A firm faces a transaction exposure whenever it has a receivable, a payable, a revenue, an expense, or a forward contract denominated in other than the functional currency in which the firm does most of its business. In all of these transactions, the firm faces a situation of uncertainty because it does not know the exact exchange rate at the time of the settlement of these transactions. Transactions that create the potential for a transaction exposure include (a) the purchase or sale of goods, services, or assets to be settled in foreign currencies; (b) the borrowing or lending of funds to be settled in foreign currencies; and (c) the buying of a forward exchange contract. Suppose that a U.S. firm sells equipment worth \$20.0 million to a French firm for FF140 million to be made in francs six months after the date of sale. The current exchange rate is FF7/\$. At the payment date, the exchange rate is FF8/\$, and the French firm remits FF140 million as contracted. The U.S. firm finds itself experiencing a transaction loss since the FF received amounted to \$17.5 million (FF140 million/FF8/\$) and is \$2.5 million shorter than the account receivable of \$20.0 million. The \$2.5 million is a transaction loss arising from a transaction expense. The U.S. firm could have avoided the loss by asking for payment in U.S. dollars. The transaction exposure is not eliminated in this case but is shifted to the French firm.

In the case of a multinational firm, each subsidiary faces transaction exposure in different currencies. Therefore the strategy of the multinational should be to determine the net transaction exposure of each subsidiary, that is, the exposure created by the transaction resulting in inflows and outflows of cash. The net transaction exposure of each subsidiary should be determined on a currency-by-currency basis. This allows the multinational firm to offset the positions between currencies and render the hedging of each position in each subsidiary unnecessary. What is necessary for the implementation of such a strategy is a centralization transaction exposure management, to allow the multinational firm to consolidate the positions of each subsidiary, offset positions between subsidiaries, and identify the net transaction exposure that needs to be managed.

HEDGING TRANSACTION EXPOSURE

The question whether or not hedging is desirable arises. It arises because hedging relies on forward contracts, and if the forward rate underestimates or overestimates the future spot rate, hedging results in higher costs in some periods and lower costs in others. If this underestimation or overestimation happens with equal frequency, hedging is not desirable. Therefore, hedging becomes desirable if the firm hedges future payables when it expects appreciation of the currency denominating the payables and hedges future receivables when it expects depreciation of the currency denominating the receivables.

Assuming that the firm finds hedging to be desirable, it has to choose among the following hedging techniques:

a. Forward contract hedge

b. Money market hedge

c. Futures contract hedge

d. Currency option hedge

FORWARD CONTRACT HEDGE

A forward contract hedge, or forward hedge or forward exchange market hedge, consists of arranging with a bank for delivery and payment, at or around the desired future date (i.e., at a "fixed" date, or during a "delivery-date option" period usually not exceeding thirty days), of an amount of foreign currency at a contractual forward rate. The contract enables the firm to avoid the uncertainty of the future spot rate by locking in the rate it will pay or receive at the forward rate. The important point to remember is that the forward contract hedge involves a contract between a firm and a bank. A firm uses the forward contract to hedge either a payable or a receivable denominated in foreign currency rather than not hedging the transaction. The two examples below illustrate the decision to hedge either a payable or a receivable. Although most forward contracts are short term, multinationals are now relying on long-term forward contracts with a maturity of up to ten years or more. In addition, given that several cash flows of the same currency are generally expected to arrive at different times during the financial year, the financial manager is advised to hedge these cash flows independently rather than include them under one integrative hedging plan.[2]

The Hedging of a Payable

Assume that a U.S. firm buys an asset for 200,000 British pounds to be paid in thirty days. The thirty-day forward rate at the time of the purchase is $1.45/£. The nominal cost of hedging is therefore $290,000 (200,000 × $1.45/£). If the spot rate at the time of payment is $1.30, the nominal cost of the payable without hedging is $260,000 (200,000 × $1.30). In other words, the real cost of hedging payables is equal to $30,000 ($290,000 − $260,000). The formula for the real cost of hedging payables is:

$$RCHR = NCHP - NCPW$$

where

$RCHP$ = real cost of hedging payables
$NCHP$ = nominal cost of hedging payables
$NCPW$ = nominal cost of payable without hedging

The above analysis of the real cost of hedging payables can only take place after the fact and at the date of payment of the payable. The management of the multinational firm may, however, develop an a priori probability distribution of the future spot rate at the time of the purchase transaction. Such probability distribution is shown in Exhibit 4.1. Notice here that the real cost of hedging the payable is different depending on the estimated future spot rate. Under these conditions of uncertainty and on the basis of the knowledge of the prior probability distribution of the future spot rate, the firm may compute the expected value of the real cost of hedging payables as follows:

$$\text{Expected value of RCHP} = \Sigma\, P_i \times RCHP_i$$

Exhibit 4.1
Probabilistic Analysis of Hedging Payables

Potential Spot Rate	Prior Probability	Nominal Cost of Payables Without Hedging	Nominal Cost of Hedging	Real Cost of Hedging
$1.35	0.20	$270,000	$290,000	$20,000
$1.30	0.15	$260,000	$290,000	$30,000
$1.34	0.22	$268,000	$290,000	$22,000
$1.41	0.18	$282,000	$290,000	$ 8,000
$1.45	0.20	$290,000	$290,000	-$ 2,000
$1.47	0.05	$294,000	$290,000	-$ 4,000

Expected value of RCHP = 0.20 ($20,000) + 0.15 ($30,000) + 0.22 ($22,000)
+ 0.18 ($8,000) + 0.20 (−$2,000) + 0.05 (−$4,000) = $4,000 + $4,500
+ $4,840 + $1,440 − $400 − $200 = $14,180

This expected value of the real cost of hedging of $14,180 coupled with the probabilistic information included in Exhibit 4.1 facilitate the decision of whether or not to hedge the payables. Exhibit 4.1 shows that there is a 25 percent chance that hedging will be better in terms of cost than no hedging. The degree of risk aversion espoused by the management of the multinational firm will determine the final decision. For an extra cost, the firm may elect to acquire additional information, update the a priori probability distribution to obtain an a posteriori probability through the use of the Baye's Theorem.

The Hedging of a Receivable

In the case of a receivable, the formula for the determination of the real cost of hedging receivables (RCHR) is equal to:

RCHR = NRWH − NRHR

where

NRWH = nominal revenues denominated in home currency received without hedging
NRHR = nominal revenues denominated in home currency received with hedging

The procedure is the same as with hedging payables in that the firm may elect to determine an a priori probability distribution of NRWH and compute an expected value of RCHR. It may also elect to use additional information to update the prior probability distribution to improve its decision of whether or not to hedge.

MONEY MARKET HEDGE

The money market hedge involves the use of surplus cash or borrowed money to hedge a receivable or payable and invest the proceeds of the transaction in a money market. Money market hedges on payables and receivables are illustrated below.

Money Market Hedge on Payables

Assume that the XYZ company, an American importer of machinery, has a payable of DM3,200,000 that comes to term in thirty days. The management of the firm decides to use its actual surplus of cash to buy a one-month German security earning 7.2 percent per year (0.6 percent per month). The amount to be used for the German security amounts to:

$$DM3,200,000/(1 + 0.6 \%) = DM3,180,914.50$$

If the German spot rate at the time of the transaction is $0.505/DM, the amount needed by the firm to buy the German security is equal to: $1,606,361.80 (DM3,180,914.50 × $0.505/DM). What happened in this money market hedge is that the XYZ firm used $1,606,361.80 of its surplus cash to invest in a DM3,180,914.50 German security that earns 0.6 percent per month and that at the end of the month will generate the DM3,200,000 needed to pay the payable.

The previous example assumes that the XYZ firm has surplus cash. In case the firm does not have surplus cash, it will proceed by (a) borrowing the amount needed through a loan and (b) investing it in the German short-term security. Using the previous XYZ example, the firm needs to (a) borrow $1,606,361.80 from a U.S. bank assuming a 7 percent interest rate,(b) convert the $1,606,361.80 into DM3,180,914.50, (c) buy a DM3,180,914.50 German security earning 0.6 percent per month, and (d) repay the loan and interest that will amount to $1,617,606.30.

Money Market Hedge on Receivables

Assume that the ABC Company, a German exporter of machinery in the Federal Republic of Germany, has a receivable of $6,336,633.60 (DM3,200,000) to be received in a month. The German firm may elect to (a) borrow U.S. dollars and convert them to marks to hedge the receivable and (b) use the proceeds of the loan to invest in short-term German securities. Hence, assuming the U.S. interest rate is 0.7 percent per month, the German firm needs to borrow the following:

$$\frac{\$6,336,633.60}{1.007} = \$6,292,585.50$$

The amount borrowed is converted to DM to cover the receivables: DM3,177,755.60. The firm then proceeds to invest the amount borrowed in a German security earning 0.8 percent per month, which at the end of the month will be worth DM3,203,177.60. What results from this transaction is that the payment of the receivable to the German firm at the end of the month will cover the loan, and the investment in a one-month German security will yield a final amount of DM3,203,177.60.

CURRENCY OPTIONS HEDGE

Currency options hedge or options market hedges may be preferable to futures, or forward hedges and money market hedges, in the event that these techniques fail due to an appreciation of the payables currency or a depreciation of the receivables currency over the hedged period. The currency options hedge consists of buying a call option to hedge payables or a put option to hedge receivables. Both option hedges protect the firm from adverse exchange rate changes and create benefits to the firm in the case of favorable exchange rate changes. The currency option hedges for payables and receivables are illustrated below.

Options Market Hedge

To hedge a payable using currency options, a firm would need to buy a currency call option that gives it the right to buy a specified amount of a particular currency at a specified price (the exercise price) within a given period. At the end of the period the firm may elect to exercise the option and buy the currency or may elect not to. The firm can buy the call option on the Philadelphia Stock Exchange or from a bank. Assume that the XYZ Company, an American importer of British machinery, has 200,000 British pounds thirty days from now. Also assume that the firm faces two alternatives:

1. Buy the call option on the Philadelphia Stock Exchange for a strike price of 1.65, a premium cost of $0.035/pound, and a contract size of 12,500
2. Buy the call option in the over-the-counter (bank) market for a strike price of 1.65 and a premium of 2 percent when the spot rate is 1.67

The cost of the first alternative is as follows:

Premium costs per option (0.035 × 12,500) = $437.50
Brokerage cost per option = 30.00
Total cost per option = $467.50

Options cost per pound ($465/12,500) = $0.0374
Number of options needed (200,000/12,500) = 16
Total cost of options (16 × $0.0374) = $7,480

The cost of the second alternative is as follows:

Size of the option $\times$ premium $\times$ spot rate $=$ cost of the option
$\$200,000 \times 0.02 \times 1.67 = \$6,680$

In this case the XYZ firm would purchase the call option with the lower cost. Given that it is a three-month option, the premium cost of the option in three months, and assuming a cost of capital of 8 percent (2 percent per quarter), will be $\$6,680 (1.2) = \$6,813.60$, or 0.034068 per pound ($\$6,813.60$).

The fate of the call option depends on the potential spot rate of the pound when the payables are due. Assume that there are three possible scenarios for the spot rate: 1.62, 1.66, or 1.68. The effects of each of the spot rates on the cost of XYZ payables differ depending on the potential spot rates:

a. Under the first scenario, the spot rate is $\$1.62$, and XYZ would prefer to let the option expire and buy pounds in the spot market at $\$1.62$. In such a case, the dollar amount paid by XYZ including the premium is $[(\$1.62 + \$0.034068) \times 200,000] = \$330,813.60$.

b. Under the second and third scenario, the spot rate is $\$1.66$ or $\$1.68$, and XYZ would prefer to exercise the option and purchase the pounds at $\$1.65$. The dollar amount paid by XYZ including the premium would be $[(\$1.65 + \$0.034068) \times 200,000] = \$336,813.60$ under both scenarios 2 and 3.

Options Market Hedge for Receivables

To hedge a payable using currency options, a firm would need to buy a currency put option that gives it the right to sell a specified amount of particular currency at a specified price (the exercise price) within a given period. At the end of the period, if the spot rate is higher than the exercise price, the firm may elect to sell the currency at the spot rate and let the option expire. If the spot rate is lower than the exercise price, however, the firm will elect to exercise the option.

Assume that the ABC company, an American exporter of machinery to the United Kingdom, has a receivable of 200,000 pounds due in three months. To avert the risks of a depreciation of the pound against the dollar, the ABC company decides to buy a put option that has an exercise price of $\$1.60$ and a premium of $\$0.04$ per unit.

Again, the fate of the put option depends on the potential spot rates when the receivables are due. Assume that there are three possible scenarios for the spot rate: $\$1.58$, $\$1.59$, or $\$1.62$. The effects of the spot rate on the cost of XYZ receivables differ depending on each of the scenarios:

1. Under the first scenario, the spot rate is $\$1.58$, and the ABC company prefers to exercise the option and sell the pounds at the exercise price of $\$1.60$. In such a case the dollar amount received from hedging the receivables after accounting for the premium paid is $(\$1.60 - \$0.04) \times 200,000 = \$312,000$.

2. Under the second scenario, the spot rate is $1.59, and the ABC company prefers to exercise the option and sell the pounds at the exercise price of $1.60. In such a case the dollar amount received from hedging the receivables after accounting for the premium paid is still ($1.60 − $0.04) × 200,000 = $312,000.

3. Under the third scenario, the spot rate is $1.62, and the ABC company prefers to let the option expire and sell the pounds at $1.62. In such a case the dollar amount received from hedging the receivables after accounting for the premium paid is ($1.62 − $0.04) × 200,000 = $316.000.

OPERATING STRATEGIES TO REDUCE TRANSACTION EXPOSURE

In certain cases hedging may not completely eliminate the transaction exposure because the firm may not know the exact amount of revenues or expenditures arising from a transaction denominated in foreign currency. Various operating strategies may be used in such cases to reduce transaction exposure. Examples of these strategies include (a) leading and lagging, (b) borrowing and lending, (c) cross-hedging, (d) currency diversification, (e) reinvoicing centers, (f) hedging against fluctuating interest rates, and (g) gold hedges. Each of those techniques is explained below.

Leading and Lagging

To offset existing foreign exchange exposure, firms sometimes elect to use the operating strategy of leading and lagging. *Leading and lagging* consists of speeding up collections or lagging payments in payables denominated in a foreign currency. It is sometimes known as an "operating hedge." The basic idea is that when a firm expects a currency to appreciate, it speeds up payments of imports and debts and slows the collection of export receipts. When it expects a currency to depreciate, it reverses the tactic, slowing import payments and accelerating collections. Leading and lagging may be (a) more feasible between affiliates given the common set of goals for the consolidated group and (b) more adaptable to a firm operating on an integrated worldwide basis. Although possible with a 100 percent-owned affiliate, it may be unfair to minority stockholders in cases in which the affiliate is not wholly owned. It also may be be unfair to 100 percent-owned profit centers when the performance evaluation of the centers is adjusted to take into account the sacrifices created by their acceptance of leading and lagging between affiliates. Leading and lagging is possible between independent firms if arrangements and adjustments are made between the firms.

Although seemingly straightforward, the leading and lagging techniques for reducing transaction exposure end up shifting the burden to one firm or affiliate in a particular country, which may explain the limits imposed by some governments on the allowed rate. Exhibit 4.2 gives examples of some of the limits on leads and lags and netting in selected countries. *Netting* refers to the process of offsetting intragroup transactions (between parent and subsidiary or subsidiary and other subsidiary) to reduce transfer values and only reflect and account for the net balance.[3]

Borrowing and Lending

Another way of minimizing translation and transaction exposure is to use foreign currency credits, such as foreign bank loans, overdrafts, and lines of credit, to finance repayables in foreign currencies. An additional way is to borrow in a local currency in anticipation of a devaluation and to convert the proceeds into a strong currency. Also, the firm may borrow in a local currency in anticipation of a devaluation and convert the proceeds into a strong currency. Finally, the firm may borrow in a local currency and use the proceeds to buy commodities from that country before their prices increase as a result of devaluation. This action is known as a "commodity hedge."

Three obstacles may arise against the use of borrowing and lending. First, some countries limit the amount of local money that foreigners can borrow. Second, companies may be holding too much foreign currency and end up scrambling to convert their local currency deposits and receivables into more usable bond currency—such as pounds, dollars, and marks—and then repatriating the cash to the United States. Third, some countries may become inclined to impose stricter controls on lending by their banks at home and through their foreign subsidiaries. One such proposal was made in February 1984 by the West German Finance Ministry to limit a bank's credit exposure to any single borrower to 50 percent of the bank's equity, down from the current 75 percent.[4] In fact, the proposal would extend Germany's banking rules to foreign subsidiaries, especially in Luxembourg where regulations specify only that a bank's lending cannot exceed thirty-three times its equity, which may have encouraged Luxembourg subsidiaries of German banks to exceed the lending norms applying at home.

Hedging Against Fluctuating Interest Rates

Corporate treasurers have started to hedge against fluctuating interest rates as much as they have been doing against currency shifts. Although some are still using the regulated financial futures markets in Chicago and London, others are going off-market through London banks. The off-market futures hedging is simpler and more flexible than the regulated markets. As an example, a corporate treasurer who has to borrow $3 million three months from now to finance inventory buildup would want to lock in low current interest rates. To do so he would find a bank willing to give him an acceptable rate. When the time comes to borrow, if interest rates have risen, the bank would pay the company any difference in the interest rates; if, on the other hand, interest rates have fallen, the company would pay the bank the difference. Under the regulated financial

Exhibit 4.2
Limits on Leads and Lags and Netting in Selected Countries

Country	Export lag	Export lead	Import lag	Import lead	Netting
Argentina	180 days for priority exports. Longer terms may be allowed under government financing arrangements. 15 days for some traditional exports (e.g. grains).	360 days. For goods stipulated under Law 21453, 180 days.	120 days. For noncapital goods originating in LAIA countries, 90 days, except for some LAIA-negotiated goods for which immediate settlement is required.	120 days to five years for 5% of the f.o.b. value of a list of capital imports costing between $50,000 and $2 million. Larger amounts require CB approval. Up to 15% of the value of these goods (less advance payments) may be prepaid if this part of the payment is made under a documentary credit. The other 85% must be amortized within six months of shipment. Some exceptions apply.	Not allowed.
Australia	Allowed—no limit.	Allowed—no limit.	Allowed—no limit.	Allowed—no limit.	Allowed.
Belgium	180 days. BLEI approval required for longer periods, usually granted, except when currency is under speculative pressure.	Allowed—no limit.	Allowed—no limit.	90 days. BLEI approval required for longer periods. Extensions may be unlimited, but only for one third of the shipment amount.	Allowed for financial transactions. BLEI approval required for bilateral netting of trade transactions over Bfr25 million and multilateral netting of trade transactions. Not allowed for netting of trade against financial transactions.
Brazil	Permission required.	Allowed—no limit. Prepayment of at least 15% of shipment's value is required when credit terms exceed two years.	180 days to eight years for foreign durable goods, raw materials and capital equipment.	Not allowed, except on some high-priority items, where a 10–20% down payment may be permitted on credit terms exceeding one year.	Not allowed.
Canada	Allowed—no limit.	Allowed—no limit.	Allowed—no limit.	Allowed—no limit.	Allowed.
Chile	90 days.	90 days.	120 days minimum. For longer periods, payment may be made five days in advance of due date.	Not allowed, but exceptions may be made for partial payment of capital imports.	Not allowed.
Denmark	30 days maximum. Must conform to usual commercial practice for particular product.	Allowed when customary within the trade.	Allowed when customary within the trade.	30 days maximum. Must conform to usual commercial practice for particular product.	Allowed.

Egypt	360 days.	Allowed—no limit.	90 days. CB will accept longer terms when stipulated in contract.	Allowed if against letter of credit.	Allowed.
Finland	Allowed—no limit.	Allowed—no limit.	360 days. Supplier credit may not exceed 180 days without authorization.	Allowed—no limit.	Allowed.
France	Allowed—no limit.	Allowed—no limit.	Allowed—no limit.	Allowed for up to 30% of the value of the import.	Permission required. Beginning to be freely granted.
Germany	Allowed—no limit.	Allowed—no limit.	Allowed—no limit.	Allowed—no limit.	Allowed.
Greece	Three years maximum. CB accepts any terms stipulated in contract. If none are stipulated, a 90-day limit is applied.	Allowed, when stipulated in the invoice.	Allowed, when stipulated in the invoice.	Allowed, when stipulated in the invoice.	Allowed.
Hong Kong	Allowed—no limit.	Allowed—no limit.	Allowed—no limit.	Allowed—no limit.	Allowed.
Ireland	180 days. Extensions are sometimes allowed.	Allowed—no limit.	Allowed—no limit.	Not allowed. Some exceptions.	Permission required.
Italy	18 months for payments from non-OECD countries. No limit for payments from OECD countries.	Five years.	Five years for imports from non-OECD countries. No limit on OECD imports.	120 days for amounts over L10 million. Up to 10% of the import's value may be prepaid 360 days in advance. 360 days for amounts under L10 million.	Allowed for bilateral netting of trade transactions. UIC approval required for bilateral netting of financial transactions. Ministry of Trade approval required for multilateral netting.
Japan	360 days.	360 days.	360 days.	360 days. Payment for plant and equipment can be made up to three years in advance.	Permission required for bilateral netting of trade transactions. Granted if between parent and wholly owned sub and cumulative sum of transactions does not exceed Y3 million. Multilateral netting is not allowed.

NOTES: CB = National central bank; LAIA = Latin American Integration Association; BLEI = Belgium Luxembourg Exchange Institute; UIC = The Italian foreign exchange authority.

Exhibit 4.2 (continued)

Country	Export lag	Export lead	Import lag	Import lead	Netting
Korea	360 days. Extensions up to three years have been allowed.	120 days. Limited to 1% of annual exports for large companies (over 300 employees) and 6% for smaller companies.	60 days. Limited to 30 days for imports from Japan, Taiwan, the Philippines and Hong Kong.	360 days.	Bilateral netting allowed under strict guidelines. Firms must register with authorized bank, hold at least 50% equity, import most raw materials and export most of the end product.
Malaysia	180 days.	Allowed—no limit.	Allowed—no limit.	Allowed—no limit.	Allowed, except for intercompany transactions involving exports from Malaysia-based companies.
Mexico	Allowed—no limit.	Allowed—no limit.	Suppliers demand payment upon delivery. 90-day minimum term for short-term import credits. 360-day minimum average amortization for long-term import credits.	Allowed at the controlled rate for up to 10% of import's value. Up to 20% allowed on long-term import credits.	Not allowed.
Netherlands	Allowed—no limit.	Allowed—no limit.	Allowed—no limit.	Allowed—no limit.	Allowed. Must be reported to the CB for statistical purposes.
Nigeria	90 days.	Allowed—no limit.	Most trade is being handled through letters of credit after prior purchase of FX by importer.	Permission required. Maximum permitted: 15%, and only on capital expenditures.	Not allowed.
Norway	One year. Commerce Ministry license required for longer terms.	Commerce Ministry license required.	Five years. Commerce Ministry license required for longer terms.	90 days. Exceptions granted for goods on special order.	Bank of Norway permission required, usually granted, except for financial transactions requiring licenses.
Philippines	60 days. Extensions granted to enable exporters to meet international competition.	Allowed—no limit.	365 days.	Not allowed.	Not allowed. Some exceptions may be made.
Portugal	180 days.	90 days. Permission required for longer terms and if payment exceeds 25% for capital equipment or 10% for other goods.	180 days.	Permission required.	Allowed.

Singapore	Allowed—no limit.	Allowed—no limit.	Allowed—no limit.	Allowed—no limit.	Allowed.
South Africa	180 days. May be increased to 360 days to capture new market or protect an existing one.	Allowed—no limit.	Allowed—no limit.	Permission required. Granted for specially designed capital goods up to a maximum of one third of the total cost. Foreign manufacturer must provide cost documentation and request payment.	Permission required.
Spain	30 days.	Allowed—no limit.	90 days, but in practice 120 days is tolerated.	90 days.	Permission required.
Sweden	Allowed—no limit.	Allowed—no limit.	Allowed within customary terms of trade.	Allowed for down payments on machinery for up to one third of shipment value, for goods worth less than Skr100,000 and for goods soon to be delivered.	Allowed for bilateral netting of trade transactions. All other netting requires CB approval.
Switzerland	Allowed—no limit.	Allowed—no limit.	Allowed—no limit.	Allowed—no limit.	Allowed.
Taiwan	360 days.	360 days.	360 days.	360 days.	Allowed.
Thailand	180 days.	Allowed within customary terms of trade.	Allowed within customary terms of trade.	Allowed within customary terms of trade.	Permission required.
UK	Allowed—no limit.	Allowed—no limit.	Allowed—no limit.	Allowed—no limit.	Allowed.
US	Allowed—no limit.	Allowed—no limit.	Allowed—no limit.	Allowed—no limit.	Allowed.
Venezuela	Not allowed.	Not allowed.	Not allowed for payments made with official-rate (B14.5:$1) dollars. Allowed without limit for payments made with free market dollars.	Not allowed for payments made with official-rate (B14.5:$1) dollars. Allowed without limit for payments made with free market dollars.	Allowed.

* Based on information obtained locally from finance ministries and central and commercial banks, and from BI's *Financing Foreign Operations*. Netting information covers bilateral and multilateral transactions unless otherwise noted.

Source: *Business International Money Report*, August 8, 1988, pp. 266–267. Reprinted with permission.

futures market, the hedger pays a little every day, whereas under the off-market he pays all of it at the end of the transaction. Most banks participating in such a hedge feel that they are offering a simpler way to hedge than the future markets.

Gold Hedge

The shortage of foreign currencies in the developing countries means that overseas subsidiaries of multinational companies may end up loaded with weak currencies like Brazilian cruzeiros and Mexican pesos. In 1982, for example, a growing number of U.S. multinational firms bought gold on the Brazilian market to protect their corporate assets against the country's runaway inflation of 107 percent and almost weekly devaluations. In the past, the companies had bought government indexed bonds to provide insurance against devaluation and inflation. A loss of confidence in these dollar-pegged government bonds led to the move to gold. Gold, in fact, presents much less political risk and yields a better return than the government indexed bonds. Moreover, gold has a tax advantage over bonds because it can be carried as an unrealized gain until resale, whereas revenues derived from bonds are immediately taxable. Another advantage of a gold hedge is the existence of a direct relationship in the short run as well as in the long run between the dollar price per unit of other major foreign currencies and the dollar price of gold, which suggests a certain degree of interchangeability of the two assets.[5]

An evaluation of the gold hedge was made as follows:

The adequacy of gold as a means to store value is limited during periods of high inflation rates since it does not pay interest or dividends. Its price fluctuations have been so great that it has either appreciated or depreciated more than the inflation rate. Despite its inability to serve as inflation hedge, the store of value function of gold had been of significant importance to investors worldwide. Its qualities as a hedge against monetary devaluations, political or economic uncertainty, and crises resulting from military confrontation, social upheaval, and terrorism have made it an insurance policy against disaster. [6]

Reinvoicing Centers

The reinvoicing center rests on the idea of creating a centralized unit that has all the transaction exposure of the multinational firms. In a sense, the affiliates of the firm are encouraged to trade among themselves and to be paid by the reinvoicing centers in their own currency. The units bought or sold are physically transferred from one affiliate to another, whereas the payment by an affiliate to another is made through the reinvoicing center. The affiliate seller receives payment from the reinvoicing center in its own currency and the affiliate buyer pays the reinvoicing center in its own currency. What results is that both the affiliate buyer and seller from different countries are allowed to deal in their own currency and avoid all transaction exposure. The transaction exposure is centralized in the reinvoicing center and is calculated at cost plus a commission for services to avoid the shifting of profits from operating affiliates.

The concept of a reinvoicing center is possible if the center acquires a non-resident status, since generally, a finance subsidiary not doing business in a country is spared some taxes such as interest withholding taxes and capital formation taxes, and it is not perceived by local authorities as a tax haven. The advantages of the reinvoicing center include (a) the centralization of foreign exchange transaction exposure and (b) the ability of affiliates to operate successfully without worrying about transaction exposure.[7]

Cross-Hedging

There are instances when the firm cannot hedge a position in a given currency X since the known hedging techniques are not possible. In that case the firm may consider determining another currency Y that is highly correlated with currency X and then set up a forward contract on the currency Y. When the forward contract is due, the firm will convert the currency Y into currency X. This technique of cross-hedging rests on the fact that the two currencies Y and X are highly correlated and the cross-hedging will actually fail if the two currencies move in different directions against the dollar as a result of an unexpected event or phenomenon.

Currency Diversification

Currency diversification is yet another technique used to reduce transaction exposure.[8] When a firm has receivables and payables from different countries that are denominated in one or two currencies, a sudden depreciation of these two currencies against the dollar will adversely affect the inflows and positively affect the outflows of cash. The firm may elect to reduce the risk associated with exposure to a few currencies by diversifying the number of currencies in which payables and receivables are denominated. This strategy of currency diversification would reduce the impact of a sudden depreciation in one of the currencies of the inflows. The diversification will work best as a strategy for reducing transaction exposure if the currencies chosen are not highly correlated.

SWAPS

A firm may use swaps to reduce foreign exchange exposure. Swaps are a set of parallel transactions in opposite directions. In other words, a swap is an agreement between two entities to exchange one currency for another now and provides dates on which to give back the original amount swapped. Types of swaps include forward swaps, ''back-to-back'' or ''parallel'' loans, currency swaps, credit swaps, and interest swaps.

Swaps have evolved over the years because of (a) financial arbitrage, (b) tax and regulatory arbitrage, (c) exposure management, and (d) competing markets.[9] Swaps take place to benefit from the differentials in cost and tax regulations of different countries; to allow firms to lower the transaction costs of managing their exposure to interest rates, currency prices, or commodity prices; and to enable market participants to fill gaps left by missing markets.

Back-to-Back Loans

A back-to-back or parallel loan is an agreement between firms to borrow each other's currency for a period and to return the borrowed currencies at a given time in the future, without at any time going through the foreign exchange market. As an example, a British firm in the United Kingdom lends a given amount in sterling to a French affiliate in the United Kingdom, while the French parent company in France lends an equal amount in French francs to the British firm's affiliate in France. Various variations exist. For example, a German parent firm lends a given amount to a French parent firm while the German firm's affiliate in the United States lends the same amount to the French parent company's affiliate in the United States. The swap appears as a loan on each company's books.

Currency Swap

A currency swap is similar to a back-to-back loan except that it does not appear in any of the firm's balance sheets and does not involve any interest. Two firms agree to exchange a given amount of two currencies for a specific period. Brokers in large banks act as middlemen for matching firms' needs and creating currency swaps, for a fee. The accounting treatment of currency swaps in the United States is that of a foreign exchange transaction. The obligation to reverse the swap at some later date is treated as a forward exchange contract.

If both interest rates are fixed, the swap is known as a *fixed currency swap*. When one of the interest rates is fixed and the other is variable, the swap is known as either a *simple interest rate swap* or a *currency coupon swap*. Swaps can also be denoted in commodities, resulting in *commodity swaps*.

Credit Swaps

A credit swap involves the exchange of currency between a firm and a bank to be reversed at a later date. For example, a French parent firm deposits a given amount in the Parisian subsidiary of a U.S. bank, and in return, the U.S. bank in New York makes an equal loan to the French firm's affiliate in New York. At a later date, the transaction is reversed with the affiliate in New York repaying the loan and the Parisian subsidiary of the U.S. bank returning the original French franc deposit. The French firm is allowed to recover its deposit no matter what happened to the exchange rate, and the U.S. bank is allowed to receive an interest free French franc deposit with the Parisian subsidiary.

Interest Rate Swap

An *interest rate swap* is an agreement between two parties for an exchange of a given interest rate for another on the same agreed-upon currency amount. The exchange may be from a fixed to a floating rate, from a floating to a fixed rate, or from a floating rate index to another. The party paying the fixed rate is known as the *fixed rate payer*, and the party paying the variable rate is known as the *floating rate payer*. The floating rate payment is generally based on the London Interbank Offered Rate (LIBOR), the Treasury bill rate, the commercial paper composite rate, the prime rate, the certificate of deposit (CD) composite rate, the federal funds rate, or the J. J. Kenny rate. The interest swap takes place because of differential information and institutional restrictions across national boundaries. As stated by James Bicksler and Andrew Chen:

For example, in contrast to the U.S. corporate bond market, there is virtually no registration of disclosure requirement for issuing new corporate bonds in the Eurobond market. As a result, it takes much less time to place a new bond issue in the Eurobond markets. However, issuing a new bond issue in the Eurobond markets requires a large underwriting cost and a larger credit premium. Thus, it is generally more difficult for a relatively small and unknown bank or business firm to issue new bonds in the Eurobond markets. In the floating-rate markets, the U.S. short term interest rates are usually lower than these in the European markets due, in part, to the presence of government insurance on deposits.[10]

As an example, suppose that a given company XYZ has outstanding 100 million noncallable bonds, which carry a fixed rate of 14 percent and have six years to maturity. The company elects to enter into an interest rate swap with a bank under which it agrees to pay the prime rate of 9.5 percent plus fifty basis points and to receive 13.0 percent from a fixed rate payer. The company benefits from the swap since it obtains a net floating rate cost of 11.0 percent and an economic gain of 3.0 percentage points in the cost of borrowed funds.

As another example, assume that an AAA-rated firm is able to obtain fixed rate financing at the lowest available market rate of 8 percent, whereas a BBB-rated firm would have to pay 12.0 percent for fixed rate financing (assuming that it could obtain it at all). The AAA-rated firm has a "comparative credit advantage." But the spread on the floating rate financing available in the capital market is not nearly as wide. The AAA-rated firm can borrow at the prime rate, and the BBB-rated firm can borrow at the prime rate plus 3.0 percent. If firm A agrees to pay firm B prime plus 2.5 percent in exchange for firm B paying firm A an 11.0 percent fixed rate, both firms will lower their cost of borrowing. Firm A will pay 250 basis points (2.5 percent) over prime for the floating rate debt received from firm B but will receive 11.0 percent for the fixed rate debt it swapped to firm B. Since firm A's cost on the fixed rate debt was only 8.0 percent, it is receiving 300 basis points (3.0 percent) over its cost. The net gain from the swap for firm A is 50 basis points (0.5 percent), computed by deducting the 250 basis points it is paying over its normal cost of borrowing at floating rates (prime) from the 300 basis points it made by swapping the fixed rate debt to firm B (11.0 percent − 8.0 percent). Firm B will receive prime plus 2.5 percent for the floating rate debt transferred to Firm A, for which it paid prime plus 3.0 percent, but will pay only 11.0 percent for the fixed rate debt, which would normally have cost it 12.0 percent. The net savings to firm B is also 50 basis points or 0.5 percent.

Hedging and speculation with regard to interest rate or currency value fluctuations can be obtained by a swap. For example, if firm A believes interest rates will rise, and firm B believes they will fall, firm A will be willing to trade its variable rate interest payments for firm B's fixed rate interest payments. If firm A expects significant devaluation of the dollar to occur, it will seek to swap its dollar-based interest payments for interest payments based on what it considers to be a more stable currency.

The swaps can be *unmatched*, when the company entering the swap has no other asset or liability related to the swap transaction. The motivations are generally speculative. "The swap agreement may have been entered into for the speculative purpose or to hedge the enterprise's overall exposure to interest rate risk (so-called macro-hedging) or as a temporary position before establishing a matched, hedged or offsetting position."[11]

In an *unmatched*, or *speculative*, position, the interest rate swap serves to create interest rate risk, and the user expects to gain from favorable changes in interest rates. In a *matched*, or *linked, swap*, the interest rate swap is specifically linked to an asset or liability. Source swaps may be unmatched but are still considered to be hedged if the firm in some way reduces or eliminates the risk posed by the agreement. An example involves offsetting the interest rate risk inherent in an unmatched swap position by purchasing or selling Treasury securities.[12]

The swap can be hedged if the firm takes any position that offsets the interest rate risk in an unmatched swap.

Another swap, called the *offsetting swap*, occurs when an intermediary arranges two swap positions that counterbalance each other, thus maintaining a "matched book" of swaps and eliminating interest rate risk. The intermediary retains the credit risk if either party should default.

Other types of swaps include the following:

a. The *commodity swap*, which is similar to the basis swap except that one of the indexes is tied to a commodity (i.e., silver).

b. The *basis swap*, whereby floating rate debt is exchanged for floating rate debt based on a different index (i.e., T-bill versus LIBOR).

c. The *circus swap*, whereby fixed rate debt is swapped for floating rate debt valued in a different currency (i.e., yen versus dollar).

d. The *reverse swap*, whereby if interest rates change so that the company could profit or escape loss by terminating the swap, it can enter into another swap that reverses or "unwinds" the original swap.

e. The *asset swap*, which converts a fixed rate asset into a floating rate asset (or vice versa) by creating a synthetic floating rate note through a swap.

f. The *amortizing swap*, whereby the national principal decreases over the term of the swap.

g. The *options or swaps* or *swaptions*, which give the purchaser of the option the right (but not the obligation) to enter into an interest rate swap at predetermined rates.

h. *Forward swaps*, which are swaps that became effective at some future time.

The advantage of interest rate swaps include the following:

• Confidentiality. The swap is a "silent" form of financing
• New funding source. Fixed rate funding is obtained without resorting to the public or private capital markets
• Flexibility. A swap contract can be sold or assigned to another party at any time
• Reduction of interest rate sensitivity. Corporations often arrange interest rate swaps to match debt costs against projected revenues
• Interest rate management. Interest rate swaps allow a company to manage its interest rate exposure actively by switching from fixed rate to floating rate debt and back again, depending on its forecast of interest rates or hedging needs
• "Cash out" convenience. Companies can use interest rate swaps to "cash out" of older, fixed rate debt when they have realized substantial gains due to a change in interest rates.[13]

Other advantages of interest swapping include the ability (a) to secure inexpensive fixed rate financing for firms with poor credit ratings, (b) to hedge against interest rate exposure by converting floating rate debt to fixed rate debt without a renegociation of the debt instrument, (c) to lock in a desired interest rate, and (d) to benefit from market imperfections and secure a low fixed or floating rate. Banks also take advantage of interest swapping to (a) chose the maturity gaps between the assets and liabilities on their balance sheets, thus eliminating interest rate exposure available; and (b) to manage basis risk by swapping floating rate debt based on one index with floating rate base on a more advantageous index.

There are, however, some risks in interest rate swaps, namely, (a) a credit risk if the counterparty required to make payments under the interest rate swap fails to do so, (b) a market risk due to changing interest rates, (c) a market liquidity risk because most interest rate swaps are over-the-counter contracts and there is limited liquidity.

Yield Curve Notes

Yield curve notes can be very useful to a multinational firm for creating debt portfolios having a stable yield. The main characteristic of these notes is that their interest rate varies inversely with the level of some key interest rates such as the LIBOR. For example, a yield curve note that pays 12 percent minus the LIBOR will have an interest rate of 2 percent if the LIBOR rises to 10 percent and an interest rate of 10 percent if the LIBOR falls to 2 percent. A firm facing a variable rate portfolio that wishes to convert to fixed rate portfolios will use the yield curve note as follows:[14] The XYZ firm has $4 million in a Eurobond paying LIBOR. If the firm uses $2 million to buy a yield curve note paying 12 percent minus LIBOR with the rest invested in LIBOR, the portfolio yield will be:

$$0.5(12 - \text{LIBOR}) + 0.5(\text{LIBOR}) = 6\% \text{ fixed.}$$

Commodity Swaps

One innovative financial instrument is the commodity swap. It is a hedging contract between buyers and sellers, with a bank acting as a middleman, where price is locked over time and the contract is ultimately settled in cash. Assume that an oil producer X wants to lock the price of his or her oil at $20 a barrel and in the process give up any profit if the price in the spot market climbs beyond $20. Also assume that an oil user Y is willing to lock the purchasing price at $20 a barrel and in the process gives up any cost savings if the price in the spot market falls under $20. A bank may be interested in acting as a middleman between X and Y in exchange for the payment of fees from both of them. Basically, the bank sets up a contract between X and Y whereby both of them agree to enter into a contract covering 20,000 barrels of oil for a locked price of $20. Two scenarios are possible:

1. If the price of oil increases to $25, for example, the contract is executed by X giving up $100,000 ($5 × 20,000) profit to the bank to be used by Y. Basically, Y is required to buy at $25 but will receive compensation of $100,000 from the bank.
2. If the price of oil decreases to $17, for example, the contract is still executed by X, who receives $40,000 ($2 × 20,000) from Y. Basically, Y buys the oil more cheaply but has to send the cost savings of 40,000 to X through the bank.

Equity Swaps

Equity swap, mostly used by multinational banks, involves exchanging long-term bonds the multinational firm is holding for equity in the firm. It is generally used by developing countries eager to cut their foreign debts. In 1988 Chile, for example, used $4.6 billion in deals to reduce its foreign debt to $19.5 billion.

In September 1988 the swap of debt for equity led to $20 million in investment by Citicorp, Scott Paper, and Royal Dutch/Shell Group in a wood products company, an unfinished pulp mill, and a eucalyptus forest. The way an equity swap works is best illustrated by the situation when Manufacturers Hanover Trust, which had loaned $2 billion to Brazil, decided to undertake an equity debt swap by exchanging some of the debt in shares in Companhia Suzano de Papel e Celulose, a pulp and paper company. What took place includes the following steps:

1. Manufacturers Hanover delivered $115 million in Brazilian government guaranteed bonds to Multuplic, a São Paulo broker.
2. A monthly debt auction at the Brazilian central banks led to the valuation of the debt at 86C on the dollar, netting $100 million worth of Brazilian cruzados for Manufacturers Hanover and $150,000 commission for the broker.
3. Manufacturers Hanover used the cruzados to buy 10 percent of the pulp and paper company.[15]

ATTITUDES AND STRATEGIES FOR MANAGING FOREIGN EXCHANGE RISK

Given the estimated trading of $150 billion a day in futures, options, swaps, money, and commodity funds,[16] the attitudes and strategies toward exchange risk management are of importance. A recent survey of corporate risk management strategies of U.S. multinational corporations revealed:

a. A strong tendency in U.S. multinationals to manage their foreign exchange risk exposure actively
b. The existence of predetermined risk hedging policies
c. The greater use of exchange rate forecasts in their operating decisions
d. The reliance on banks as the prime source of a country risk forecast.
e. The exchange risk aversion of U.S. exporting companies, regardless of their extent of overseas involvement
f. The continuous use of leading and lagging internal funds transfer, transfer pricing adjustment, leading and lagging external receivables and payables, the use of credit terms and factoring, the use of local debt, the covering of an exposed position with the purchase or sale of a counterbalancing contract such as forward contracts, swaps, and investment insurance.[17]

CONCLUSION

This chapter dealt with the problems of managing transaction exposure. The methods available are both imaginative and useful to the multinational firm that elects to hedge transaction exposure. They include (a) the forward contract hedge, (b) the money market hedge, (c) the currency options, (d) various operating strategies, and (e) various forms of currency and interest rate swaps. The multinational firm has to first make a cost/benefit analysis about the desirability of hedging and then a secured cost/benefit analysis to determine the best hedging techniques to be used for every particular situation and environment.

NOTES

1. Pat Wilder, "Currency Trading Skyrockets in U.S. to $128.9 Billion a Day," *Chicago Tribune*, September 15, 1989, Sec. 3, p. 3.

2. Chuck C. Y. Kwok, "Hedging Foreign Exchange Exposure: Independent vs. Integrative Approaches," *Journal of International Business Studies*, Summer 1987, pp. 33–52.

3. International Federation of Accountants, *Foreign Currency Exposure and Risk Management*, Study no. 2 (New York, 1986), p. 17.

4. This may be an effort to prevent severe exposures, such as the one that caused the near collapse of Schweder, Nueuchmeyer, Hengst and Company in 1983 when it overextended itself on loans to IBH Holding AG, which eventually was forced into bankruptcy proceedings.

5. L. J. Johnson and C. H. Walther, "The Effectiveness of Forward and Gold Market Hedges Against Currency Risk," *Management International Review* 4 (1985): 5–16.

6. Ibid., p. 6.

7. D. K. Eiteman and A. I. Stonehill, *Multinational Business Finance* (Reading, Mass.: Addison-Wesley, 1989), p. 205.

8. Mark R. Eaker, "Denomination Decision for Multinational Transactions," *Financial Management*, Autumn 1980, pp. 23–29.

9. C. W. Smith, Jr., C. W. Smithson, and L. M. Wakeman, "The Evolving Market for Swaps," *Midland Corporate Finance Journal*, Winter 1986, pp. 24–27.

10. James Bicksler and Andrew H. Chen, "An Economic Analysis of Interest Rate Swaps," *The Journal of Finance*, July 1986, p. 646.

11. Keith Wilshon and Lorin S. Chevalier, "Interest Rate Swaps—Your Rate or Mine?" *The Journal of Accountancy*, September 1985, p. 74.

12. Ibid.

13. Anthony J. Gambino, "Cash Management, Interest Rate Swaps, Risk Management Addressed by CPA's in Industry," *The Journal of Accountancy*, August 1985, pp. 66, 68.

14. John Edmonds and S. E. Moeller, "Interest Rate Swaps and Yield Curve Notes: Innovative Techniques in International Finance," *Issues in International Business*, Summer 1988, pp. 75–78.

15. J. Ryser and E. Weiner, "How an Equity Swap Works," *Business Week*, October 3, 1988, p. 116.

16. "Round the World on $150 Billion a Day," *The Economist*, November 30, 1985, p. 10.

17. Y. A. Choudry and ABM Saiful Huq, "Managing Foreign Exchange Risks: Currency Attitudes and Strategies," *Issues in International Business*, Summer–Fall 1986, pp. 1–10.

REFERENCES

Arak, Marcelle, Arturo Estrella, Laurie Goodman, and Andrew Silver. "Interest Rate Swaps: An Alternative Explanation." *Financial Management*, Summer 1988, pp. 12–18.

Arnold, Tanya S. "How to Do Interest Rate Swaps." *Harvard Business Review*, September/October 1984, pp. 96–101.

Babbel, Dabid F. "Determining the Optimum Strategy for Hedging Currency Exposure." *Journal of International Business Studies*, Spring/Summer 1983, pp. 133–139.

Batra, Raveendra N., Shabtai Donnenfeld, and Josef Hadar. "Hedging Behavior by Multinational Firms." *Journal of International Business Studies*, Winter 1982, pp. 59–70.

Beidleman, Carl R., John L. Hillary, and James A. Greenleaf. "Alternatives in Hedging Long-Date Contractual Foreign Exchange Exposure." *Sloan Management Review*, Summer 1983, pp. 45–54.

Bicksler, James, and Andrew H. Chen. "An Economic Analysis of Interest Rate Swaps." *The Journal of Finance*, July 1986, pp. 646–655.

Booth, Laurence D. "Hedging and Foreign Exchange Exposure." *Management International Review* 22, no. 1 (1982): 26–42.

Calderon-Rossel, Jorge R. "Covering Foreign Exchange Risks of Single Transactions: A Framework for Analysis." *Financial Management*, Autumn 1979, pp. 78–85.

Choudry, Y. A., and ABM Saiful Huq. "Managing Foreign Exchange Risks: Currency Attitudes and Strategies." *Issues in International Business*, Summer-Fall 1986, pp. 1–10.

Eaker, Mark R. "Denomination Decision for Multinational Transactions." *Financial Management*, Autumn 1980, pp. 23–29.

———. "The Numeraire Problem and Foreign Exchange Risk." *Journal of Finance*, May 1981, pp. 419–426.

Eaker, Mark R., and Dwight M. Grant. "Cross-Hedging Foreign Currency Risk." *Journal of International Money and Finance*, March 1987, pp. 85–105.

Edmonds, John, and S. E. Moeller. "Interest Rate Swaps and Yield Curve Notes: Innovative Techniques in International Finance." *Issues in International Business*, Summer 1988.

Eiteman, D. K., and A. I. Stonehill. *Multinational Business Finance*. Reading, Mass.: Addison-Wesley, 1989.

Folks, William R., Jr. "Decision Analysis for Exchange Risk Management." *Financial Management*, Winter 1972, pp. 101–112.

———. "Optimal Foreign Borrowing Strategies with Operations in the Forward Exchange Markets." *Journal of Financial and Quantitative Analysis*, June 1978, pp. 245–254.

———. "The Optimal Level of Forward Exchange Transactions." *Journal of Financial and Quantitative Analysis*, January 1973, pp. 105–110.

Gambino, Anthony J. "Cash Management, Interest Rate Swaps, Risk Management Addressed by CPA's in Industry." *The Journal of Accountancy*, August 1985, pp. 66, 68.

Giddy, Ian H. "The Foreign Exchange Option as a Hedging Tool." *Midland Corporate Finance Journal*, Fall 1983, pp. 32–42.

International Federation of Accountants. *Foreign Currency Exposure and Risk Management*. Study no. 2. New York, 1986.

Jacque, Laurent L. "Management of Foreign Exchange Risk: A Review Article." *Journal of International Business Studies*, Spring/Summer 1981, pp. 81–99.

Johnson, L. J., and C. H. Walther. "The Effectiveness of Forward and Gold Market Hedges Against Currency Risk." *Management International Review* 4 (1985): 5–16.

Kaufold, Howard, and Michael Smirlock. "Managing Corporate Exchange and Interest Rate Exposure." *Financial Management*, Autumn 1986, pp. 64–72.

Kwok, Chuck C. Y. "Hedging Foreign Exchange Exposure: Independent vs. Integrative Approaches." *Journal of International Business Studies*, Summer 1987, pp. 33–52.

Madura, Jeff, and E. Theodore Veit. "Use of Currency Options for International Cash Management." *Journal of Cash Management*, January–February 1986, pp. 42–48.

Makin, John H. "The Portfolio Method of Managing Foreign Exchange Risk." *Euromoney*, August 1976, pp. 58–64.

———. "Portfolio Theory and the Problem of Foreign Exchange Risk." *The Journal of Finance* 33 (May 1978): 517–534.

Naidu, G. W., and Tai Shim. "Effectiveness of Currency Futures Market in Hedging Foreign Exchange Risk." *Management International Review* 21, no. 4 (1981): 5–16.

Park, Yoon S. "Currency Swaps as a Long-Term International Financing Technique." *Journal of International Business Studies*, Winter 1984, pp. 47–54.

"Round the World on $150 Billion a Day." *The Economist*, November 30, 1985, p. 10.

Ryser, J., and E. Weiner. "How an Equity Swap Works." *Business Week*, October 3, 1988, p. 116.

Shapiro, Alan C., and David P. Ruttenberg. "Managing Exchange Risks in a Floating World." *Financial Management*, Summer 1976, pp. 48–58.

Shepherd, Sidney A. "Forwards, Futures, and Currency Options as Foreign Exchange Risk Protection." *Canadian Banker*, December 1983, pp. 22–25.

Smith, C. W., Jr., C. W. Smithson, and L. M. Wakeman. "The Evolving Market for Swaps." *Midland Corporate Finance Journal*, Winter 1986, pp. 20–32.

Soenen, Luc A., and E.G.F. van Winkel. "The Real Costs of Hedging in the Forward Exchange Market." *Management International Review* 22, no. 1 (1982): 53–59.

Swanson, Peggy E., and Stephen C. Caples. "Hedging Foreign Exchange Risk Using Forward Foreign Exchange Markets: An Extension." *Journal of International Business Studies*, Spring 1987, pp. 75–82.

Turnbull, S. M. "Swaps: A Zero Sum Game?" *Financial Management*, Spring 1987, pp. 15–21.

Wheelright, Steven. "Applying Decision Theory to Improve Corporate Management of Currency-Exchange Risks." *California Management Review*, Summer 1975, pp. 41–49.

Wilder, Pat. "Currency Trading Skyrockets in U.S. to $128.9 Billion a Day." *Chicago Tribune*, September 15, 1989, Sec. 3, p. 3.

Wilshon, Keith, and Lorin S. Chevalier. "Interest Rate Swaps—Your Rate or Mine?" *The Journal of Accountancy*, September 1985, pp. 63–84.

III

Organization and Controlling

5

Organizational Structures of Foreign Operations

Multinational corporations face unique opportunities and unique obstacles in their quest for achieving an adequate return on investment. One way of benefiting from these opportunities and fending off obstacles is to achieve the appropriate fit between organizational systems and environmental characteristics. The decisions of importance are the choice of the proper organizational design in terms of the extent of decentralization and the choice of organizational structure. This chapter elaborates on the organizational designs and structures options available to multinational corporations and the strategies used to achieve the "best" structure.

ORGANIZATIONAL DESIGN OF FOREIGN CORPORATIONS

To Centralize or Decentralize

Forms of Organizational Design: The design of a formal organizational structure should contribute to the attainment of corporate objectives. Such a design should take into account four process criteria and a design criterion. The process criteria necessary in the design of a formal organizational structure include the following:

1. *Steady-state efficiency* is achieved when the unit cost of output is minimized for a given level of activity. This involves analyzing factors such as economies of scale, skills, and overhead.

2. *Operating responsiveness* measures an organization's ability to make efficient changes in its production level in response to environmental changes. It involves inventory control and accents all information.

3. *Strategic responsiveness* measures an organization's ability to make efficient changes in the nature of its production process in response to environmental changes. It involves a possible expense for technological and market related changes.

4. *Structural responsiveness* measures the ability of a firm to design and implement new structures when the first three criteria cannot be met.[1]

Each of these criteria should be applied toward the evaluation of an organizational design's potential success in meeting the objectives of the firm.

The criteria just described can be met by at least two possible types of organizational designs: the centralized functional form and the decentralized divisional form.

The *centralized functional form* consists primarily of a departmentalization by function. In a manufacturing firm, such functions include production, finance, sales, accounting, personnel, purchasing, and research and development. Centralization has been described as follows: "Centralization is the tightest means of coordinating decision making in the organization. All decisions are made by one person, in one brain, and then implemented through direct supervision. Other reasons have been given for centralized structures, but aside from the well-known one of lust for power, most of them amount to the need for coordination."[2] Such design is justifiable in terms of steady-state efficiency by allowing for economies of scale, overhead, and skills. It results, however, in relatively low strategic and structural responsiveness.

The *decentralized divisional form* consists primarily of a series of organizational units, or divisions, responsible for a specific product market under the direction of a manager having strategic and operating decision prerogatives. This form achieves steady-state efficiency and operating responsiveness, because departmentalization by function is used within each division. This design is justifiable mainly in terms of strategic and structural responsiveness. In general, the transition of the corporation from the functional to the divisionalized form has four stages:

We begin with the large corporation that produces all its products through one chain and so retains what we call the integrated form—a pure functional structure, a Machine bureaucracy or perhaps an Adhocracy. As the corporation begins to market some of the intermediate products of its production processes, it makes the first shift toward divisionalization, called the by-product form. Further moves in the same direction to the point where the by-products become important than end products, although a central theme remains the product-market strategy, lead to a structure closer to the divisionalized one, which is called the related product form. And finally, the complete breakdown of the production chain, to the point where the different products have no relationship with each other, takes the corporation to the conglomerate form, a pure divisional structure. Although some corporations may move though all these stages in sequence, we shall see that others stop at one stage along the way because of the very high fixed cost technical systems (typical in the case of the integrated form), operations based on a single raw material (typical in the case of the by-product form), or focus on a core technology or market theme (typical in the case of the related product form).[3]

Since World War II, the decentralized divisional form had become the most frequent in large firms. It is accomplished most often through either a departmentalization by location (geographical diversifaction) or a departmentalization by-product.

Various types of organizational growth require the creation of decentralized organizational structures. Ideally, management will choose the degree of decentralization that will help achieve corporate goals. "Decentralization" should not be confused with "divisionalization," which is a major organizational device for decentralization, although it does not indicate to what degree. *Decentralization* is essentially the freedom to make decisions.

Theories of Organizational Change and the Genesis of the Multidivisional Firm: Five theories of organizational change may be used to explain the genesis of the multidivisional form, namely, (1) strategy-structure, (2) transaction cost analysis, (3) population-ecology theory, (4) control theory based on power, and (5) organizational homogeneity theory.[4]

The first theory, strategy-structure, was enunciated in A. D. Chandler's seminal work *Strategy and Structure*.[5] *Strategy* is defined as "the determination of long-term goals and objectives of an enterprise, and the adoption of courses of action and the allocation of resources necessary for carrying out these goals."[6] These strategies include either horizontal, vertical, or diversification in related or unrelated markets. Chandler maintained that a horizontal strategy called for a *unitary structure*, one characterized by manufacturing, sales and marketing, and finance departments; a vertical strategy called for a *functional structure*, one characterized by departments along discrete task lines; and a diversification strategy called for a *multidivisional structure*, one in which a firm is organized into product divisions and each division contains a unitary structure.

The second theory, transaction cost analysis, was enunciated by O. Williamson.[7] His work on understanding the economics of organization relied on three related concepts: transaction costs, bounded rationality, and opportunism. *Transaction cost* is the cost of performing an economic exchange, *bounded rationality* is a view that constrains individuals in their ability to process their knowledge, and *opportunism* is a view that people not only act out of self-interest but also act with guile. Given high transaction costs, bounded rationality, and opportunism in the market (referred to as the "market failures approach"), firms choose to contract activities with the markets or build hierarchies to perform the same task. Williamson concluded that firms may be inclined to choose the multidivisional form because the continuous expansion of the unitary or functional structure creates "cumulative control loss" effects, which have "internal efficiency consequences."[8] As size increases, people reach their limits of control as a result of bounded rationality and start resorting to opportunism, thereby threatening efficiency and profitability. The multidivisional form is one solution for these problems.

The third theory, population-ecology, was enunciated by M. Hamman and J. Freeman.[9] They elaborated on the link between organizational niche, age, inertia, and the possibility of organizational change. As organizations age and reach high reliability of performance and high levels of accountability, they move to a state of "structural inertia." N. Fligstein pointed out that if the population-ecology argument is used, one would expect that younger and smaller firms would be more likely to adopt the multidivisional form than older and larger ones.[10]

The fourth theory, control based on power, was enunciated by several authors and most recently by Jeffrey Pfeffer.[11] In the allocation of scarce resources in an organization, no optimal mechanism exists. Power enters in all important organization decisions and must be based on some structural claim over resources. When it comes to profit orientated organizations, there has been over time a shift of power from production to sales and marketing and finance personnel. Therefore, the multidivisional form would be favored by these new power holders, sales and marketing and finance personnel, since the multidivisional form allows for growth through product-related and unrelated strategies.

The fifth theory, organizational homogeneity, was enunciated by Paul Di-Maggio and Walter Powell.[12] They argued that large organizations begin to resemble one another as a result of three kinds of environmental pressures: (1) the cultural expectations of competitors, suppliers, and the state; (2) environmental uncertainty; and (3) a particular world view of appropriate behavior created by the professionalization of managers. As a result of these three kinds of environmental pressures, large organizations start mimicking one another structurally by adopting the multidivisional form (MDF). Fligstein stated: "The MDF spreads to various organizations as a response to other firms' behavior. The examples of successful firms such as DuPont or General Motors provided the role models for other firms. The MDF has also become the accepted form for large firms. Business schools have taught the MDF as an important organizational tool, and managers have come to implement it."[13]

The M Form Hypothesis: The multidivisional (M Form) structure has evolved as a better solution to the problems of managing growth and diversity within a centralized (U Form) structure. In a major historical study of American enterprise, A. D. Chandler noted that in the early 1920s, the M Form was adopted as a response to the increasingly complex administrative problems encountered within a U Form as firm size and diversity increased.[14] Building on Chandler's analysis, Williamson suggested that because of two problems encountered by expanding multiproduct firms—cumulative control loss and the compounding of strategic and operating decision making—there is the risk of failure to achieve least cost profit maximization behavior.[15,16] He maintained that as size increases, people reach their limits of control as a result of bounded rationality and start resorting to opportunism, thereby threatening efficiency and profitability. The M Form is presented as a unique structural framework that overcomes these difficulties and favors goal pursuits and least cost behavior more nearly associated with the neoclassical profit making hypothesis.

Building on Williamson, researchers investigated a hypothesis of links between the M Form and better performance. Results to date have provided either a support of the proposition that the M Form implementation affects performance regardless of other contingencies or mixed results. The studies did not differentiate between the firms on the basis of their diversification strategy. One exception by Hoskisson provided evidence in support of a contingency view of the relationship between performance and implementation of an M Form structure.[17] The type of diversification strategy—vertical, related, or unrelated—is assumed to mediate the results. The impact of these strategies is examined below:

First, firms may opt for vertical integration. A strategy of vertical integration is used by firms to increase the economies of scale and efficiency.[18] Each stage of the production process is organized as a separate division that must, however, buy or sell from other separate divisions of the firms. The need to coordinate these transfers requires the use of a system of transfer prices and most often top-level operational control. Top management of the firm keeps a hands on approach. It requires that incentives be based on overall economic performance rather than based on objective financial performance criteria and implementation of an internal capital market.[19] Because the investment opportunities affect the whole corporation rather than one or some of the divisions, top management would formulate the investment opportunities.[20] In vertically integrated firms, the corporate strategic control as well as the operational controls keep a certain dose of centralization in the implementation of the M Form structure.

Second, firms may also opt for an unrelated diversification. The implementation of the M Form following a strategy of unrelated diversification requires both divisionalization—the creation of distinct divisions—and decentralization—the delegation of managerial and operating responsibility to the divisions. Because the divisions are operating in different businesses, top management may feel the need for an integrative effort. In such a case it was found that too much integrative effort will disturb the divisional autonomy and accountability resulting in poorer performance.[21] A successful performance is more likely if the M Form enterprise was implemented following a strategy of unrelated diversification and is managed as a holding company.[22]

Third, firms may opt for a related diversification. A strategy of related diversification is used by firms to increase its economies of scope, or the sharing of resources and capabilities among a related set of businesses.[23,24] As in vertically integrated firms, each division needs to coordinate its activities with the other related divisions through a system of transfer prices and information transfer. Similarly, the incentives need to be based on both objective and subjective criteria rather than just on an objective financial performance criteria and the implementation of an internal capital market.[25,26] Top management needs to centralize information flows and have a certain knowledge of the operating activities of the divisions to be able to formulate opportunities in the division that may have some benefits for other divisions. This activity can be handled at the corporate level or at the intermediate level of strategic business unit (SBU) structures to insure the development of synergy among divisions. In firms pursuing a strategy of related diversification, the information flows need to be centralized to achieve the economies of scope in the implementation of the M Form structure. The management of the divisions find themselves pursuing two objectives: one of sharing information with top management for coordinating purposes and another of pursuing independent opportunities in the marketplace.

Organizational Structure and Multinational Firms

Various conventional structures have been proposed as adequate for multinational firms. They include (a) the use of a separate international division; (b) the use of a product division structure, (c) the use of a geographical division structure, (d) the use of a functional division structure, (e) the matrix organization, and (f) the use of a strategy matrix. Each of these types of structures is discussed below, including the strategy and structure of multinational firms.

The Use of a Separate International Division: Multinational firms may rely on a separate division to handle all the international activities. This is ideal for those firms whose international activities and assets are still immaterial compared to the domestic activities.[27] This form of organizational structure is more prevalent in the United States than in Europe since the U.S. firms are generally more concerned about the impact of their domestic divisions.[28] The creation of a separate international division gives it equal footing and power with its domestic counterparts, although it may have to compete and even depend on the same domestic divisions for crucial resources in terms of personnel, technology, and other resources. With the creation of an international division, international expertise, data on foreign opportunities, as well as the freedom to make international decisions are centralized in a semiautonomous unit. The major manufacturing and related functions remain in the hands of the domestic divisions to allow for more economies of scale. Coordination between the domestic and international divisions is necessary to avoid the conflict arising from the geographical orientation of the international division and the product or functional orientation of the domestic divisions.[29]

Product Division: Various multinational firms opted instead for a product-oriented organizational structure, with the product divisions operating in different countries and completely independent of one another. They basically opted for a global organizational structure that gives product divisions the international responsibility for production and marketing. Cost efficiency is assumed to be obtained by the centralization of production activities and the ability to react quickly to needed product specific changes.[30] This type of structure is particularly useful in those cases in which the products are technologically sophisticated, custom designed, and requiring extensive capital investment. As R. W. Drake and L. M. Caudill stated: "The product groups of these companies often represent worldwide businesses which lend themselves to a limited number of product development and production facilities, worldwide marketing strategies, and (following from these conditions) centralized planning."[31]

Geographical (Area) Division: Various multinational firms with very large foreign operations, not concentrated in a single country, have opted for a geographic divisional structure. They opted for a global organizational structure that gives complete manufacturing and marketing responsibilities to geographical or area divisions.

Having narrow product lines geared to be used by specific foreign users is the main motivation behind the geographical divisional structure. Witness the following comments from a survey of multinational firms:

For geographic markets of significance and/or importance, at great distance from the parent headquarters, special organizational and reporting arrangements typically have been established. These arrangements give recognition to unique marketing and business conditions, distinctive managerial styles, the intensity of local competition, and the problem of managing a local company from afar. Brazil, Japan, and (for European-based companies) the United States are three markets in which the need for such arrangements is particularly evident.[32]

Functional Division: Various multinational firms have opted for a functional divisions structure, with each functional division operating in different countries or geographic areas. They opted for a global organization structure that gives international responsibilities to the various functional areas of production, marketing, finance, and personnel. Strategy emanates from the top or strategic apex.[33] The consequence is a low participation of subunits in foreign subsidiaries in the strategic formulation process. As stated by W. G. Egelhoff: "The functional structure should be most suitable when the information required to formulate strategy already exists in the strategic apex of the parent and when strategy can be formulated more on a worldwide than a subsidiary-by-subsidiary basis (e.g. where a product tends to sell more in a uniform worldwide market than undifferentiated, local markets)."[34]

Matrix Organization: Some multinational firms have opted for a matrix organization to allow all the major perspectives, groups, functions, or areas to be represented in strategic as well as operational decision making. The matrix organization is basically an integration of the functional, geographical, and product structures. The functional, geographical, and product structures constitute different and multiple commands that still have to report to the matrix structure manager, who serves as coordinator, facilitator of communications, and potential arbiter in case of conflicts. The matrix organization favors the creation of a network global organization whereby the various subsidiaries report not only to headquarters but to other subsidiaries. A variety of matrix patterns has been found to be used by multinational companies:

- The current matrix pattern in each company reflects present needs and particular circumstances.
- Each company's matrix pattern reflects the managerial style and culture of headquarters, as well as of its foreign-based management terms.
- The matrix pattern is influenced by the special emphasis given to large and particularly attractive geographic markets.
- The matrix is inherently unstable; it must shift continually in response to new business, environmental and competitive conditions.[35]

Strategy Matrix: Some multinational companies have opted for the style of management known as a strategy matrix, a participatory planning and management system involving the integration of matrix management and strategic planning.[36] Matrix management involves team building and a multiple command system, whereas strategic planning involves the determination of corporate and business unit objectives, goals, and strategies in response to environmental scanning. Therefore, the strategy matrix as adopted by a multinational involves (a) an extension of the scope of matrix management beyond short-term project management to long-term international strategic management and (b) the extension of strategic planning not only within business units but across multiple business units.[37] The international strategy matrix is seen as inevitable to the running of multinational companies even if the formal structure adopted is a divisional management structure. As Thomas Naylor stated:

The international strategy matrix can accommodate the multidimensional nature of international management problems much more easily than traditional single-dimensional hierarchical approaches can. Indeed, it can be argued that when companies attempt to force divisionalized management structures as their international business, success often comes only by virtue of the fact that informal teams and matrices emerge among the interdependent businesses and countries. Thus, whether or not senior management formally introduces the matrix into a multinational company, there remains the strong possibility that an informal matrix structure will eventually evolve as a natural response to the multinational interdependencies.[38]

STRATEGY AND STRUCTURE OF MULTINATIONAL FIRMS

Mix of Centralization and Decentralization

The preceding discussion concerned various types of organizational structures. There is, however, no consensus about the best form for multinational corporations. What has been noted in practice are various experimentations in general and five basic patterns of organization in particular. The five basic patterns are:

1. Functionally organized—with foreign operations integrated into the functional units (Tata Chemicals Limited, India; Inocenti, Italy)

2. Functionally organized—with foreign operations assembled into one separate overall international unit (AKU, Netherlands; Volkswagen, Germany)

3. Product organization—with foreign operations integrated into product divisions or groups (Imperial Chemicals Limited, United Kingdom; Fiat, Italy)

4. Product organization—with foreign operations reporting directly to top management or assembled as a separate international unit (Ericsson Telephone, Sweden; Dunlop Rubber Co., United Kingdom)

5. Regional organization—with foreign and domestic operations grouping into components under regional heads (Singer, United States; Standard Oil Company, United States)[39]

What seems to be taking place is a search for a form of organizational structure most efficient for operating and financial control purposes. A rise of centralized and decentralized activities has appeared more recently as a way of meeting the different objectives of the various functions and goals of multinational companies. Centralization in production and logistics, for example, is easier with the advent of international computer-linked communications systems. Similarly, centralized purchasing or "common sourcing" may make it easier to obtain purchaser quantity discounts, greater bargaining power for supplies, benefits from price differentials, and other economies of scale.[40] Naturally, the right mix of centralized and decentralized activities differs from one multinational company to another because of different industries and environments. There seem to be, however, common factors in the search for the mix:

1. The major decisions affecting the entire system that previously may well have been made locally now tend to be made centrally in a coordinated fashion. For example, foreign affiliates typically now have decreased discretion over reinvestment of their earnings; headquarters, aware of all competing alternatives, allocates resources in a balanced fashion for the global system.

2. Local managers retain considerable authority in largely local matters and in other matters where it is necessary to maintain flexibility and immediacy of response at the operating levels.

3. Financial control systems are changing from the emphasis on profits under the profit-center concept to control via budgets and budget variances; additionally, other evaluation techniques are increasingly used supplementally. These new control systems are designed to permit control centrally even though a great deal of authority is left at the local level.

4. New systems for centralized coordination and for cooperative management are emerging. That is, a levy of new central coordination techniques, many requiring extensive interaction with cooperation from local managers, is emerging. As examples, Operations Research techniques (particularly simulation and network analysis) are used for coordination; formal, frequent, and lengthy meetings of managers from around the world are reaching new heights of sophistication as a coordination technique; top-management policy guidelines have been refined for extensive use as a means to guide local managers in decision making in situations important for global coordination but

too complex to permit promulgation of rigid decision rules; behind each of these new developments, the accounting and management information system must be redesigned, altered, and expanded to accommodate information flows resulting from the use of the new techniques.[41]

Organizational Characteristics of Multinational Firms

Multinational firms are known to experiment with various organizational structures. Various organizational characteristics are believed to influence multinational structure.

1. After showing that diversity influenced organizational design,[42] Chandler hypothesized that foreign involvement is also an influencing variable.[43] Both variables were later found to be strong predictors of multinational structure.[44,45]

2. Case studies of U.S. multinationals showed that changes in organizational parameters such as size, diversity, foreign activity, and personnel deployment may lead to a change of structure.[46]

3. Following a case of isomorphism, multinational firms have been formed to change their structure to imitate a leader.[47]

4. In evaluating important fits between elements of strategy and type of organizational structure, W. G. Egelhoff formed the following elements of strategy to differentiate significantly between types of structure: (a) foreign product diversity, (b) product modification differences between subsidiaries, (c) product change, (d) size of foreign operations, (e) size of foreign manufacturing, (f) number of foreign subsidiaries, (g) extent of outside ownership in foreign subsidiaries, and (h) extent of foreign acquisitions.[48] The fits are summarized as follows:

   Five fits are important for firms with worldwide functional divisional structures: a narrow and highly consistent worldwide product line, a limited number of foreign subsidiaries, a low level of outside ownership in foreign subsidiaries, and few foreign acquisitions. . . .

   The international division structure has a single dominant fit with the firm's international strategy. It is appropriate when foreign operations are relatively low. . . .

   For companies with geographical region structures, the most important fits are a sufficiently large foreign operation and a high percentage of foreign manufacturing. . . .

   Companies with worldwide product division structures also have large foreign operations and are distinguished from other structures by high level of product diversity and product change.[49]

5. Multinational firms are constantly evolving in their search of the best organizational design. Over time, specific trends emerge. Davis reported on the following trends:

   • Worldwide functional structures show definite instabilities.

   • Corporations organized by country are exploring how and where to place product management more adequately in their framework.

   • Firms with worldwide product groups require better coordination within countries and regions than their structures provide.

   • Corporate planning and development activities have led some companies to organize around markets, not geography.

   • Some companies experiment with global matrix management and structure.[50]

6. U.S. multinationals go through three phases as their foreign business becomes material: (1) a phase of "ignoring the systems potential" in which international financial management is left to a small staff that monitors quasi-independent affiliates, (2) a phase of "exploiting the system's potential" in which the international financial management is centralized in a more coherent and capable and experienced unit, and (3) a phase of "compromising with flexibility" in which the large central international unit is now delegating responsibility to foreign based subsidiaries through detailed "rule books."[51]

CONCLUSION

This chapter elaborates on the types of organizational design and structure options open for a multinational corporation eager to deal with varieties of opportunities and difficulties. What appears from the literature is a mood of experimentation by multinational corporations to find the appropriate fit between organizational design and structure and specific environmental variables.

NOTES

1. H. I. Ansoff and R. G. Brandenburg, "A Language for Organizational Design: Parts 1 and 2," *Management Science* 17 (1971): 705–731.

2. H. Mintzberg, *Structure in Firms: Designing Effective Organizations* (Englewood Cliffs, N.J.: Prentice-Hall, 1983), pp. 95–96.

3. Ibid., p. 233.

4. Neil Fligstein, "The Spread of the Multidivisional Firm Among Large Firms," *American Sociological Review,* June 1985, pp. 377–391.

5. A. D. Chandler, Jr., *Strategy and Structure* (Cambridge, Mass.: MIT Press, 1962).

6. Ibid., p. 13.

7. O. Williamson, *Markets and Hierarchies* (New York: The Free Press, 1975).

8. Ibid., p. 133.

9. M. Hamman and J. Freeman, "The Population Ecology of Organizations," *American Journal of Sociology* 92 (1977): 929–964. See also idem, "Structural Inertia and Organizational Change," *American Sociological Review* 49 (1984): 149–164.

10. Fligstein, "The Spread of the Multidivisional Firm Among Large Firms," p. 379.

11. Jeffrey Pfeffer, *Power in Organizations* (Marshfield, Mass.: Pitman, 1981). See also idem, *Organizations and Organization Theory* (Marshfield, Mass.: Pitman, 1982); J. Pfeffer and G. Salanick, *The External Control of Organizations: A Resource Dependency Perspective* (New York: Harper and Row, 1978).

12. Paul DiMaggio and Walter Powell, "Institutional Isomorphism," *American Sociological Review* 48 (1983): 147–160.

13. Fligstein, "The Spread of the Multidivisional Firm Among Large Firms," p. 380.

14. Chandler, *Strategy and Structure.*

15. Williamson, *Markets and Hierarchies.*

16. Ibid.

17. R. E. Hoskisson, "Multidimensional Structure and Performance: The Contingency of Diversification Strategy," *Academy of Management Journal* 30 (1987): 625–644.

18. K. R. Harrigan, "Vertical Integration and Corporate Strategy," *Academy of Management Journal* 28 (1985): 397–425.

19. J. L. Kerr, "Diversification Strategy and Managerial Rewards: An Empirical Study," *Academy of Management Journal* 28 (1985): 155–179.

20. R. W. Ackerman, "Influence of Integration and Diversity on the Investment Process," *Administrative Science Quarterly* 15 (1970): 341–351.

21. J. W. Lorsch and S. A. Allen, *Managing Diversity and Independence* (Boston: Division of Research, Graduate School of Business Administration, Harvard University, 1973).

22. K.N.M. Dundas and P. R. Richardson, "Implementing the Unrelated Product Strategy," *Strategic Management Journal* 3 (1982): 287–301.

23. D. J. Teece, "Economies of Scope and the Scope of the Enterprise," *Journal of Economic Behavior and Organization* 1 (1980): 223–247.

24. Hoskisson, "Multidimensional Structure and Performance."

25. M. E. Porter, *Competitive Advantage: Creating and Sustaining Superior Performance* (New York: The Free Press, 1985).

26. Kerr, "Diversification Strategy and Managerial Rewards."

27. Richard D. Robinson, *Internationalization of Business: An Introduction* (Hinsdale, Ill.: Dryden, 1984), p. 84.

28. W. G. Egelhoff, "Strategy and Structure in Multinational Corporations: An Information Processing Approach," *Administrative Science Quarterly* 27 (1982): 435–458; J. D. Daniels, R. A. Pitts, and M. J. Tretter, "Strategy and Structure of U.S. Multinationals: An Exploratory Study," *Academy of Management Journal* 27, no. 2 (June 1984): 292–307.

29. M. Z. Brooke and H. L. Remmers, *The Strategy of the Multinational Enterprise* (New York: Elsevier, 1970).

30. W. H. Davidson and P. Hasjeslagh, "Shaping a Global Product Organization," *Harvard Business Review*, March–April 1982, pp. 69–76.

31. Rodman Drake and Lee M. Caudill, "Management of the Large Multinational: Trends and Future Challenges," *Business Horizons* 24 (May–June 1981): 85.

32. Ibid., p. 86.

33. H. Mintzberg, *The Structuring of Organizations* (Englewood Cliffs, N.J.: Prentice-Hall, 1978).

34. Egelhoff, "Strategy and Structure in Multinational Corporations," p. 440.

35. Drake and Caudill, "Management of the Large Multinational," p. 87.

36. Thomas H. Naylor, "The International Strategy Matrix," *Columbia Journal of World Business*, Summer 1985, pp. 11–19.

37. Ibid., p. 11.

38. Ibid., p. 12.

39. H. Stieglitz, *Organizational Structures of International Companies*, Studies in Personnel Policy no. 198 (New York: National Industrial Conference Board, 1965), p. 5.

40. Committee on International Accounting, "Report," *The Accounting Review*, suppl. 48 (Summer 1973): 135.

41. Ibid., p. 136.

42. A. D. Chandler, Jr., *Strategy and Structure* (Garden City, N.Y.: Anchor, 1966).

43. A. D. Chandler, Jr., "The Multi-Unit Enterprise: A Historical and International Comparative Analysis and Summary," in *Evolution of International Management Struc-*

tures, ed. H. F. Williamson (Newark: University of Delaware Press, 1975), pp. 222–254.

44. Daniels, Pitts, and Tretter, "Strategy and Structure of U.S. Multinationals," pp. 292–307.

45. J. M. Stopford and L. T. Wells, *Managing the Multinational Enterprise* (New York: Basic Books, 1972).

46. C. K. Prabolad, "Strategic Choices in Diversified Multinational Corporations," *Harvard Business Review* 55 (1977): 127–136.

47. F. T. Knickerbocker, *Oligopolistic Reaction and Multinational Enterprise* (Cambridge, Mass.: Harvard University, Graduate School of Business, Division of Research, 1974).

48. Egelhoff, "Strategy and Structure in Multinational Corporations," pp. 435–458.

49. Ibid., pp. 453–454.

50. Stanley M. Davis, "Trends in Organization of Multinational Organizations," *Columbia Journal of World Business,* Summer 1976, p. 59.

51. Sidney M. Robbins and Robert B. Stobaugh, "Evolution of the Finance Function," *Money in the Multinational Enterprise* (New York: Basic Books, 1973), reprinted as "Growth of the Financial Function," *Financial Executive,* July 1973, pp. 24–31.

REFERENCES

Ackerman, R. W. "Influence of Integration and Diversity on the Investment Process." *Administrative Science Quarterly* 15 (1970): 341–351.

Ansoff, H. I., and R. G. Brandenburg. "A Language for Organizational Design: Parts 1 and 2." *Management Science* 17 (1971): 705–731.

Brooke, M. Z., and H. L. Remmers. *The Strategy of the Multinational Enterprise.* New York: Elsevier, 1970.

Chandler, A. D., Jr. "The Multi-Unit Enterprise: A Historical and International Comparative Analysis and Summary." In *Evolution of International Management Structures.* Edited by H. F. Williamson. Newark: University of Delaware Press, 1975, pp. 222–254.

———. *Strategy and Structure.* Garden City, N. Y. Anchor, 1966.

———. *Strategy and Structure.* Cambridge, Mass.: MIT Press, 1962.

Committee on International Accounting. "Report." *The Accounting Review,* suppl. 48 (Summer 1973): 120–136.

Daniels, J. D., R. A. Pitts, and M. J. Tretter. "Strategy and Structure of U.S. Multinationals: An Exploratory Study." *Academy of Management Journal* 27, no. 2 (June 1984): 292–307.

Davidson, W. H., and P. Hasjeslagh. "Shaping a Global Product Organization." *Harvard Business Review,* March–April 1982, pp. 69–76.

Davis, Stanley M. "Trends in Organization of Multinational Organizations." *Columbia Journal of World Business,* Summer 1976, pp. 59–71.

DiMaggio, Paul, and Walter Powell. "Institutional Isomorphism." *American Sociological Review* 48 (1983): 147–160.

Drake, Rodman, and Lee M. Caudill. "Management of the Large Multinational: Trends and Future Challenges." *Business Horizons* 24 (May–June 1981): 83–91.

Dundas, K.N.M., and P. R. Richardson. "Implementing the Unrelated Product Strategy." *Strategic Management Journal* 3 (1982): 287–301.

Egelhoff, W. G. "Strategy and Structure in Multinational Corporations: An Information Processing Approach." *Administrative Science Quarterly* 27 (1982): 435–458.

Fligstein, Neil. "The Spread of the Multidivisional Firm Among Large Firms." *American Sociological Review,* June 1985, pp. 377–391.

Hamman, M., and J. Freeman. "The Population Ecology of Organizations." *American Journal of Sociology* 92 (1977): 929–964.

———. "Structural Inertia and Organizational Change." *American Sociological Review* 49 (1984): 149–164.

Harrigan, K. R. "Vertical Integration and Corporate Strategy." *Academy of Management Journal* 28 (1985): 397–425.

Hoskisson, R. E. "Multidimensional Structure and Performance: The Contingency of Diversification Strategy." *Academy of Management Journal* 30 (1987): 625–644.

Kerr, J. L. "Diversification Strategy and Managerial Rewards: An Empirical Study." *Academy of Management Journal* 28 (1985): 155–179.

Knickerbocker, F. T. *Oligopolistic Reaction and Multinational Enterprise.* Cambridge, Mass.: Harvard University, Graduate School of Business, Division of Research, 1974.

Lorsch, J. W., and S. A. Allen. *Managing Diversity and Independence.* Boston: Division of Research, Graduate School of Business Administration, Harvard University, 1973.

Mintzberg, H. *Structure in Firms: Designing Effective Organizations.* Englewood Cliffs, N.J.: Prentice-Hall, 1983.

———. *The Structuring of Organizations.* Englewood Cliffs, N.J.: Prentice-Hall, 1978.

Naylor, Thomas H. "The International Strategy Matrix." *Columbia Journal of World Business,* Summer 1985, pp. 11–19.

Pfeffer, Jeffrey. *Organizations and Organization Theory.* Marshfield, Mass.: Pitman, 1982.

———. *Power in Organizations.* Marshfield, Mass.: Pitman, 1981.

Pfeffer, J., and G. Salanick. *The External Control of Organizations: A Resource Dependency Perspective.* New York: Harper and Row, 1978.

Porter, M. E. *Competitive Advantage: Creating and Sustaining Superior Performance.* New York: The Free Press, 1985.

Prabolad, C. K. "Strategic Choices in Diversified Multinational Corporations." *Harvard Business Review* 55 (1977): 127–136.

Robbins, Sidney M., and Robert B. Stobaugh. "Evolution of the Finance Function." *Money in the Multinational Enterprise.* New York: Basic Books, 1973. Reprinted as "Growth of the Financial Function." *Financial Executive,* July 1973, pp. 24–31.

Robinson, Richard D. *Internationalization of Business: An Introduction.* Hinsdale, Ill.: Dryden, 1984.

Stieglitz, H. *Organizational Structures of International Companies.* Studies in Personnel Policy no. 198. New York: National Industrial Conference Board, 1965.

Stopford, J. M., and L. T. Wells. *Managing the Multinational Enterprise.* New York: Basic Books, 1972.

Teece, D. J. "Economies of Scope and the Scope of the Enterprise." *Journal of Economic Behavior and Organization* 1 (1980): 223–247.

Williamson, O. *Markets and Hierarchies.* New York: The Free Press, 1975.

6

Performance Evaluation of Multinational Operations

Performance evaluation of international operations is a more complex issue than it is for domestic operations since multinational companies face a host of uncertainties and opportunities. This chapter elaborates on the models, techniques, and issues facing multinational corporations as they attempt to implement a management control system for their worldwide operations.

CONTROL MODELS FOR MULTINATIONAL OPERATIONS

The Baliga and Jaeger Model

As stated by J. T. Child, "Control is essentially concerned with regulating the activities within an organization so that they are in accord with the expectations established in policies, plans and targets."[1] The activities or phenomena assumed to be monitored and evaluated are behavior and output.[2] They are the two objects of control. At the same time the instruments of control are either (a) pure bureaucratic/formalized control relying predominately on accounting control instruments such as budgets, variances, and performance reports; or (b) cultural controls relying on an informal socialization process better known as corporate culture. A comparison of bureaucratic and cultural control mechanisms, provided by B. A. Baliga and A. M. Jaeger,[3] is shown in Exhibit 6.1. In their article, Baliga and Jaeger proposed that the type of control system chosen, cultural or bureaucratic, dictates a different level of delegation and is itself a function of the type of interdependence, environmental uncertainty, and cultural proximity. The model is shown in Exhibit 6.2.

The types of interdependence, as based on the work of J. D. Thompson, include (a) pooled interdependence, whereby the autonomous subsidiaries share

Exhibit 6.1
Comparison of Bureaucratic and Cultural Control Mechanisms

	TYPE OF CONTROL	
OBJECT OF CONTROL	Pure bureaucratic/ formalized control	Pure cultural control
Output	Formal performance reports	Shared norms of performance
Behavior	Company manuals	Shared philosophy of management

Source: B. A. Baliga and A. M. Jaeger, "Multinational Coporations: Control Systems and Delegation Issues," *Journal of International Business Studies*, Fall 1984, p. 28. Reprinted with permission.

common resources; (b) sequential interdependence, whereby the output of one system is fed into another part of the system; and (c) reciprocal interdependence, whereby segments of firms feed their work back and forth among themselves.[4] The three types are illustrated in Exhibit 6.3.

The environmental uncertainty is either high or low. The greater uncertainty is created by a highly dynamic, complex, diverse, and hostile environment that leads the firms to adopt low levels of formalization and centralization.[5,6]

Finally, *cultural proximity* is defined as "the extent to which the host cultural ethos permits adoption of the home organization culture";[7] it is either high or low.

The rationale for the model rests on (a) the maximum need for control, co-ordination, and consistency in decision making under reciprocal interdependence, which amounts to more centralization than under sequential interdependence first and pooled interdependence second; and (b) the need for more decentralization under high environmental uncertainty than under low environmental uncertainty and under a high level of cultural proximity than under a low level of cultural proximity. As stated by Baliga and Jaeger:

Regardless of the type of interdependence, under conditions of high environmental uncertainty some degree of delegation should be provided to subsidiary management so that they may be more responsive to their local environment. Conversely, centralization could be extensive under conditions of low uncertainty. Under conditions of low cultural prox-

Exhibit 6.2
Control System and Level of Delegation Appropriate to Subsidiaries Under Various Conditions

Type of Interdependence	Environmental Uncertainty	Cultural Proximity	Type of Control System	Extent of Delegation
POOLED	H	H	Cultural	Highly decentralized
		L	Bureaucratic	Highly decentralized
	L	H	Cultural	Moderately decentralized
		L	Bureaucratic	Highly decentralized
SEQUENTIAL	H	H	Cultural	Moderately decentralized
		L	Bureaucratic	Moderately decentralized
	L	H	Cultural	Centralized
		L	Bureaucratic	Centralized
RECIPROCAL	H	H	Cultural	Highly decentralized
		L	Cultural	Moderately decentralized
	L	H	Cultural	Centralized
		L	Cultural	Centralized

Key: H — High
L — Low

Source: B. A. Baliga and A. M. Jaeger, "Multinational Coporations: Control Systems and Delegation Issues," *Journal of International Business Studies*, Fall 1984, p. 38. Reprinted with permission.

Exhibit 6.3
Types of Interdependence within Organizations

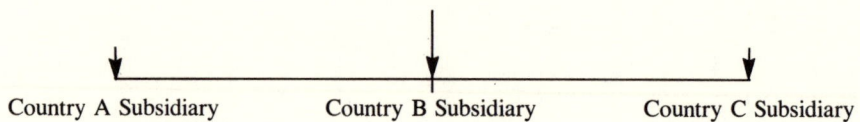

POOLED INTERDEPENDENCE

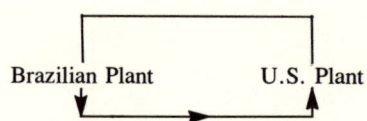

SEQUENTIAL INTERDEPENDENCE

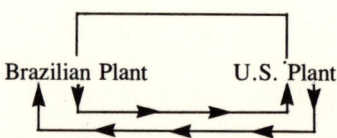

RECIPROCAL INTERDEPENDENCE

Key: ──▶──▶── indicates direction of flow of materials.

Source: B. A. Baliga and A. M. Jaeger, "Multinational Corporations: Control Systems and Delegation Issues," *Journal of International Business Studies*, Fall 1984, p. 32. Reprinted with permission.

imity, employment of cultural control systems would probably not be worth the expenditure. Where cultural proximity is high, socialization and indoctrination can be carried out more effectively, and use of cultural control would permit a higher level of delegation.[8]

The Hill and Hoskisson Model

Multinational, multiproduct firms differ in their diversification strategies, choosing (a) vertical integration to achieve vertical economies, (b) related diversification to achieve synergistic economies, and (c) unrelated diversification to achieve financial economies. Given the differences in the diversification strategies, Charles Hill and Robert Hoskisson suggested that the "control arrangements within the basic M-Form framework must be consistent with (fit) a strategy in order to realize the economic benefits associated with that strategy."[9]

Although the realization of financial economies in the case of unrelated diversification dictates a certain high degree of divisional autonomy, both the realization of vertical economies and synergistic economies require a certain degree of central coordination and linkages between division. It follows that the control characteristics will depend on (1) the degree of decentralization, (2) the degree of decomposition between divisions, and (3) the degree of divisional profit accountability, where the degree of divisional profit accountability is a function of the first ten dimensions.[10] As a result, two propositions are suggested as follows:

Control systems consistent with realizing financial economies are characterized by relatively high degrees of decentralization of decisions to divisions, decomposition between divisions and consequently high accountability for divisional profits.[11]
Control systems consistent with realizing vertical and synergistic economies will be characterized by relatively low degrees of decentralization to divisions, decomposition between divisions, and consequently, low accountability for divisional profits.[12]

The first part of the model is depicted in Exhibit 6.4. The second level of the Hill and Hoskisson Model deals with the information processing requirements of each diversification strategy. The information processing requirement IP is defined as follows:

$$IP = f(N, C, U, U*C)$$

where

N = number of divisions
C = the amount of interdependence or connectedness
U = product market uncertainty
$U*C$ = interaction terms

Exhibit 6.4
A Model of Control for a Multinational Corporation

```
                          Unrelated Diversification ←————  →High Decentralization
                                                           →High Decomposition Among
                                                              Divisions
┌──────────┐                                               →High Accountability for
│ Choice of│                                                  for Divisional Profit
│ Control  │
│ Systems  │                                               →Low Decentralization
└──────────┘              Related and Vertical ————————    →Low Decomposition Among
                          Diversification                     Divisions
                                                           →Low Accountability for
                                                              Divisional Profit
```

The degree of connectedness will vary between diversification strategies as follows, for vertical diversification:

$$C_v = N - 1 \tag{1}$$

For related diversification:

$$C_s = \tfrac{1}{2}(N^2 - N) \tag{2}$$

As a result the information processing requirements will be as follows, for vertical diversification:

$$IP_v = aN + b(N - 1) + cU + dU(N - 1) \tag{3}$$

For related diversification:

$$IP_s = aN + b[\tfrac{1}{2}(N^2 - N)] + cU + dU[\tfrac{1}{2}(N^2 - N)] \tag{4}$$

For unrelated diversification:

$$IP_f = aN + cU \tag{5}$$

What appears is that for a given number of divisions and a given level of market uncertainty, $IP_s > IP_v > IP_f$.[13] As stated by Hill and Hoskisson:

Information processing needs in the vertical and synergistic cases increase not only because of the direct effects managing linkages, but also because of indirect effects. Realizing vertical or synergistic gains requires many decisions to be shared or made by a coordinating body. . . . When this occurs, divisional autonomy is violated, which can lead to a loss of control. Again, this is a disadvantage of focusing upon vertical and/or synergistic economies. The loss of control can be attenuated, however, by installing more detailed information processing systems and relying on bureaucratic, as well as output controls.[14]

As a result, two more propositions are advanced as follows:

As firms grow by vertical integration or related diversification they will become increasingly constrained by information processing requirements to focus on attaining financial economies.[15]

The level of any changes in product market uncertainty will affect the extent to which the firm focuses on realizing various economic gains. Under conditions of either high or increasing uncertainty, vertically integrated and related firms will focus on realizing financial economies. Under conditions of either low or decreasing uncertainty, such firms will focus on realizing vertical or synergistic economies.[16]

CHARACTERISTICS AND OBJECTIVES OF
INTERNATIONAL PERFORMANCE EVALUATION

The control process is made difficult internationally by the factors of (a) geographic and cultural distance separating countries; (b) diversity of operations between countries in terms of market size, type of competition, product, labor cost, currency, and other factors; (c) uncontrollable factors such as dictates of outside stockholders and government regulations; and (d) degree of uncertainty in the setting of plans and the realization of results internationally.[17] The geographic and cultural distance separating countries makes it difficult to observe foreign environmental changes and to control for them adequately.[18,19] The closer a subsidiary is to headquarters, the less autonomy it will have compared to others that are in distant countries. This was particularly observed in the case of the Canadian subsidiaries of U.S. firms.[20]

Multinational firms have been found to expand and modify their domestic profitability measures when evaluating foreign operations.[21] They relied on the following specific objectives when using evaluation procedures internationally:

1. To insure adequate profitability
2. To have an early warning system if something is wrong
3. To have a basis for allocation of resources
4. To evaluate individual managers[22]

Performance evaluation for multinational operations has also been viewed as having four major purposes:

1. To insure that actual performance of the subsidiary agrees with expected performance
2. To facilitate comparison between subsidiaries in meeting some predetermined set of criteria
3. To assist top management in making resource allocation decisions so that corporate resources are directed to subsidiaries when expected profits are the highest
4. To motivate decision makers (foreign subsidiary managers) in achieving their goals, which should not be in conflict with top-management goals[23]

Performance evaluations for multinational operations depend on the attitude taken by the corporate management's multinational business policies and on a pattern of control that has been labeled "waxing and waning."[24]

Maximizing the type of attitude taken by top management toward multinational business policies, Howard Perlmutter used three classifications: ethnocentric (home-country oriented), polycentric (host-country oriented), and geocentric (world oriented).[25] As a result, performance evaluation in a centralized ethnocentric company will be tightly controlled by the parent company, but in a decentralized polycentric or geocentric company it will be controlled less by the parent company.

Waxing and waning was noticed by S. M. Robbins and R. B. Stobaugh, who found that the performance evaluation function for multinational operations depended mainly on the degree of foreign experience that the firm had and the size of the firm's foreign operations.[26] In fact, they noticed three phases of the evolutionary process of performance evaluation. In the first phase, given the small scale of foreign operations and the lack of foreign experience, relatively little control is exercised by the parent company, and each subsidiary is practically left on its own to improve its performance with the possible result of suboptimization. The performance evaluation systems of the firm in general are far from being coordinated. In the second phase, the foreign operations expand and top management starts getting closer control in foreign operations. The result is a strong and coordinated performance evaluation system dominated by the parent company. In the third phase, the scale of operations is so large and complex that the control exercised by headquarters begins to diminish in favor of a more decentralized performance evaluation system. Headquarters keeps a hand in the situation, however, by formulating guidelines for the foreign subsidiaries to follow.

EVALUATING DIVISIONAL PERFORMANCE

Organization of a Decentralized Concern

Cost centers, profit centers, and investment centers are the types of segments used by a decentralized concern in creating the type of organization structure most suitable to the efficient conduct of its activities.

A *cost center* is the smallest segment of activity or area of responsibility for which costs can be accumulated. Responsibility in a cost center is restricted to cost. For planning purposes, the budget estimates are cost estimates; for control purposes, performance evaluation is guided by a cost variance equal to the difference between the actual and the budgeted costs for a given period. In general, cost centers are associated with segments of the firm that provide tangible or intangible services to live departments. For example, cost centers may include departments providing services such as legal advice and accounting, personnel, and data processing services. Cost centers may also be found in producing or line departments. When a production process requires different types of machines and operations, cost centers are created to enhance the accumulation of costs by operation.

A *profit center* is a segment of activity or area of responsibility for which both revenues and costs are accumulated. The manager holds responsibility for both revenues and expenses. For planning purposes, the budget estimates include both revenues and expenses. For control purposes, performance is guided by both a revenue variance and a cost variance. In short, the objective function of a profit center's manager is to maximize the center's profit.

Although the profit center concept is vital to the implementation of decentralization, it can be used in firms with centralization. In other words, the profit center concept leads essentially to a divisionalized firm but not necessarily to a decentralized firm. Decentralization implies the relative freedom to make decisions.

An *investment center* is a segment of activity or area held responsible for both profits and investment. For planning purposes the budget estimate is a measure of the rate-of-return-on-investment (ROI) estimate. For control purposes, performance evaluation is guided by an ROI variance. In short, the objective function of an investment center is to maximize the center's ROI. The merits of the ROI measure and the possible problems associated with such a measure are illustrated later in the chapter (see Exhibit 6.5).

Rate of Return on Investment

Measurement of the Rate of Return on Investment: E. I. duPont de Nemours and Company is generally credited with the development of the ROI concept. Alfred P. Sloan evaluated the principle of ROI as follows:

I am not going to say the the rate of return is a magic word for every occasion in business. There are times when you have to spend money just to stay in business, regardless of the visible rate of return. Competition is the final price determinant and competitive prices may result in profits which force you to accept a rate of return less than you hoped for, or for that matter to accept temporary losses. And, in times of inflation the rate-of-return concept comes up against the problem of assets undervalued in terms of replacement. Nevertheless, no other financial principle with which I am acquainted serves better than rate of return as an objective aid to business management.[27]

The ROI is found by dividing the net income by the amount of investment. It relates the profit to invested capital, both of which are important areas of management responsibility. The rationale lies in the belief that there is an optimal investment level in each asset leading to optimal profit level. The ROI is the product of two components: profit margin and investment turnover. The *profit margin* equals net income divided by sales and indicates the segment's ability to transform sales into profit. The *investment turnover* equals sales divided by invested capital. Thus the ROI can be expressed as follows:

$$\text{ROI} = \frac{\text{Net income}}{\text{Invested capital}} = \frac{\text{Sales}}{\text{Invested capital}} \times \frac{\text{Net income}}{\text{Sales}}$$

This formula shows that the ROI can be increased by an increase in either the profit margin or the investment turnover, and it can be decreased by a decrease

Exhibit 6.5
Relationship of Factors Influencing the Rate of Return on Investment

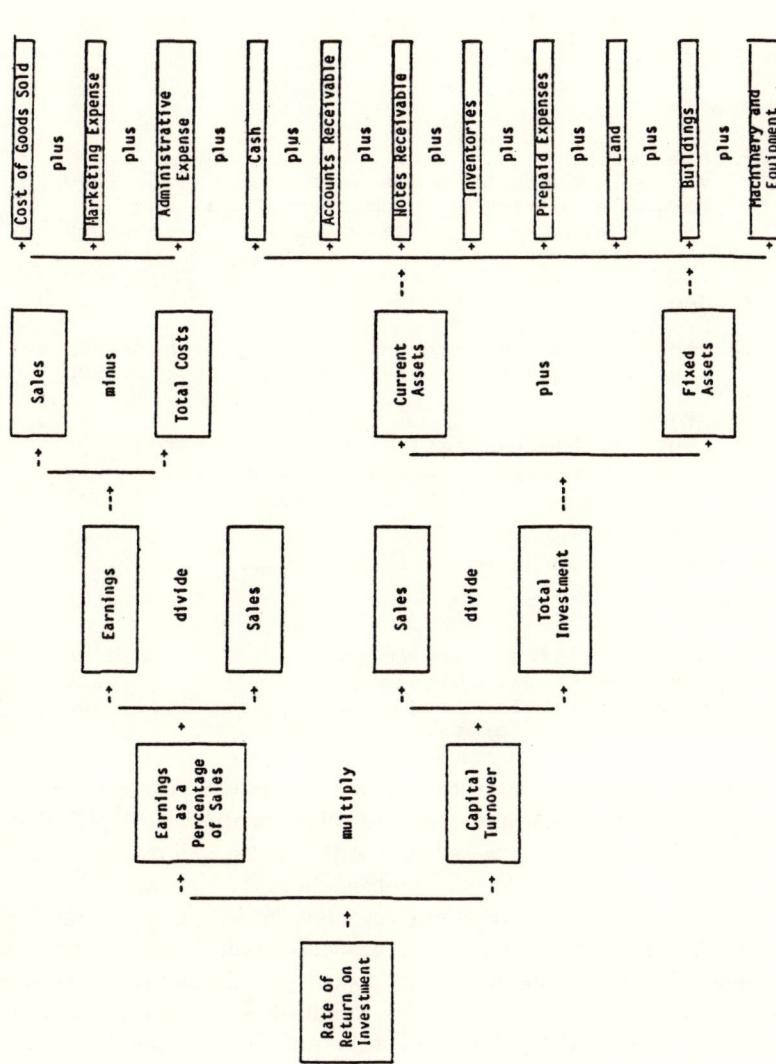

Exhibit 6.6
Format and Content of a Divisional Income Statement (in thousands)

```
Revenues.............................................12000
     External sales..........................5000
     Internal sales (transfer price equal to
          market value).......................6000
     Internal sales (transfer price different from
          market value).......................1000
```

Minus

```
Variable costs......................................5000
     Variable costs of goods sold.............2000
     Variable selling and administrative
          divisional expense..................3000
Total contribution margin...........................7000
```

Add (Deduct)

```
Fixed costs allocated to other divisions for transfers
     made at other than market value...........500
```

(Deduct)

```
     Controllable discretionary and committed
          fixed costs.........................200
```

Equals

```
Controllable operation income.......................6300
```

(Deduct)

```
     Uncontrollable fixed costs...............300
Operating income before taxes.......................6000
Income taxes..................................500
Net income (after taxes)............................5500
```

in either the profit margin or the investment turnover. These are not the only alternatives. Exhibit 6.5 shows the factors that can affect the final ROI outcome.

Rate of Return on Investment Issues: Although the ROI may qualify as a good management tool, some potential problems must be recognized.

The net income figure used in calculating the ROI may require certain adjustments that do not conform with generally accepted accounting principles. Exhibit 6.6 illustrates the format and content of a divisional income statement. Distinctions are made between sales to outside customers and sales to other divisions, between controllable and uncontrollable costs, and between variable and fixed costs. This format allows for the possibility of distinguishing between the performance of the manager and the performance of the division. Two rates of return can be computed—the controllable ROI and net ROI—as follows:

Controllable ROI = Controllable income/Controllable capital investment
Net ROI = Net income after taxes/Total capital investment

Another problem with the ROI is that the investment figure used in calculating the ROI may lead to an "unrealistic" ROI. Hence the most obvious figure is the *net book value of assets,* which is the original cost minus depreciation to date. Such a measure has inherent weaknesses. For example, it enables divisions with the older assets to earn a higher rate of return than divisions with newer assets, given the low book value resulting from greater depreciation charges.

Several solutions can overcome this limitation of the ROI method:

First, gross book value can be used. This approach, however, still enables a divisional manager to increase the ROI by scrapping nonprofitable assets that may be detrimental to the company.

Second, four nonhistorical cost valuation methods can be used to determine the economic value, the replacement cost, the net realizable value, and the general price level adjusted historical cost. The first three methods approximate the current value, whereas the last one merely adjusts historical cost. The *replacement cost* represents the amount of cash or other consideration that would be required to obtain the same asset or its equivalent. The *net realizable value* represents the amount of cash for which an asset can be sold. The *capitalized value* refers to the present value of net cash flows expected to be received from the use of the asset. The three current values are relevant to different types of decisions. Although the capitalized value appears to be dominant, it is a subjective value based on the present value of expected cash flows. Replacement cost and net realizable value may be more available and constitute a better alternative to historical cost.

Third, the use of an increasing-charge depreciation (annuity depreciation), the compound-interest depreciation, can lead to a lower income being related to a smaller investment base. Sinking-fund depreciation is based on the financial concept that depreciation represents the return of investment. Suppose that a company is considering buying an asset with a two-year life and no salvage value. If the cost of the asset is estimated to be \$8,680 and the yearly cash flow to be \$5,000, the ROI, using a discounted cash flow method, can be obtained by solving the following equation for r:

$$\$8,680 = \sum_{t=1}^{2} \frac{\$5,000}{(1 + r)^t}$$
$$r = 10\%$$

Given the knowledge of the ROI, compound-interest depreciation assumes a capital recovery factor. Exhibit 6.7 presents the results of sinking-fund depreciation, showing each cash payment to be equal to interest on investment plus principal. Exhibit 6.8 shows the superiority of compound-interest depreciation with the income statement and the ROI computations using either constant, increasing, or decreasing depreciation. The compound-interest depreciation method results in a stable, constant ROI figure compared to the fluctuating results obtained by the straight-line and accelerated methods. Therefore, compound-

Exhibit 6.7
Example of Compound-Interest Depreciation

Year	Initial Investment (a)	Cash Earnings (b)	Return of 10% (c = 10%a)	Depreciation (d = b - c)	Unrecovered Investment (e = a - d)
0	$8,680	$5,000	$868.0	$4,132.0	$8,680
1	4,548	5,000	454.8	4,545.2	$4,548
2					2.8[*]

*Due to rounding.

Exhibit 6.8
Depreciation Methods and Rate-of-Return Computations

	Methods of Depreciation					
	Straight-Line		Accelerated Depreciation		Compound Interest Depreciation	
Year	1	2	1	2	1	2
Cash Earnings	$5,000	$5,000	$5,000	$5,000	$5,000	$5,000.0
Depreciation	4,340[a]	4,340[a]	5,786[b]	2,893[b]	4,132	4,545.2
Net Income	$ 660	$ 660	$ (786)	$2,107	$ 868	$ 454.8
Investment Base	$8,680	$4,340	$8,680	$2,894	$8,680	$4,548.0
Rate of Return on Investment	7.6%	15.2%	-9%	72%	10%	10%

[a]$8.680 ÷ 2 = $4,340.
[b]$8.680 ÷ ⅔ = $5,786. $8.680 × ⅓ = $2,983.

interest depreciation is preferred by many companies to measure divisional profitability.

An appropriate allocation of assets to divisions makes the ROI more meaningful and contributes to goal congruence. Such allocation differs from one company to another, given that some companies elect to centralize certain activities and decentralize others. For instance, in most decentralized companies the home office centralizes cash management, billing, or receivable collections.

As a general rule, the basis of allocation of assets to divisions should be controllability. That is, the amount of assets controllable by any given segment in its managerial activities should be the rate of return on divisional investment.

To summarize, the ROI limitations can be corrected if the investment base is at current value net of depreciation and if a sinking-fund depreciation method is used.

Residual Income

Developed in the 1950s by General Electric Company, the concept of *residual income* to measure divisional performance is defined operationally as divisional income in excess of prescribed interest on investment. This concept directs the manager toward the maximization of income above a charge for assets used. The interest rate used corresponds conceptually to the firm's cost of capital. For example, if a divisional income were $50,000 for a budgeted investment of $200,000 with a cost of capital of 10 percent, the residual income would be computed as follows:

Divisional net income	$50,000
Minus	
Imputed interest at 10 percent of assets	20,000
Equals	
Residual income	$30,000

There are two advantages to the residual-income method for divisional performance evaluation:

1. The method enables the division to continue to expand as long as it meets the cost of capital requirements. For the previous example, the cost of capital was 10 percent, whereas the ROI was 25 percent ($50,000/$200,000). In other words, using the ROI of 25 percent as an investment criterion would eliminate projects whose returns might exceed the cost of capital and, consequently, would eliminate projects acceptable from the point of view of the corporation as a whole.
2. The method requires setting a rate-of-return target for every type of asset, regardless of the division's profitability. The end result is a yardstick for comparisons between divisions. However, the adequate determination of the cost of capital or the rate of return of individual assets is a possible problem.

TECHNIQUES USED FOR PERFORMANCE EVALUATION INTERNATIONALLY

As might be expected, multinational firms use a variety of techniques for performance evaluation internationally in order to adapt to different contexts. Various surveys attempted to determine the nature of these techniques:

The first survey conducted by F.D.S. Choi and I. J. Czechowicz identified multiple criteria used in performance evaluation.[28] Both financial and nonfinancial criteria were used for the evaluation of the performance of overseas units and subsidiary managers. The firms indicated that the primary purpose of a performance evaluation system is to issue adequate profitability. Of the multiple criteria used, the budget compared to actual profit was indicated as the most important financial criterion followed by the return on investment, budget compared to actual sales, return on sales, return on assets, budget compared to actual return on investment, and operating cash flows. One noticeable result is that U.S. based multinationals preferred cash flows to the parent company rather than cash flows to the subsidiary, indicating a more global perspective than the non-U.S. based multinationals. Of the multiple nonfinancial criteria used, the market share was judged to be the most important, followed by productivity improvements, relationships with host governments, quality control, employee development, and safety.

The second survey conducted by William Persen and Van Lessig,[29] cited earlier, also found the actual performance compared to the budget as the most important financial criteria used in performance evaluation internationally. Other criteria included, by order of importance, the following:

1. Operating budget comparison

2. Contribution to earnings per share

3. Return on investment

4. Contribution to corporate cash flow

5. Return on sales

6. Return on assets

7. Asset/liability management

8. Nonaccounting data such as market share, quality control, and labor turnover

9. Long-term plan comparisons

10. Return of investment—inflation adjusted

What is noticeable from both surveys is the dominant importance of operation budget comparisons and variance analysis in performance evaluation internationally.

Finally, the Committee on International Accounting of the American Accounting Association provided the following list of performance evaluation approaches:

1. No formal evaluation of operations exists: the general manager's performance evaluation for salary, bonus and promotion purposes is entirely subjective on the basis of personality and other personal traits. This approach cannot be considered desirable and typically is found in domestic operations; however, it is rather more frequently encountered in evaluation of foreign subsidiaries and their managers.

2. Operating results are evaluated in absolute terms which are generally profit or return-on-investment (ROI). Here, a subjective evaluation is made about what is good performance and the general manager is rewarded accordingly. This approach also in-

cludes a large subjective element and is found only where more sophisticated approaches have not been developed.

3. Operating results of the entity are compared to operating results of other entities in the same family; resource utilization and the entity general manager are both evaluated on this basis since an entity is assumed to exist between the two for evaluation purposes. This approach is called "the comparison of entities" approach, and it has merit where the most important environmental variables are much the same for the entities compared.

4. Operating results are evaluated relative to operating results for the same entity in preceding periods and an identity between the general manager and the entity is assumed. This approach is called the "temporal comparison." A major problem here is that an improvement over the preceding period's poor results still may not represent good performance in absolute terms.

5. Operating results are evaluated on the basis of how closely they conform to planned operating results. Although this is potentially an excellent evaluation approach, in practice the evaluation is less than satisfactory. For example, performance is often based on actual results compared to budget for only key factors such as profit and ROI, the constituents of which may not be entirely controllable by the general manager. Another common problem with this approach is that the plan becomes obsolete because of the factors beyond the general manager's control and the plan is not revised in consideration of this. With this approach too, an identity is generally assumed between operating results and the general manager's performance.[30]

There are, however, various factors that may affect the usefulness of currently used techniques of performance evaluation.

1. The interaction of organizational structures and environmental factors in a complex network may cause profit indicators of performance evaluation to be misleading.[31]

2. The reliance on a companywide ROI measure may not portray important aspects of the subsidiary.[32]

3. Comparisons of ROIs may be misleading given the difficulties associated with the determination of an appropriate investment base for the computation of the ROI.[33]

4. The fluctuations of the exchange rates of the different countries housing the subsidiaries must become the responsibility of the managers of the foreign subsidiaries. The assignment of such responsibility is difficult.[34]

5. Wide variations in multinational corporations exist in order to approach and secure an overall balance between control and attention to local conditions as evidenced by a summary of organizational and control characteristics of nine of the world's most successful multinational corporations shown in Exhibit 6.9.

6. In comparing actual results with budgeted figures, there is a need to consider the explicit assumptions that are incorporated in the budget and the knowledge of how changes in these assumptions are likely to affect the budgeted numbers.[35] For example, Exhibit 6.10 indicates the impact of exchange rate changes depending on the sector of the economy in which a firm is operating (export, domestic-import-competing, domestic nonimport-competing) and the source of its inputs (imports, domestic traded goods and services, domestic nontraded goods and services).

Exhibit 6.9

Organizational and Control Characteristics of Nine Multinational Corporations

	Parent Company Characteristics	
Company	**Dominant Organizational Concept**	**Planning and Control**
American Cyanamid Company (U.S.)	Product divisions with global responsibility	Heavy reliance on strategic planning: under guidance of Corporate Planning and Development Department; plans prepared by designated business units; accompanied by annual profit plan: investment priority matrix to facilitate allocation of funds
Ciba-Geigy Limited (Switzerland)	Product divisions with global responsibility, but gradual strengthening of key regional organizations	Moderate reliance on strategic planning by global product divisions: gradual buildup of the role of key regional companies in the planning process; operational plans and capital budgets by country organizations and their product divisions, with the latter playing the more active role
The Dow Chemical Company (U.S.)	Decentralized geographically into six regional companies: central coordination through World Headquarters Group	Coordination of geographic regions through World Headquarters Group, particularly the Corporate Product Department; strategic planning at the corporate level on a product basis, and in the operating units on a regional basis; operational plans and capital budgets by geographic region; control function at the corporate level
General Electric Company (U.S.)	Product-oriented strategic business units on a worldwide basis	Heavy reliance on strategic planning; under guidance of Corporate Planning and Development Department; plans prepared by designated strategic business units; priority matrix to facilitate allocation of funds
Imperial Chemical Industries Limited (U.K.)	Product divisions with global responsibility, but gradual strengthening of regional organizations	Coordination of planning through Central Planning Department; strategic planning at the divisional and regional levels; tight financial reporting and control by headquarters

Exhibit 6.9 (continued)

	Parent Company Characteristics	
Research and/or Product Development	**U.S. Companies: Handling of International Business**	**European Companies: Handling of U.S. Business**
Research and product development activities carried out by product divisions at five separate centers, each concentrating on a particular technology and/or market	Separate international operating divisions organized into two geographic areas; limited authority, serving primarily in staff capacity	(not applicable)
Research and product development activities carried out by domestic product divisions and certain product divisions in key geographic areas	(not applicable)	Dual reporting relationship, with U.S. company reporting directly to headquarters and its local divisions also reporting to their counterpart domestic divisions
Research and development activities heavily process-oriented and usually associated with manufacturing facilities reporting to geographic regions; central coordination by World Headquarters Group	Highly decentralized organization of six geographic areas, each with almost complete authority over planning operations	(not applicable)
Centralized research, with supportive product development activities at the operating level	International business sector, together with overseas activities in other sectors; nine country strategic business units, which prepare an international integration plan to coordinate activities with product SBUs	(not applicable)
Research and product development activities carried out by headquarters and selected regional organizations	(not applicable)	U.S. organization oversees ICI activities in the Americas, and reports directly to headquarters; U.S. board has considerable authority regarding local decisions and activities

Exhibit 6.9 (continued)

| Company | Parent Company Characteristics | |
	Dominant Organizational Concept	Planning and Control
Nestlé S.A. (Switzerland)	Decentralized regional and country organizations	Increasing emphasis on strategic planning, with recent formation of Central Planning and Information Services Department; annual plans (budgets) by each major company; tight financial reporting and control by headquarters
N. V. Philips (The Netherlands)	Product divisions with global responsibility, but gradual strengthening of geographic organizations; U.S. company financially and legally separate from parent	Moderate to heavy reliance on strategic planning by planning units in product divisions, selected national organizations, and Central Planning Department; operational plans by division and national organizations, with initiative from the former; monthly review of performance
Rhône-Poulenc S.A. (France)	Product divisions with global responsibility, but major country organizations regain special status	Moderate reliance on strategic planning by Central Strategy and Planning Department; in addition, strategic planning at the operational level, primarily by product divisions; operational plans and capital budgets by divisions and country organizations; monthly review of performance
Solvay & Cie S.A. (Belgium)	Product divisions with global responsibility, but national and subsidiary organizations allowed to exercise a reasonable degree of autonomy	Increasing emphasis on strategic planning with the recent formation of Central Planning Department; operational plans and capital budgets by country organizations

Exhibit 6.9 (continued)

Parent Company Characteristics

Research and/or Product Development	U.S. Companies: Handling of International Business	European Companies: Handling of U.S. Business
Highly centralized research, but local product development by regional and country organizations	(not applicable)	U.S. activities divided among three main companies, each with special reporting relationship to headquarters
Highly centralized research, but with product development by product divisions and large national organizations; other research centers located in four key countries	(not applicable)	No formal chain of command between headquarters and U.S. organization; latter operating under direction of U.S. Philips Trust
Research and product development activities carried out by product divisions; several large centers, each focusing on different specializations	(not applicable)	Special reporting relationship directly to headquarters; U.S. company coordinates activities with product divisions at headquarters
Centralized research and product development activities; major national organizations also carry out product development	(not applicable)	U.S. organization functions as legal entity, overseeing Solvay's activities in the United States; however, several of the U.S. businesses report independently to headquarters

Source: Rodman Drake and Lee M. Caudill, ''Management of the Large Multinational: Trends and Future Challenges,'' *Business Horizons* 24 (May–June 1981): 88–90. Reprinted with permission.

Exhibit 6.10
Characteristic Economic Effects of Exchange Rate Changes of Multinational Corporations

Cash-flow categories	Relevant economic factors	Devaluation impact	Revaluation impact
Revenue		*Parent-currency revenue impact*	*Parent-currency revenue impact*
Export sales	Price sensitive demand	Increase (+ +)	Decrease (− −)
	Price insensitive demand	Slight increase (+)	Slight decrease (−)
Local sales	Weak prior import competition	Sharp decline (− −)	Increase (+)
	Strong prior import competition	Decrease (−) (less than devaluation %)	Slight increase
Costs		*Parent-currency cost impact*	*Parent-currency cost impact*
Domestic inputs	Low import content	Decrease (− −)	Increase (+ +)
	High import content/ inputs used in export or import competing sectors	Slight decrease (−)	Slight increase (+)
Imported inputs	Small local market	Remain the same (0)	Remain the same (0)
	Large local market	Slight decrease (−)	Slight increase (+)
Depreciation		*Cash-flow impact*	*Cash-flow impact*
Fixed assets	No asset valuation adjustment	Decrease by devaluation % (− −)	Increase by revaluation % (+ +)
	Asset valuation adjustment	Decrease (−)	Increase (+)

Note: To interpret the above chart, and taking the impact of a devaluation on local demand as an example, it is assumped that if import competition is weak, local prices will climb slightly, if at all; in such a case there would be a sharp contraction in parent-company revenue. If imports generate strong competition, local-currency prices are expected to increase, although not to the full extent of the devaluation; in this instance only a moderate decline in parent-company revenue would be registered.

Source: Alan Shapiro, ''Evaluation and Control of Foreign Operations,'' *The International Journal of Accounting Education and Research* 14, no. 1 (Fall 1978): 93. Reprinted with permission.

7. The purpose of evaluation—appraisal of an economic entity or appraisal of managerial performance—should dictate the selection of the information to be used and the choice of the basis of comparison as shown in Exhibit 6.11.[36]

CURRENCY CONSIDERATIONS IN PERFORMANCE EVALUATION

Centralization/Decentralization Dilemma

The control process of firms with foreign operations may be exercised as for domestic operations by a comparison between the actual profit performance and a budgeted profit performance based on forecasted sales and expenses. Unlike the domestic operations and because the basic operating budget of the subsidiary must be expressed in the parent company's currency for intercountry comparability, the future course of exchange rates and the choice of exchange rates in the control process have a definite impact on the performance evaluation of subsidiaries. Given this impact of the choice of exchange rates on performance evaluation, the first decision may be who should set these exchange rates in the budgeting and control process. If, as suggested by various normative models, these exchange rates are set centrally, it may create negative behavioral patterns in subsidiaries where operating managers may think that their performances are being influenced by exchange risk policies over which they have no control. A more practical and behaviorally sound solution is to give the subsidiaries' operating managers responsibility for financial decisions in general and for setting foreign exchange rates in particular. If this decentralized solution is chosen, the problem is to control any attempt by the operating managers to "suboptimize," that is, choose policies that may not be optimal from a corporate point of view as a result of an overreaction to exchange risks. This dilemma may be solved by determining the appropriate exchange rate for use in the budgeting and control processes. A good solution is provided by the Lessard/Lorange Model, which is examined next.

The Lessard/Lorange Model

The Lessard/Lorange Model examines nine theoretical combinations of exchange rates in the control process. These combinations are the result of using three possible rates for determining the budget and for tracing performance relative to the budget. These rates are the actual (spot) rate (the initial rate) at the time the actual budget is created, the projected rate at that time for the end of the period, and the ending rate obtained by continuously updating it as exchange rates change. The nine combinations obtained are shown in Exhibit 6.12.

Of the nine combinations, four are undesirable or illogical. The remaining five combinations—A–1, A–3, P–2, P–3, and E–3—are then analyzed to determine the appropriate exchange rate to use in the budgeting and control process.

Exhibit 6.11
Interrelations Involved in the Evaluation of Investment Centers

Purposes of the Evaluation	Information to be Used	Bases of Comparison
Decide whether to expand or contract the investment in the division	Present value of future incremental cash flows	Risk-adjusted cost of capital
Capital budgeting or expenditure analysis	Special purpose information gathered for a particular decision	Target rate of return by top management
Prospective investment analysis	Not a periodic information need	
Periodically measure the profitability of the resources invested in the center	Separable income/ separable investment	Cost of capital
Performance of the center as an economic entity	Source is financial accounting records of income and investment	Budgeted rate of return set by top management
Retrospective investment analysis	Attention directing information to spot weak areas and unfavorable trends	Other divisions (lack of comparability because of differences in age of plant)
	Periodic surrogate for a detailed present value	Past periods (ROI may rise over time)
		Not company-wide rate of return or independent free-standing companies (would have to allocate common costs and common investments)
Appraise the performance of division managers	Controllable income/ controllable investment	Budgeted rate of return set by top management
Managerial evaluation	Source is periodic accounting figures from control reports	Past periods
		Not cost of capital (would have to allocate noncontrollable income and investment)
		Not company-wide rate of return
		Not other divisions (lack of comparability in economic environment)

Source: Earl A. Spiller, Jr., ''Return on Investment: A Need for Special Purpose Information,'' *Accounting Horizons*, June 1988, p. 5. Reprinted with permission.

Exhibit 6.12
Possible Combinations of Exchange Rates in the Control Process

Rates Used to Determine Budget	Rates Used to Track Performance Relative to Budget Actual Time of Budget	Projected at Time of Budget	Actual at End of Period
Actual Time of Budget	A-1,	A-2	A₃
Projected at time of Budget	P-1	P-2	P₃
Actual at end of period (through updating)	E-1	E-2	E₃

Source: Donald R. Lessard and Peter Lorange, "Currency Changes and Management Control: Resolving the Centralization/Decentralization Dilemma," *The Accounting Review*, July 1977, p. 630. Reprinted with permission.

To show the differences among the five combinations and determine the appropriate exchange rate, we can use the following income statement, which may result from the performance of a foreign subsidiary (FC = foreign currency):

Sales	FC120,000
Cost of sales	30,000
Operating expenses	3,000
Operating income	FC 87,000

Assume that the subsidiary has exposed assets of FC60,000 and an initial exchange rate at the time of budget setting of FC20 = $1; there are two equally likely possibilities for the dollar value of the foreign currency in the next period— a 50 percent chance that it will remain the same (FC20 = $1) and a 50 percent chance that it will move to FC30 = $1. Thus the projected exchange rate is FC25 = $1. Based on this example, the acceptable five combinations of budget and performance measurement are shown as Exhibit 6.13.

Combination A–1—Budget at Initial; Track at Initial: It is assumed that there will be no exchange rate changes and no need to forecast them or include them in the budget and control process. As a result, the project appears profitable.

Combination P–2—Budget at Projected; Track at Projected: This approach requires a projection of exchange rates. The profitability of the project changes from $4,350 in combination A–1 to $2,880, showing that it rests on the accurate forecast of exchange rate changes by the corporate treasurer. However, given

Exhibit 6.13

Effects of Performance from Possible Combinations of Exchange Rates in Budgeting

	A-1 Budget at initial FC20= $1	A-1 Track at initial (FC20=$1)		A₃ Budget at initial (FC20=$1)	A₃ Track at ending rate (FC20=$1)	A₃ Track at ending rate (FC30=$1)
Sales	$6,000	$6,000		$6,000	$6,000	$4,000
Cost of Sales	1,500	1,500		1,500	1,500	1,000
Operating Expenses	150	150		150	150	100
Loss of Expired Assets	0	0		0	0	1,000
Operating Income (loss)	$4,350	$4,350		$4,350	$4,350	$1,900
Variance from Budget		0			0	-$2,450

	P-2 Budget at projected (FC25=$1)	P-2 Track at projected (FC25=$1	P₃ Budget at projected (FC20 = $1)	P₃ Track at ending rate (FC20=$1)	P₃ Track at ending rate (FC30=$1)
Sales	$4,800	$4,800	$4,800	$6,000	$4,000
Cost of Sales	1,200	1,200	1,200	1,500	1,000
Operating Expenses	120	120	120	150	100
Loss of Expired Assets	600	600	600	0	1,000
Operating Income (loss)	$2,880	$2,880	$2,880	$4,350	$1,900
Variance from Budget		0		$1,470	-$ 980

	E₃ Budget at ending (FC20=$1)	E₃ Track at ending (FC20=$1)	E₃ Budget at ending (FC30=$1)	E₃ Track at ending (FC30=$1)
Sales	$6,000	$6,000	$4,000	$4,000
Cost of Sales	1,500	1,500	1,000	1,000
Operating Expenses	150	150	100	100
Loss of Expired Assets	0	0	1,000	1,000
Operating Income (loss)	$4,350	$4,350	$1,900	$1,900
Variance from Budget		0	0	0

Note: Loss on exposed assets: Beginning exposed assets = FC60,000 ÷ 20 = $3,000.

ᵃWhen ending rate is FC25 = $1, ending exposed assets = FC60,000 ÷ 25 = $2,400. Loss = $600.

ᵇWhen ending rate is FC30 = $1, ending exposed assets = FC60,000 ÷ 30 = $2,000. Loss = $1,000.

the zero variance, the operating manager is freed of the responsibility of forecasting the exchange rate changes.

Combinations E–3—Budget at Ending; Track at Ending: As in combination A–1 or P–2, this combination allows the operating manager to ignore the effects of both anticipated and unanticipated fluctuations in exchange rates. Notice the zero variance. Again the profitability of the project appears, however, to rest on the treasurer's forecast of future exchange rates.

Combination A–3—Budget at Initial; Track at Ending: Unlike the previous combinations, this combination makes the operating manager responsible for the foreign exchange risk. The profitability of the project depends on the ending rate. It is equal to a loss of $2,450 if it changes to the local currency of 30 = $1. This combination is perceived to be the worst of all possible worlds. Donald Lessard and Peter Lorange explained it as follows: "In the budgeting stage, no account will be taken of possible exchange fluctuations, yet their full impact will be attributed to the manager at the tracking state. The harmful effects of such a system can be expected to include 'padding' of budgets or decentralized hedging actions by managers to reduce exchange risks which are likely to loom very large from their narrower local perspective."[37]

Combination P–3—Budget at Projected; Track at Ending: This combination also makes the operating manager responsible for the foreign exchange risk. The profitability is either significantly above the budget when the ending rate is FC20 = $1 (positive variance $1,470) or under the budget when the ending rate is FC30 − $1 (negative variance of − $980). This combination may be attractive in cases in which operating plans should and can be changed in response to exchange rate fluctuations.

Appropriate Combinations: Lessard and Lorange favored combination P–2, which incorporated the projected exchange rates in both the budgeting and control processes. These rates are viewed as "internal forward rates" since their use is analogous to the treasurer's acting as a backer and "buying forward" receipts in foreign currencies at a guaranteed rate. As a result, combination P–2 excludes unplanned exchange fluctuations but acknowledges expected fluctuations at the budgeting stage and appears as the dominant combination. Management control criteria used to support the choice of internal forward exchange rates as the basis to decision making and performance evaluation are goal congruence and fairness. As stated by Lessard and Lorange:

Goal-congruence is restored because a corporate-wide point of view has been brought to bear on the currency exchange rate, eliminating decisions taken on the basis of the expectations and risk-preferences of local managers who necessarily have a narrower horizon on the currency risk problem than the corporate headquarters. Fairness is restored, at least in regard to the exchange rate fluctuations, by the establishment of a standard under which the local decision maker gets no blame or credit for currency fluctuations outside of the division manager's control.[38]

Improvements on the Lessard/Lorange Model

The Lessard/Lorange Model, however, has been found to be inadequate in evaluating affiliates located in countries experiencing hyperinflation and rapid exchange rate devaluation since it may yield distorted results.[39] Laurent Jacque and Lorange suggested that under these extreme operating conditions of monetary hyperinflation, multinational firms should upgrade or "environmentalize" their control systems by removing variance in an affiliate's operating results that is due to economic exposure and therefore uncontrollable.

Another improvement to the Lessard/Lorange Model is the use of a Purchasing Power Parity-Normalized Approach. G. Bennett Stewart suggested the use in performance evaluation of a "normalized" exchange rate computed as the exchange rate that would exist if the market properly adjusted for the purchasing power parity over the short run.[40] The rationale is that in the short run the exchange rate fluctuates and fails to return to the purchasing power parity conditions as a result of nonmarket factors. The suggested adjustment of the exchange rate can correct for the distortions caused by the fluctuating exchange rate. An illustration of such an adjustment follows:

	Period 1	Period 2
Jordanian price index	100	140
U.S. price index	100	120
Ratio: Jordanian to U.S.		1.166
Actual exchange rate	JDO.600/$	JDO.700/$
PPP-normalized rate	JDO.600/$	JDO.7056/$

The use of the PPP normalized rate for the translation of assets and profits and the computation of the rate of return are judged the most appropriate measures of foreign operating performance for the following reasons:

(1) it reflects the underlying real performance of the local economy and of local operating managers; (2) it reflects the cost of sustaining real holding losses on monetary assets that must be compensated for by a higher return in the business; (3) it includes holding gains which, after translation, would be commensurate with U.S. inflation, making it directly comparable to costs of capital experienced in dollars (which, of course, implicitly incorporates U.S. inflation); (4) it is equally applicable for countries that experience appreciating exchange values realized by investors; and finally, (5) the use of normalized exchange rates forces management, both local and corporate, to see through distortions caused by the temporary suspension of fundamental economic forces, and to incorporate anticipated currency changes into forward planning.[41]

CONCLUSION

The control of foreign operations appears to be a complex issue when multinational firms have to experiment with various options that fit the specific characteristics of their operations. This chapter identified various issues and questions in need of further research and investigation for a better implementation of management control systems internationally.

NOTES

1. J. Child, "Strategy and Control and Organizational Behavior," *Administrative Science Quarterly*, March 1973, p. 117.

2. W. G. Ouchi, "The Relationship Between Organizational Structure and Control," *Administrative Science Quarterly*, March 1977, pp. 95–112.

3. B. A. Baliga and A. M. Jaeger, "Multinational Corporations: Control Systems and Delegation Issues," *Journal of International Business Studies*, Fall 1984, pp. 25–40.

4. J. D. Thompson, *Organizations in Action* (New York: McGraw-Hill, 1967).

5. P. R. Lawrence and J. W. Lorsch, *Organization and Environment* (Homewood, Ill.: Irwin, 1967).

6. T. Burns and G. M. Stalker, *The Management of Innovation*, 2d ed. (London: Tavistock, 1964).

7. Baliga and Jaeger, "Multinational Corporations," p. 33.

8. Ibid., p. 34.

9. Charles W. Hill and Robert E. Hoskisson, "Strategy and Structure in the Multiproduct Firm," *Academy of Management Review* 12, no. 2 (1987): 333.

10. Ibid., p. 334.

11. Ibid.

12. Ibid., p. 335.

13. Ibid., p. 337.

14. Ibid.

15. Ibid., p. 338.

16. Ibid., p. 340.

17. John D. Daniels and Lee H. Radebaugh, *International Business: Environments and Operations* (Reading, Mass.: Addison-Wesley, 1989), p. 526.

18. W. R. Fannin and A. E. Rodriguez, "National or Global? Control vs. Flexibility," *Long Range Planning* 19, no. 5 (October 1986): 84–88.

19. Jacques Picard, "How European Companies Control Marketing Decisions Abroad," *Columbia Journal of World Business*, Summer 1977, pp. 113–121.

20. Rodman Drake and Lee M. Caudill, "Management of the Large Multinational: Trends and Future Challenges," *Business Horizons* 24 (May–June 1981): 84.

21. William Persen and Van Lessig, *Evaluating the Financial Performance of Overseas Operations* (New York: Financial Executive Research Foundation of the Financial Executives Institute, 1979), pp. 11–12.

22. Ibid., p. 16.

23. Wagdy Abdullah, *Internal Accountability: An International Emphasis* (Ann Arbor, Mich.: UMI Research Press, 1984), p. 3.

24. Jeffrey S. Arpan and Lee H. Radebaugh, *International Accounting and Multinational Enterprises* (Boston: Warren, Gorham and Lamont, 1981), p. 312.

25. Howard Perlmutter, "The Tortuous Evolution of the Multinational Corporation," *Columbia Journal of World Business,* January–February 1969, pp. 9–18.

26. Sidney M. Robbins and Robert B. Stobaugh, *Money in the Multinational Enterprise: A Study in Financial Policy* (New York: Basic Books, 1973).

27. Alfred P. Sloan, Jr., *My Years with General Motors* (Garden City, N.Y.: Doubleday, 1964), p. 140.

28. F.D.S. Choi and I. J. Czechowicz, "Assessing Foreign Subsidiary Performance: A Multinational Comparison," *Management International Review* 4 (1983): 14–25.

29. Persen and Lessig, *Evaluating the Financial Performance of Overseas Operations.*

30. Committee on International Accounting, "Report," *The Accounting Review,* suppl. 48 (Summer 1973): 120–135.

31. Abdullah, *International Accountability,* p. 4.

32. Paul S. Tse, "Evaluating Performance in Multinationals," *Management Accounting,* June 1979, pp. 21–25.

33. Sidney M. Robbins and Robert B. Stobaugh, "The Best Measuring Stick of Foreign Subsidiaries," *Harvard Business Review,* September–October 1973, p. 81.

34. Alan Shapiro, "Evaluation and Control of Foreign Operations," *The International Journal of Accounting Education and Research* 14, no. 1 (Fall 1978): 85.

35. Ibid., p. 92.

36. Earl A. Spiller, Jr., "Return on Investment: A Need for Special Purpose Information," *Accounting Horizons,* June 1988, pp. 1–9.

37. Donald R. Lessard and Peter Lorange, "Currency Changes and Management Control: Resolving the Centralization/Decentralization Dilemma," *The Accounting Review,* July 1977, pp. 633–634.

38. Ibid., p. 634.

39. Laurent L. Jacque and Peter Lorange, "The International Control Conundrum: The Case of Hyperinflationary Subsidiaries," *Journal of International Business Studies,* Fall 1984, pp. 185–201.

40. G. Bennett Stewart, "A Proposal for Measuring International Performance," *Midland Corporate Finance Journal,* Summer 1983, pp. 57–71.

41. Ibid., p. 71.

REFERENCES

Abdullah, Wagdy. *Internal Accountability: An International Emphasis.* Ann Arbor, Mich.: UMI Research Press, 1984.

Arpan, Jeffrey S., and Lee H. Radebaugh. *International Accounting and Multinational Enterprises.* Boston: Warren, Gorham and Lamont, 1981.

Baliga, B. A., and A. M. Jaeger. "Multinational Corporations: Control Systems and Delegation Issues." *Journal of International Business Studies,* Fall 1984, pp. 25–40.

Burns, T., and G. M. Stalker. *The Management of Innovation,* 2d ed. London: Tavistock, 1964.

Child, J. "Strategy and Control and Organizational Behavior." *Administrative Science Quarterly,* March 1973.

Choi, F.D.S., and I. J. Czechowicz. "Assessing Foreign Subsidiary Performance: A Multinational Comparison." *Management International Review* 4 (1983): 14–25.

Committee on International Accounting. "Report." *The Accounting Review,* suppl. 48 (Summer 1973): 120–135.

Daniels, John D., and Lee H. Radebaugh. *International Business: Environments and Operations.* Reading, Mass.: Addison-Wesley, 1989.

Drake, Rodman, and Lee M. Caudill. "Management of the Large Multinational: Trends and Future Challenges." *Business Horizons* 24 (May–June 1981): 84–90.

Fannin, W. R., and A. E. Rodriguez. "National or Global? Control vs. Flexibility." *Long Range Planning* 19, no. 5 (October 1986): 84–88.

Hill, Charles W., and Robert E. Hoskisson. "Strategy and Structure in the Multiproduct Firm." *Academy of Management Review* 12, no. 2 (1987): 331–341.

Jacque, Laurent L., and Peter Lorange. "The International Control Conundrum: The Case of Hyperinflationary Subsidiaries." *Journal of International Business Studies,* Fall 1984, pp. 185–201.

Lawrence, P. R., and J. W. Lorsch. *Organization and Environment.* Homewood, Ill.: Irwin, 1967.

Lessard, Donald R., and Peter Lorange. "Currency Changes and Management Control: Resolving the Centralization/Decentralization Dilemma." *The Accounting Review,* July 1977, pp. 628–637.

Ouchi, W. G. "The Relationship Between Organizational Structure and Control." *Administrative Science Quarterly,* March 1977, pp. 95–112.

Perlmutter, Howard. "The Tortuous Evolution of the Multinational Corporation." *Columbia Journal of World Business,* January–February 1969, pp. 9–18.

Persen, William, and Van Lessig. *Evaluating the Financial Performance of Overseas Operations.* New York: Financial Executive Research Foundation of the Financial Executives Institute, 1979.

Picard, Jacques. "How European Companies Control Marketing Decisions Abroad." *Columbia Journal of World Business,* Summer 1977, pp. 113–121.

Robbins, Sidney M., and Robert B. Stobaugh. "The Best Measuring Stick of Foreign Subsidiaries." *Harvard Business Review,* September–October 1973, pp. 80–88.

———. *Money in the Multinational Enterprise: A Study in Financial Policy.* New York: Basic Books, 1973.

Shapiro, Alan. "Evaluation and Control of Foreign Operations." *The International Journal of Accounting Education and Research* 14, no. 1 (Fall 1978): 83–104.

Sloan, Alfred P., Jr. *My Years with General Motors.* Garden City, N.Y.: Doubleday, 1964.

Spiller, Earl A., Jr. "Return on Investment: A Need for Special Purpose Information." *Accounting Horizons,* June 1988, pp. 1–9.

Stewart, G. Bennett. "A Proposal for Measuring International Performance." *Midland Corporate Finance Journal,* Summer 1983, pp. 57–71.

Thompson, J. D. *Organizations in Action.* New York: McGraw-Hill, 1967.

Tse, Paul S. "Evaluating Performance in Multinationals." *Management Accounting,* June 1979, pp. 21–25.

IV

Management Accounting Issues

7

International Financial Analysis

Both foreign investors and U.S. investors favor international portfolio diversification because of known potential benefits.[1] But to reap these benefits, the financial analyses of the foreign firms demand a different use of the popular financial ratios to take into account differences in accounting principles between countries as well as different attitudes about financial soundness. This is particularly important to U.S. investors who are faced with an array of foreign stocks that are increasingly being listed in the United States in order to increase corporate visibility and product image in the United States. This chapter elaborates on the use and potential misuse of ratios in financial analysis and other predictive models.

CONVENTIONAL FINANCIAL ANALYSIS

Financial analysis is a methodology designed to provide data for decision makers. It is intended to be flexible enough to assist different users in their decision making. Financial analysis rests entirely on the use of financial ratios. Financial ratios are more convenient to interpret than the financial statement accounts. This convenience is possible because the financial ratios represent "significant relationships" between various items in the financial statements. These financial ratios are then compared to establish standard ratios for the firm or other firms in the industry. If the comparison is with similar ratios of the firm over a certain number of years, the analysis is referred to as *time-series analysis*. If the comparison is with similar ratios of other firms over a certain number of years, the analysis is referred to as *cross-sectional analysis*. Whatever the type of analysis chosen, ratio analysis is intended to evaluate important financial aspects of the firm that depict its financial strengths. Examples include liquidity, leverage, profitability, and turnover dimensions. Some of the types of ratios used to measure these dimensions are presented next. They are classified into four major categories: (1) the firm's ability to meet its short-term obligations, (2) the capital structure of the firm and its ability to meet its long-term obligations, (3) the profitability and efficiency resulting from the use of capital, and (4) the efficiency resulting from the operational use of its assets.

Liquidity Ratios

Liquidity ratios are used to assess the ability of the firm to meet its short-term financial obligations when and as they fall due. These ratios are of prime interest to short-term lenders.

Current Ratio: The current ratio may be expressed as:

$$\frac{\text{Current assets}}{\text{Current liabilities}}$$

Current assets are composed mainly of cash, short-term marketable securities, accounts receivable, inventories, and prepaid expenses. *Current liabilities* are composed mainly of accounts payable, dividends, taxes payable, and short-term bank loans. The current ratio has been considered for a long time as a good indicator of a firm's liquidity. It is, however, susceptible to "window dressing," that is, susceptible to manipulation intended to approximate a "desirable" current ratio.

Quick (Acid Test) Ratio: The quick ratio may be expressed as:

$$\frac{\text{Quick assets}}{\text{Current liabilities}}$$

Quick assets are composed of cash, short-term marketable securities, and receivables. The quick ratio is intended to be a focus on immediate liquidity. Both the quick ratio and the current ratio have been criticized for failure to incorporate information about timing and magnitude of future cash flows.[2]

Defensive Interval Measure: The defensive interval measure was presented as a better replacement of both the current ratio and the quick ratio:

$$\frac{\text{Total defensive assets}}{\text{Projected daily operating expenditures}}$$

The *total defensive assets* have been appropriately defined as follows:

Defensive assets include cash, short-term marketable securities and accounts receivable. Inventories are not included in the total, nor are current liabilities deducted from the total. The denominator includes all projected operating costs requiring the use of defensive assets. Ideally, this would be based on the cash budget for the next year or shorter period.

Since this information is unlikely to be available to external analysts, the total of operating expenses on the income statement for the prior period will usually serve as a basis for calculating the projected expenditures. The adjustments must be made to the total expense figure on that statement:

(1) Depreciation, deferred taxes and other expenses that do not utilize defensive assets must be subtracted.

(2) Adjustments should be made for known changes in planned operations.[3]

Other measures of liquidity based on a fund flow concept include: (a) the ratio of net working capital to funds provided by operations, (b) the ratio of funds provided from operations to current debt, and (c) a liquidity index based on projected fund flows. Each of these fund flow based ratios reflects the idea that liquidity depends on the ability of liquid assets and cash inflows to cover the cash outflow by a material margin.

A measure of future liquidity may be expressed as follows: the five-year cash flow as a percentage of five-year growth needs is equal to the five-year sum of: (1) net income available for common stockholders plus (2) depreciation and amortization plus (3) income from discontinued operations and extraordinary items net of taxes, divided by the five-year sum of (1) capital expenditures plus (2) changes in inventories during the most recent five years plus (3) common dividends.

Leverage/Capital Structure Ratios

Leverage ratios are used to assess the long-term solvency risk of the firm, that is, its ability to meet interest and principal payments on long-term obligations as they become due. These ratios are of prime interest to long-term lenders and bondholders.

Debt to Equity Ratio: There are two possible debt-to-equity ratios:

$$\text{Long-term debt-to-equity} = \frac{\text{Long-term debt}}{\text{Shareholders' equity}} \tag{1}$$

$$\text{Total debt to equity} = \frac{\text{Current liabilities} + \text{Long-term debt}}{\text{Shareholders' equity}} \tag{2}$$

Both debt-equity ratios press the degree of leverage in the capital structure of the firm. They are also used as a measure of the financial risk associated with the common stocks of the firm.

Times Interest Earned: The times interest earned ratio may be expressed as:

$$\frac{\text{Net income (from continuing operations) before interest and income taxes}}{\text{Interest expense}}$$

or

$$\frac{\text{Net income plus total interest (adjusted by the tax rate)}}{\text{Interest expense (adjusted by the tax rate) plus preferred dividend requirement}}$$

Profitability Ratios

The profitability ratios portray the ability of the firm to use the capital committed by stockholders and lenders efficiently to generate revenues in excess of expenses. These ratios are consequently of interest to both stockholders and bondholders.

Rate of Return on Assets: The rate of return on assets, also known as the rate of return on investment, is computed as follows:

$$\text{ROI} = \frac{\text{Net income } + \text{ Interest expense net of income tax savings } + \text{ Minority interest in earnings}}{\text{Average total assets}}$$

This ratio measures the efficient use of the assets by the firm to generate earnings. One way of explaining the changes in ROI over time is to disaggregate the ratio as follows:

$$\text{ROI} = \text{Profit margin ratio} \times \text{Assets turnover ratio}$$

or

$$\text{ROI} = \frac{\text{Net income } + \text{ Interest expense net of income tax savings } + \text{ Minority interest in earnings}}{\text{Sales}}$$
$$\times \frac{\text{Sales}}{\text{Average total assets}}$$

where the profit margin ratio reflects the firm's ability to control the level of costs corresponding to the sales realized and the assets turnover ratio corresponds to the ability to generate sales from the assets used. The improving ROI may be realized either by improving the profit margin ratio or the assets turnover ratio or by improving both.

Return on Equity: The return on equity is computed as follows:

$$\frac{\text{Income available for common stockholders}}{\text{Common stockholders' equity}}$$

This ratio indicates how efficiently the capital supplied by the common stockholders was employed within the firm.

Other examples of profitability ratios used by some analysts include the expense-to-revenue ratio, the operating income ratio ([sales − cost of goods sold − selling and administrative expenses]/sales), the earnings-per-share (presented earlier) ratio, the price-earnings ratio (market price of a common stock/earnings per share), the dividends-to-net-income or payout ratio, and the operating income-to-operating assets ratio.

Turnover Ratios

Turnover or efficiency ratios are intended to convey various aspects of operational efficiency. They are generally computed on the basis of a sales figure in the numerator and the balance of an asset in the denominator. The previously mentioned total assets turnover ratio is one example of turnover ratios. Other examples include the following ratios:

Inventory Turnover: The inventory turnover is computed as follows:

$$\frac{\text{Cost of goods sold}}{\text{Average inventory}}$$

It is used as an indicator of operational efficiency.

Accounts Receivable Turnover: The accounts receivable turnover is computed as follows:

$$\frac{\text{Sales}}{\text{Average (net) accounts receivable}}$$

By dividing the accounts receivable turnover by 360 days, one also obtains the average collection period for accounts receivable. It is an indicator of the efficiency in the collection efforts of accounts receivable.

Plant Assets Turnover: The plant assets turnover is computed as follows:

$$\frac{\text{Sales}}{\text{Average plant assets}}$$

It is used as a measure of the relationship between sales and the plant assets used by the firm for its operations.

PROBLEMS WITH CONVENTIONAL FINANCIAL ANALYSIS APPLIED DOMESTICALLY

Various problems need to be recognized before conventional financial analysis can be effectively used domestically. Some of these problems include the following:

1. Ratio analysis is generally based on historical cost/generally accepted accounting principle (GAAP) numbers. Constant-dollar or current-cost information may be able to correct some of the inflationary problems by their recognition of general price level and specific price level changes.

2. Various important information is disclosed only in the footnotes and needs to be included in the analysis.

3. A better computation of leverage ratios needs to account for some of the off-balance sheet financing. For example, Standard & Poor's reports the following:

   Off-balance sheet items that are factored in the leverage analysis include:

   —Operating leases

   —Pension obligations

   —Debts of joint ventures and unconsolidated subsidiaries

   —Guarantees

   —Take-or-pay contracts and obligations under through-put and deficiency agreements

   —Receivables that have been factored or transferred

   S & P uses various methodologies to determine the proper capitalized value for each of the off-balance sheet items. In general, the relevance of the activity financed to the mainstream business of the organization and the likelihood of its needs for financial support are key considerations. Thus, debt of joint ventures which are sound, stand-alone credits may be viewed as much less onerous liability than capitalized operating results.[4]

4. The use of computerized financial statement data bases may be fraught with problems including (a) the exclusion of some small, not actively trusted or privately held firms; (b) the exclusion of bankrupt firms; (c) the exclusion of recent data; (d) the exclusion of vital information; (e) the inconsistent classification of statement items across firms; and (f) the inclusion of recording errors.[5,6]

5. The normality of the distribution of financial statement numbers has been recognized in the United States[7,8] and abroad.[9,10] Reducing normality includes either a "trimming" of the sample or a transformation of the financial ratios. Logarithm transformation or square root transformation is generally used.

6. Ratios are generally correlated, creating problems of multicollinearity when used in a multiple regression model. Reducing the number of variables may be one of the solutions.

7. Firms in the United States resort to different alternative accounting methods so that adjustments may be needed. The frequency of changes is most evident in the cases of firms facing potential distress.[11,12,13]

8. Firms all over the world use a variety of fiscal year endings, which can create problems for making an inference about any financial dimension.

9. Line of business data, although disclosed and available, may be affected by structural and organizational changes such as acquisitions, divestitures, organizational changes, and changes in internal reporting system, to name only a few.[14]

10. The comparison of financial firms may be affected by (a) differences in industrial classification;[15,16] (b) differences in fiscal year endings and stock exchange membership,[17] and (c) differences in the economic sector classification: core versus the periphery sector.[18]

PROBLEMS WITH FINANCIAL ANALYSIS
APPLIED INTERNATIONALLY

The analysis of foreign financial statements and the use of financial ratios for such an analysis are fraught with several problems: First, although the situation in some developed countries is characterized by data availability and accessibility, various countries in the world suffer from the lack of either timely reliable accounting information or computerized data bases. The timeliness of the information is best characterized by the time delay between the year-end date and the date of the auditor's report averaging from 31 to 60 days in countries like Brazil, Canada, and the United States to 121 days and over in countries like Austria and Italy.[19]

Second, it is generally agreed that the most important means of communication with stockholders is the annual report. The extent of disclosure adequacy in the annual report may be a major determinant of the quality of investment decision making in particular and economic resource allocation in general. Research studies indicate a marked difference in disclosure adequacy from one country to another.[20,21,22]

Third, beside requiring language translation, there is a need for currency translation of financial statements to a domestic currency. In December 1981 the Financial Accounting Standards Board (FASB) issued statement no. 52 (FAS 52).[23]

The FAS 52 requirements follow:

1. Foreign currency financial statements must be in conformity with the GAAP before being translated to the reporting currency.

2. Foreign currency financial statements must be expressed and, if necessary, remeasured in the functional currency before being translated to the reporting currency. The statement provides some guidelines based on certain indicators to be used in determining the functional currency. These indicators are as follows:

a. Cash flow

b. Sales price indicators

c. Sales market indicators

d. Expense indicators

e. Financing indicators

f. Intercompany transaction and arrangements indicators

If the foreign operation's cash flows are usually in foreign currency and do not affect the parent company's cash flows, if the sales price of its products depends on local conditions rather than on fluctuations in the exchange rates, if it has an active local sales market for its product, if most of its costs are incurred locally, if it services its debt obligations through local resources, and if it has little relationship with the parent company except for competitive advantages, the functional currency is the foreign currency. Otherwise, the functional currency is the parent company's currency.

3. The translation process may be divided into two categories. In category one the U.S. dollar is the functional currency. In that case the temporal method of FAS 8 will be used, with one major exception: Whereas deferred taxes are translated in FAS 8 using the historical exchange rates, they are translated in FAS 52 using the current rate. In addition, the translation gains or losses are reported in the income statement as a nonoperating item. In category two the foreign currency is the functional currency. In that case the current method will be used. In addition, the translation gains or losses are reported in the stockholders' equity section of the balance sheet as a translation adjustment.

4. The only exception to the above translation process relates to the financial statements of a foreign entity in a country that has had cumulative inflation of approximately 100 percent or more over a three-year period (highly inflationary). In this case the reporting currency is the functional currency.

5. The usefulness of financial statement information seems to differ from one country to another. In the United Kingdom context the evidence is in support of the usefulness of financial statement information.[24,25] A comparison of the institutional investors, individual investors, and financial analysts from the United States, the United Kingdom, and New Zealand showed intercountry differences in the importance attached to some parts of the corporate annual report.[26,27]

6. There is definitely a need to restate financial statistics. The need arises because of (a) difference in accounting principles used in the countries; (b) difference in taxation rates and in the relationship between the accounting principles used and those used for financial reporting; (c) differences in the financing, operations, and other business arrangements in the country; and (d) differences in the cultural, institutional, and political environment in each country.[28] For example, the reconciliation between Volvo 1986 net income in accordance with Swedish accounting principles and net income in accordance with the U.S. GAAP needs to account for untaxed reserves, deferred taxes, and others are as follows:[29]

	Kr(m)
Net Income in Accordance with Swedish Accounting Principles	2,551
Add: Allocations to Untaxed Reserves	2,694
Less: Deferred Income Taxes	(1,574)
Other Adjustments	(742)
Net Income in Accordance with U.S. GAAP	2,956

The same rationale applies to stockholders' equity.[30]

Stockholders' Equity in Accordance	10,214
Add: Untaxed Reserves	20,980
Less: Deferred Income Taxes	(11,950)
Other Adjustments	938
Equity in Accordance with U.S. GAAP	20,092

Examples of the various types of reserves used by Volvo include:

Inventory Reserves: In Sweden and certain other countries, companies are permitted to make allocation to inventory reserves. In accordance with the general rule of Swedish tax legislation, the general inventory reserve may amount to a maximum of 50% of the value of a company's year-end inventories, after deductions for obsolescence. In the case of inventories of securities, allocations may be made in amounts considered reasonable, due account being taken of the risk of a decline in price and other factors.

Payroll Reserve: Companies in Sweden may make allocations to a payroll-based reserve in a maximum amount of 20% of wages and salaries paid in the tax year. If an allocation is made to this reserve, the inventory reserve, described above, may not exceed 35% of the year-end inventories.

Investment Reserve: The investment reserve was established by Swedish law to stimulate investments during recessionary periods, and has also been used as an instrument of labor market policy and to promote balance in industrial plant siting.[31]

7. There is definitely a need to translate the financial statements to the language of the potential analyst. In making the linguistic translation from one language to another one has to be aware of (a) the different world view that can be created by the newly translated financial statements as espoused in the Hypothesis of Linguistic Relativism,[32] (b) the different social classes or different professional affiliations as espoused by the sociolinguistic thesis in accounting,[33] and (c) the special needs and capabilities of bilinguals as espoused by the bilingual thesis in accounting.[34,35,36,37]

8. Countries differ in terms of the level of conservatism used in their profits measurement. There is a need to standardize the reports for adequate comparison. A standardized method of analysis and presentation of company accounts has been developed by the European Federation of Financial Analysts Societies (EF-FAS) "to arrive at a figure which can be used as a basis for earning forecasts and for the calculation of ratios."[38] What has been done is an exclusion from the profit of various discretionary transfers to or from reserves and of any expectational provisions. S. J. Gray used these figures for a sample of companies from France, West Germany, and the United Kingdom to compute a conservatism index as follows:

$$1 - \frac{R_A - R_D}{|R_A|}$$

where R_A = adjusted profit and R_D = disclosed profit.[39] A negative index implies a conservative approach in the measurement of profit. The results showed intensive conservatism in Germany and a similar tendency toward conservatism in France. The following explanation is provided:

All of the foregoing suggests that the discretion is likely to be the preserve of the United Kingdom with its emphasis on flexibility. But although uniform accounting principles and forms of presentation are specified in France and Germany, there remains considerable scope for flexibility in application and for such discretion to manifest itself in a more conservative view of profits. The most significant areas of flexibility are indeed those identified by the analysts and concern transfers to and from reserves, and the creation and write-back of provisions for various risks and special purposes including those which are designed to gain tax advantages. These can be used to create hidden or secret reserves and to smooth out bias fluctuations in profits.[40]

9. Ratios can be misused when they do not take into account the specific institutional characteristics of each country. This misuse was best illustrated in a study by F.D.S Choi and associates[41] that undertook a comparison of firms from Japan, Korea, and the United States using ratio analysis. Exhibit 7.1 illustrates a comparison of aggregate financial ratios for a large sample of manufacturing firms in the three countries. Before any adjustment, the ratios suggest that Japanese and Korean firms are less profitable and efficient and bear a higher financial risk than their U.S. counterparts. In fact, the high leverage of Japanese firms is acceptable in Japan because the *Keiretsu* network allows for higher interdependencies between banks and their industrial borrowers. As stated by Choi and associates:

Interdependence was fostered among *Keiretsu* group companies through financial, commercial and personal ties. Under such arrangements, the relationships between the borrowing company, related companies, and their banks were very close. Cross shareholdings between borrower, related companies, and the bank were common. Today, their relationship has evolved to the point where a bank would seldom impose financial penalties on delayed interest payments nor call a delinquent loan from a related company; instead, the lending bank would typically postpone interest and principal repayments and, in some instances, even refinance the loan on more liberal terms. It is common practice for the lending bank to install a bank official as president or board member of the troubled company to provide it with helpful managerial assistance.[42]

Similarly, the high leverage of Korean firms is attributed to the larger role assumed by government in corporate finance, which includes tax and trade privileges, special financing, foreign currency loans secured by bank guarantees, and subsidized interest rates. The role of Korean banks is also different:

Another feature of Korean lending practice is that corporate borrowers are not classified into credit risk categories with interest rates scaled accordingly. Rather, the more bank debt a company has, the greater the bank's stake in the success of the enterprise, and the

Exhibit 7.1

Mean Differences in Aggregate Financial Ratios, 1976–1978, for Japan, Korea, and the United States

Enterprise category (number of firms)	Current ratio	Quick ratio	Debt ratio	Times Interest earned	Inventory turnover	Collection period	Fixed assets turnover	Total assets turnover	Profit margin	Return on total assets	Return on net worth
ALL MANUFACTURING											
Japan (976)	1.15	0.80	0.84	1.60	5.00	86	3.10	0.93	0.013	0.012	0.071
Korea (354)	1.13	0.46	0.78	1.80	6.60	33	2.80	1.20	0.023	0.028	0.131
U.S. (902)	1.94	1.10	0.47	6.50	6.80	43	3.90	1.40	0.054	0.074	0.139
CHEMICALS											
Japan (129)	1.30	0.99	0.79	1.80	7.10	88	2.80	0.90	0.015	0.014	0.065
Korea (54)	1.40	0.70	0.59	2.40	7.10	33	1.60	0.90	0.044	0.040	0.100
U.S. (n.a.)	2.20	1.30	0.45	6.50	6.50	50	2.80	1.10	0.073	0.081	0.148
TEXTILES											
Japan (81)	1.00	0.77	0.81	1.10	6.20	66	3.50	0.92	0.003	0.003	0.017
Korea (34)	1.00	0.37	0.83	1.30	4.90	30	2.20	1.00	0.010	0.011	0.064
U.S. (n.a.)	2.30	1.20	0.48	4.30	6.50	48	5.80	1.80	0.027	0.049	0.094
TRANSPORTATION											
Japan (85)	1.20	0.86	0.83	1.90	3.90	116	4.50	0.90	0.017	0.015	0.092
Korea (14)	0.95	0.40	0.91	1.90	18.60	18	1.10	0.80	0.026	0.021	0.221
U.S.	1.60	0.74	0.52	8.70	5.60	31	6.50	1.60	0.049	0.078	0.161

Source: Adapted from Frederick D. S. Choi, Hisaaki Hino, Sang Kee Min, Sang On Nam, Junichi Ujiie, and Arthur I. Stonehill, "Analyzing Foreign Financial Statements: The Use and Misuse of International Ratio Analysis," *Journal of International Business Studies*, Spring/Summer 1983, p. 116. Reprinted with permission.

Note: Data on Japan from the Bank of Japan, data on Korea from the Bank of Korea, and data on the United States from the U.S. Federal Trade Commission.

n.a. Not applicable.

higher the probability that the bank will come to the firm's rescue in times of economic adversity. Thus, rather than being viewed with alarm, high debt ratios in Korea signify a company's close ties with its bank which, in turn, signify a company's favorable association with the government.[43]

The situation in Exhibit 7.1 shows higher liquidity in the United States than in Japan and Korea. The Japanese situation is explained by (a) their preference for short-term debt, (b) the tendency to sell their accounts receivable without recourse, and (c) the potential understatement of marketable securities compared to market values. The Korean situation is due to their continuous use of short-term financing as a substitute for long-term financing. In the process, short-term debt is a misnomer in the Korean context and is in fact long term. The situation in Exhibit 7.1 also shows higher turnover ratios in the United States than in Japan and Korea. For example, the collection period is 86 days for Japan, 33 days for Korea, and 43 days in the United States. The reason may be related to the 60 to 120 additional days given to Korea to cope with the scarcity of capital and to the Japanese tradition of lifetime employment. As stated by Choi and associates: "Thus, during business downturns, repayment extensions are granted to avoid putting the buyer in a financial bind and thereby threatening an otherwise stable employment base. In return, continued future patronage helps assure employment stability for the enterprise."[44]

Another example relates to the high fixed asset turnover in the United States compared to Japan and Korea. The situation in Korea is due to the enormous investments made in plant and equipment and to the understatement of sales revenues caused by government price controls imposed on domestic goods to stem inflation and imposed on exports to penetrate overseas markets. Finally, the situation in Exhibit 7.2 shows higher profit margins and return on total assets in the United States compared to Japan and Korea. The focus on long-term profits in Japan and low pricing and margins in Korea is the potential explanation.

10. The assumption of nonnormality for the distribution of ratios was also verified in the case of a United Kingdom sample.[45] In addition, the deletion of outliers had a stronger impact on the data, in terms of improving approximation of normality, than did square root and natural logarithm transformation.

ALTERNATIVE FORECASTING IN AN
INTERNATIONAL SETTING

Because security analysts and most forecasting agencies focus on the U.S. environment, management accountants and financial managers of multinational corporations (MNCs) may have to rely on their own efforts to forecast other companies' earnings and to provide forecasts of their own earnings. Their choice of techniques may be mechanical or nonmechanical and univariate or multivariate. Mechanical univariate forecasting approaches include moving average models and Box-Jenkins univariate models. Mechanical multivariate forecasting

Exhibit 7.2
Coefficients of Discriminant Functions for the Predictions of Canadian Takeovers

Ratios	Year 1	Year 2	Year 3	Year 4	Year 5
x_1	-0.05699	-0.04873	-0.07209	-0.12516	-0.10842
x_2	0.06193	0.00819	0.15693	0.33359	0.23390
x_3	0.05251	0.03903	0.03587	0.08908	0.07953
x_4	-0.03333	-0.19860	-0.08349	-0.17424	-0.13008
x_5	-0.00317	-0.01890	0.11576	-0.01842	-0.02801
x_6	-0.03280	-0.00583	-0.05502	0.16184	0.07621
x_7	0.11758	0.15185	0.12712	0.15114	-0.23027
x_8	-0.02427	-0.05758	0.02146	-0.30738	-0.18708
x_9	0.04061	0.05671	-0.15501	-0.21040	-0.03840
x_{10}	0.00286	0.00824	-0.00323	0.00628	0.00566
x_{11}	-0.01080	-0.01212	0.03049	0.01923	-0.00831
x_{12}	0.00431	0.00470	-0.01461	-0.01725	0.03342
x_{13}	-0.00255	-0.01728	0.02637	-0.00153	-0.00639
x_{14}	-0.00102	-0.00031	-0.04474	-0.00409	-0.01536
x_{15}	0.00458	0.01253	-0.01134	0.00326	0.02200
x_{16}	-0.00941	-0.01057	-0.04834	0.00726	-0.05233

The zones of ignorance and cut-off point score were:
-0.10998 to 0.08565 and -0.02051 for Year 1.
-0.14146 to 0.02957 and -0.02365 for Year 2.
-0.13668 to 0.08098 and -0.00243 for Year 3.
-0.14245 to 0.07651 and -0.00921 for Year 4.
-0.16617 to 0.04876 and -0.02543 for Year 5.

models include regression models, Box-Jenkins transfer function models, and econometric models. Finally, nonmechanical models include univariate models such as visual curve extrapolation and multivariate models such as security analyst approaches.[46] These forecasts may be evaluated in terms of either dispersion or bias. Dispersion of forecast errors is generally measured by the mean square error (MSE) as follows:

$$MSE = \frac{1}{n} \sum_{i=1}^{n} [ax_{it} - fx_{it}]^2$$

where

ax_{it} = actual value of the variable in period t for firm i
fx_{it} = forecasted value of the variable in period t for firm i
n   = number of forecasts examined

Bias is measured by the expected value of the error (EVE):

$$EVE = \frac{1}{n} \sum_{i=1}^{n} [ax_{it} - fx_{it}]$$

Various research questions arise in the international setting:

1. What are the properties of security analysts' forecasts internationally?[47]
2. How reliable are the forecasts of security analysts in the international context compared to time-series models?
3. What are the properties of management forecasts of multinational corporations?
4. What are the characteristics of foreign and domestic multinational firms that voluntarily disclose forecasts?
5. How reliable are the management forecasts in multinational firms compared to security analysts and time-series models.[48]

CORPORATE RESTRUCTURING INTERNATIONALLY

The prominence of takeovers all over the world has prompted several studies. R. N. Marris's study of managerial capitalism showed that the companies acquired are those that are undervalued by the market.[49] Similarly, Michael Gort supported a related hypothesis that the level of takeover activity varies with the degree of share underdevaluation in the market.[50] This type of analysis relies heavily on a meaningful share price valuation model. More explicitly, the parameters measuring the relationship between the market prices of shares and relevant factors should be reasonably constant. M. D. Bonford found that the market will sometimes attach different weights to those factors.[51] Similarly, J. T. Tzoannos and J. M. Samuels, in experimenting with a number of valuation models, found that the variables, whether explaining earning yield or divided yield, were not significant.[52] Thus the type of analysis based only on share valuation might lack external validity.

Because of the difficulties of appraising the "true" value of a share, most of the other studies have attempted to identify the financial characteristics of the acquired firms. Accordingly, R. J. Chambers examined the undervaluation of net assets as a result of conservative accounting policies.[53] The undervaluation of net assets was seen as a key factor for predicting takeovers. These findings were later contested by R. A. Taussig and S. L. Hayes on the basis of the absence of a control group in the Chambers study.[54] They rejected the hypothesis of a statistically significant relationship between understated asset values and the possibility of a takeover. Both studies were univariate, however, and considered only in voluntary mergers. The first limitation with regard to the univariate nature of the analysis was corrected by J. S. Vance.[55] He developed the "raider's index" composed of four financial ratios. The second limitation was first corrected by various studies that considered companies acquired through voluntary mergers in England and the United States.[56,57,58]

In fact, the corporate restructuring internationally also included mergers, consolidations, divestitures, going private transactions, leveraged buyouts (LBOs), and spinoffs, aimed at either (a) maximizing the market value of equities held by existing shareholders or (b) maximizing the welfare of existing management.[59,60] It is, however, the modes of takeovers that are mostly the subject of empirical analysis. The analyses taking place in the U.S. context include those by R. P. Boisjoly and T. M. Corsi,[61] R. S. Harris and associates,[62] W. P. Rege,[63] J. K. Dietrich and E. T. Sorensen,[64] and Krisna Palepu.[65]

Palepu's multivariate logit model was based on the following ten variables:

x_1 = average excess security return per day over prior four years

x_2 = average market adjusted security return per day over prior four years

x_3 = 0/1 dummy variable with 1 for low growth/high liquidity/low leverage combinations and 0 for all other combinations and high growth/low liquidity/high leverage combinations and 0 for all other combinations.

x_4 = average annual sales growth rate over prior three years

x_5 = ratio of net liquid assets to total assets averaged over prior three years

x_6 = ratio of long-term debt to total equity averaged over prior three years

x_7 = 0/1 dummy variable with 1 if there is at least one acquisition in a firm's four-digit SIC industry in prior year

x_8 = net book assets of firm ($ millions)

x_9 = ratio of firm's market price to book value of common equity in prior year

x_{10} = ratio of firm's market price to earnings at end of fiscal year of prior year of prior year

A likelihood ratio of 9.93 percent to 12.45 percent was obtained.

The Meeks study focused on the profitability of mergers of U.K. firms in the 1964–1972 period. The acquiring firms were examined using a standardized profitability measure E, called "the profitability of the amalgamation (standardized for industry and year) less three-year average premerger profitability of the amalgamation (similarly standardized)."[66] An average decline was reported leading the author to title his study *Disappointing Marriage: A Study of the Gains from Merger*.

Studies of mergers in Belgium, the Federal Republic of Germany, France, the Netherlands, Sweden, the United Kingdom, and the United States show little improvement in profitability as measured by accounting profitability measures. As concluded by D. C Mueller:

No consistent pattern of either improved or deteriorated profitability can be claimed across the seven countries. Mergers would appear to result in a slight improvement here, a slight worsening of performance there. If a generalization is to be drawn, it would have to be that mergers have hit modest effects, up or down, on the profitability of the merging firms in the three to five years following merger. An economic efficiency gain from the merger would appear too small.[67]

In the context of the United Kingdom, Paul Barnes estimated the following discriminant function:

$$Z = -1.91218 - 1.61605x_1 + 4.99448x_2 + 1.11363x_3 - 0.70484x_4 - 0.11345x_5$$

where

x_1 = quick assets/current liabilities
x_2 = current assets/current liabilities
x_3 = pretax profit margin
x_4 = net profit margin
x_5 = return on shareholders' equity

The model was able to predict accurately 74.3 percent of a holdout sample.[68]

Ahmed Belkaoui's study focused on predicting Canadian takeovers on the basis of linear combinations of sixteen ratios.

x_1 = cash flow/net worth
x_2 = cash flow/total assets
x_3 = net income/net worth
x_4 = net income/total assets
x_5 = long-term debt + preferred stock/total assets
x_6 = current assets/total assets
x_7 = cash/total assets
x_8 = working capital/total assets
x_9 = quick assets/total assets
x_{10} = current assets/current liabilities
x_{11} = quick assets/current liabilities
x_{12} = cash/current liabilities
x_{13} = current assets/sales
x_{14} = quick assets/sales
x_{15} = working capital/sales
x_{16} = cash/sales[69]

Five discriminant functions were produced for each of the five years preceding the takeover of Canadian firms. They are shown in Exhibit 7.2.

DEBT RATINGS INTERNATIONALLY

Firms resort to financial leverage through debt financing as a way of financing growth more readily and more efficiently. For firms to be able to accomplish this financing task readily and efficiently, their bond issues need to have interesting investment features of profitability, stability, and liquidity, to name only a few. Above all, the investors need to assume themselves that the issuers will be able to fullfill their obligations. Fortunately, the market provides the investor one way of judging the quality of a bond through the unbiased opinions of informed and experienced professionals working for the bond rating agencies. These professionals rate bonds by assigning to them known bond ratings designed essentially to rank the issues in order of the probability of default, that is, the inability to meet interest obligations, sinking-fund payments, or repayments of principal. This is reflected in the wording used by the agencies to describe what a rating represents: "Ratings are designed exclusively for the purpose of grading bonds according to their investment qualities."[70] "A Standard & Poor's corporate or municipal debt rating is a current assessment of the credit worthiness of obligor with respect to a specific obligations."[71]

The functions of these ratings have been to provide a superior low-cost source of information on the ability of the firms to make timely repayments of principal and interest. The implications are as follows. First, they are intended to be an indicator of the probability of default or loss of market value that may be experienced by a firm facing degrees of financial difficulties. Second, they have been found to be good predictors of default and of the magnitude of the losses at default. Third, the bond ratings were found to be consistent with the systematic risk of securities.

Various recent bond rating models have shown the importance of profit based measures as well as other measures of financial fitness in the explanation and prediction of bond ratings. For example, Belkaoui developed a discriminant analysis based bond rating model on the basis of following variables:

x_1 = total assets
x_2 = total debt
x_3 = long-term debt/total invested capital
x_4 = short-term debt/total invested capital
x_5 = current assets/current liabilities
x_6 = fixed change coverage ratio
x_7 = five-year cash flow divided by five-year sum of (1) capital expenditure, (2) change in inventories during most recent five years, and (3) common dividends
x_8 = stock price/common equity per share
x_9 = subordination (0–1 dummy variable), 1 if the bond being rated is subordinated[72]

Six discriminant functions are proposed to explain or predict bond ratings, including the following for an AAA rating:

$$Z = -31.6004 + 0.000737x_1 + 0.000119x_2 + 0.44234x_3 + 0.62823x_4 \\ + 7.26898x_5 + 0.68425x_6 + 0.06102x_7 + 0.01802x_8 + 10.26302x_9$$

For an AA rating:

$$Z = -26.0425 + 0.000431x_1 - 0.000147x_2 + 0.49299x_3 + 0.67906x_4$$
$$+ 6.80279x_5 + 0.54641x_6 + 0.06600x_7 + 0.01687x_8 + 9.76648x_9$$

For an A rating:

$$Z = -26.1304 + 0.00269x_1 - 0.000149x_2 + 0.58069x_3 + 0.60516x_4$$
$$+ 7.83642x_5 + 0.48850x_6 + 0.06777x_7 + 0.00809x_8 + 8.18782x_9$$

For a BBB rating:

$$Z = -29.3824 + 0.000250x_1 - 0.000233x_2 + 0.71530x_3 + 0.79864x_4$$
$$+ 8.5763x_5 + 0.50766x_6 + 0.07116x_7 + 0.00235x_8 + 4.27079x_9$$

For a BB rating:

$$Z = -31.3397 + 0.000265x_1 - 0.000295x_2 + 0.76589x_3 + 0.80544_4$$
$$+ 9.15411x_5 + 0.48010x_6 + 0.05952x_7 + 0.00705x_8 + 1.69732x_9$$

For a B rating:

$$Z = -34.8229 + 0.000242x_1 - 0.000357x_2 + 0.85499x_3 + 0.84459x_4$$
$$+ 9.24043x_5 + 0.49208x_6 + 0.06970x_7 + 0.00099x_8 - 1.73660x_9$$

The classification method consists simply of using the discriminant functions on new data as follows. For each firm that needs to be classified into a bond rating category, compute the classification score for each rating category from the discriminant function coefficients (multiply the data by the coefficients and add the constant term). The firm is then classified into the group for which the classification score is highest.

To illustrate the classification procedure, consider the following 1980 data for Frontier Airlines (the ratings given by Standard & Poor's was B).

$x_1 = \$312.8$ (in millions)

$x_2 = 116.1$ (in millions)

$x_3 = 48.7$

$x_4 = 4.1$

$x_5 = 0.9$

$x_6 = 3.5$

$x_7 = 52.8$

$x_8 = 104.7$

$x_9 = 1$ (subordinated debt)

The classification scores for each rating category from the discriminant functions obtained by multiplying the coefficients by the data and adding the constant term are the following:

$$Z_{AAA} = 18.50916$$
$$Z_{AA} = 26.208$$
$$Z_{A} = 30.37737$$
$$Z_{BBB} = 38.72666$$
$$Z_{BB} = 41.09244$$
$$Z_{B} = 43.51933$$

Given that Z_B gives the highest classification score, the firm is classified by the model in the bond rating category B.

Various questions arise in the international context:

1. Are bond rating models, like Belkaoui's model, applicable to the prediction of the bond ratings of the obligations of foreign multinational companies residing in countries where such ratings do exist?
2. Are the same bond rating models applicable to the prediction of the bond ratings or investment quality of the obligations of foreign multinational companies residing in countries where such ratings do exist?
3. For both preceding cases, should the bond rating models be revised to include specific variables geared to the specific international context in which these firms operate?

DISTRESS ANALYSIS INTERNATIONALLY

Predicting financial distress is of utmost importance to lenders, investors, regulatory authorities, government officials, auditors, and management. Various univariate and multivariate models have been used in the United States for the prediction of bankruptcy. The best known discriminant analysis model, by E. I. Altman, is as follows:

$$Z_i = 1.2x_{1i} + 1.4x_{2i} + 3.3x_{3i} + 0.6x_{4i} + 1.0x_{5i}$$

where

$x_{1i} = $ (current assets − current liabilities) /total assets
$x_{2i} = $ retained earnings/total assets
$x_{3i} = $ earnings before interest and taxes/total assets
$x_{4i} = $ market value of preferred and common equity/book value of liabilities
$x_{5i} = $ sales/total assets[73]

The discriminant rule used is that any firm with a Z score below 1.8 is considered to be a prime candidate for bankruptcy and a Z score above 2.99 is a safe candidate. Because some firms do not have publicly traded securities, Altman's reestimation of the model, with x_{4i} as the book value of preferred and common equity/book value of total liabilities, was as follows:[74]

$$Z_1 = 0.717x_{1i} + 0.847x_{2i} + 3.10x_{3i} + 0.420x_{4i} + 0.998x_{5i}$$

The prediction rule was that any company with a Z score below 1.20 was a candidate for bankruptcy and with a Z score above 2.90 a safe candidate.

The success of these models led Altman and associates to develop a commercial model: THE ZETA® CREDIT RISK.[75] It is reported to include the following seven variables:

1. Size as total assets
2. Profitability as earnings before interest and taxes/total assets
3. Debt service as earnings before interest and taxes/total interest payments
4. Liquidity as current ratio
5. Cumulative profitability as retained earnings/total assets
6. Market capitalization as five-year coverage of market value of common equity/five-year average of market value of total capital (includes preferred stock, long-term debt, and capitalized leases)
7. Earnings stability as a normalized measure of the standard error of estimate around a ten-year trend in the overall profitability table

Because it is a commercial product, the coefficients of each variable have not been disclosed. However, the promotional literature provided by ZETA® Services includes the following description:

ZETA is a risk evaluation model developed by ZETA Services Inc. For the development of ZETA, risk was defined as the inability of a company to meet its obligations. The ZETA SCORE tells a user how much a company resembles firms that have been poor credit risks, i.e., firms that have recently filed bankruptcy petitions. We are not interested in bankruptcy per se but we feel that it is an unequivocal credit standard. Prior to bankruptcy, companies have a strong tendency to pass common and preferred dividends, go into technical defaults and engage in forced sales of assets, all to the detriment of securities values. The ZETA model does not forecast failure or nonfailure and ZETA Services Inc. did not design it to do so. Rather, it compares a company's operations and financial characteristics to those of over 50 firms which have already failed. The test sample [used to develop the model] was composed of 53 industrial corporations which filed for bankruptcy or were taken over by their banks. No banks, finance companies, real estate companies or railroads were included. All firms were required to have at least $20 million in reported assets in the two years prior to bankruptcy. These firms were paired with other randomly selected. nonbankrupt firms in similar industries. The ZETA SCORE is a result of a linear combination of all seven variables (weighted by the discriminant analysis technique) plus a constant. Zero was the dividing line between nonfailing (positive scores) and failing firms (negative scores).

In addition to the Z-score model and the ZETA model, we should also cite the gambler-ruin model.[76,77] The question remains, how useful are these models internationally? The Z-score model was applied successfully to Japanese bankruptcy cases, with a "Japanese cut-off score" of 1.0, lower than Altman's score of 1.8.[78] In addition, C. J. Ko developed a unique Z-score model of the following form.

$$Z_j = 0.868x_1 + 0.198x_2 - 0.048x_3 + 0.436x_4 + 0.115x_5$$

where

x_1 = earnings before interest and taxes/sales
x_2 = inventory turnover two years prior/inventory turnover three years prior
x_3 = standard error of net income (four years)
x_4 = working capital/total debt
x_5 = market value of equity/total debt
Z_j = Z-score for the Japanese model

The model yielded an 82.9 percent correct classification rate.

The Altman Z-score model with modifications on x_2 and x_4 were used in the Brazilian context.[79] Calculations for x_2 are:

$$x_2 = \frac{\text{Total equity} - \text{Capital contributed by shareholders}}{\text{Total assets}}$$

and x_4 was computed as book value of equity divided by total liabilities. Two are derived with one excluding x_1 and one excluding x_2. They are as follows:

$$Z_1 = 1.44 + 4.03x_2 + 2.25x_3 + 0.14x_4 + 0.425x_5$$

and

$$Z_2 = -1.84 - 0.51x_1 + 6.23x_3 + 0.71x_4 + 0.56x_5$$

The vertical cut-off score was chosen to be zero, with any firm with a score lower than zero defined as a potentially bankrupt firm. The failure prediction models were provided by A. D. Castagna and Z. P. Matobesy[80] for Australia, and R. M. Kinglit[81] and E. I. Altman and M. T. R. Lavallee[82] for Canada. Altman and Lavallee's model was as follows:

$$Z_c = -1.626 + 0.234x_1 - 0.531x_2 + 1.002x_3 + 0.972x_4 + 0.612x_5$$

where

Z_c = Canadian Z-score
x_1 = sales/total assets
x_2 = total debt/total assets
x_3 = current assets/current liabilities
x_4 = net profits after tax/total debt
x_5 = rate of growth—rate of asset growth

Two prediction models are used for the case of the Netherlands. J. B. Bilderbeek's five-ratio model is as follows:

$$Z_{NB} = 0.45 - 5.03x_1 - 1.57x_2 + 4.55x_3 + 0.17x_4 + 0.15x_5$$

where

Z_{NB} = Z-score for the Netherlands
x_1 = retained earnings/total assets
x_2 = added value/total assets
x_3 = accounts payable/sales
x_4 = sales/total assets
x_5 = net profit/equity[83]

The model yielded a 70–80 percent accuracy score for one year before bankruptcy and remained stable during a five-year period preceding bankruptcy.

The Van Fredrikslust model is as follows:

$$Z_{NF} = 0.5293 + 0.4488x_1 + 0.2863x_2$$

where

Z_{NF} = Z-score for the Netherlands
x_1 = liquidity ratio for internal coverage
x_2 = profitability ratio as rate of return on equity[84]

The prediction of bankruptcy in France included attempts by Altman and associates,[85] P. O. Bontemps,[86] Yves Collongues,[87] and F. R. Mader.[88, 89] The usefulness of these models are best summarized as follows: "The application of statistical credit scoring techniques in the French environment appears to be problematic but the potential remains. One problem usually is the quality of the data and the representativeness of it. But this is a problem in all countries and is not unique to France."[90]

P. F. Weibel used cluster analysis to arrive at six ratios that best predict bankruptcy in the Swiss case. [91] G. T. Weinrich's factor analysis[92] and K. B.

Beerman's discriminant analysis[93] were used in the German case. Other German efforts include the one by G. L. Gebhardt.[94]

These models cover selected developed countries and omit completely most of the Asian countries and all of the developing world. It is clear that a lot remains to be done in the area of business failure models internationally.

CONCLUSION

The use of ratio analysis in an international context is fraught with a lot of problems. Variable adjustments presented in this chapter need to be made before there can be an effective use of financial analysis internationally. In addition, predictive models of economic events need to be adjusted to be useful in an international context. To date, various attempts have been made to develop predictive models of economic events in an international context.

NOTES

1. H. Levy and M. Sarnat, "International Diversification of Investment Portfolios," *American Economic Review*, September 1970, pp. 66–82.

2. J. E. Walter, "Determination of Technical Solvency," *Journal of Business*, January 1957, pp. 30–34; K. W. Lemke, "The Evaluation of Liquidity: An Analytical Study," *Journal of Accounting Research*, Spring 1970, pp. 47–77.

3. S. Davidson, G. H. Sorter, and H. Kalle, "Measuring the Defensive Position of a Firm," *Financial Analyst Journal*, January–February 1964, p. 23.

4. Standard & Poor's, *Credit Overview: Industrial Ratings* (New York, 1983), p. 22.

5. A. P. Gale, "Computerized Research: An Advanced Tool," *The Journal of Accountancy*, January 1982, pp. 73–84.

6. George Foster, *Financial Statement Analysis*, 2d ed. (Englewood Cliffs, N.J.: Prentice-Hall, 1986), pp. 80–83.

7. E. B. Deakin, "Distributions of Financial Accounting Ratios: Some Empirical Evidence," *The Accounting Review*, January 1976, pp. 90–96.

8. T. J. Frecka and W. S. Hopwood, "The Effects of Outliers on the Cross-Sectional Distributional Properties of Financial Ratios," *The Accounting Review*, January 1983, pp. 115–128.

9. P. D. Bougen and J. C. Drury, "U.K. Statistical Distributions of Financial Ratios, 1975," *Journal of Business Finance and Accounting*, Spring 1980, pp. 39–47.

10. W. Buijink and M. Jegers, "Cross-Sectional Distributional Properties of Financial Ratios, Belgian Manufacturing Industries: Some Empirical Evidence," Working paper (Belgium: University of Antwerp, 1984).

11. Steven Lilian, Martin Mellman, and Victor Pastena, "Accounting Changes: Successful vs. Unsuccessful Firms," *The Accounting Review*, October 1988, pp. 642–656.

12. K. B. Schwartz, "Accounting Changes by Corporations Facing Possible Insolvency," *Journal of Accounting, Auditing and Finance*, Fall 1982, pp. 32–34.

13. W. G. Bremser, "The Earnings Characteristics of Firms Reporting Discretionary Accounting Changes," *The Accounting Review*, July 1975, pp. 563–573.

14. Foster, *Financial Statement Analysis*, p. 186.

15. R. P. Magee, "Industry-Wide Commonalities in Earnings," *Journal of Accounting Research*, Autumn 1974, pp. 270–287.

16. R. N. Clarke, "SIC's as Delineators of Economic Markets," *Journal of Business* 1 (1989): 17–31.

17. David B. Smith and Susan Pourciau, "A Comparison of the Financial Characteristics of December and Non-December Year-End Comparisons," *Journal of Accounting and Economics,* December 1988, pp. 335–366.

18. Ahmed Belkaoui and Philip Karpik, "A Comparison of the Financial Characteristics of Companies in the Core and Periphery Economies," Working Paper (Chicago: University of Illinois at Chicago, 1990).

19. F.D.S. Choi and G. G. Mueller, *International Accounting* (Englewood Cliffs, N.J.: Prentice-Hall, 1984), p. 300.

20. Alfred Kahl and Ahmed Belkaoui, "Bank Annual Report Disclosure Adequacy," Summer 1981, pp. 196–198.

21. A. Belkaoui and A. Kahl, "What Canadian Bank Financial Statements Don't Tell," *The Chartered Accountant Magazine,* June 1977, pp. 32–35.

22. A. Belkaoui and A. Kahl, *Corporate Financial Disclosure in Canada* (Vancouver: Canadian Certified General Accountants, 1978), parag. no. 1.

23. Financial Accounting Standards Board, "Foreign Currency Translation," *Statement of Financial Accounting Standards No. 52* (Stamford, Conn., December 1981).

24. J. Arnold and P. Moizer, "A Survey of Methods Used by UK Investment Analysis to Appraise Investments in Ordinary Shares," *Accounting and Business Research,* Summer 1984, pp. 195–207.

25. J.F.S. Day, "The Use of Annual Reports by U.K. Investment Analysts," *Accounting and Business Research,* Autumn 1986, pp. 295–307.

26. L. S. Chang, K. S. Most, and C. W. Brain, "The Utility of Annual Reports: An International Study," *Journal of International Business Studies,* Spring/Summer 1983, pp. 63–84.

27. A. Belkaoui, A. Kahl, and J. Peyrard, "Information Needs of Financial Analysis: An International Comparison," *Journal of International Education and Research in Accounting,* Fall 1977, pp. 19–27.

28. Foster, *Financial Statement Analysis.*

29. Stuart J. McLeay, "International Financial Analysis," in *Issues in Multinational Accounting*, ed. C. Nobes and R. Parker (Oxford: Philip Allan, 1988), p. 132.

30. Ibid., p. 132.

31. John N. Slipkowski, "The Volvo Way of Financial Reporting," *Management Accounting,* October 1988, p. 23.

32. "Linguistic Relativity in Accounting," *Accounting Organizations and Society,* October 1978, pp. 97–104.

33. A. Belkaoui, "The Interprofessional Linguistic Communication of Accounting Concepts: An Experiment in Sociolinguistics," *Journal of Accounting Research,* Fall 1980, pp. 362–374.

34. J. Monti-Belkaoui and A. Belkaoui, "Bilingualism and the Perception of Professional Concepts," *Journal of Psycholinguistic Research* 12 (1983): 111–127.

35. A. Belkaoui, "Accounting and Language," *Journal of Accounting Literature* 8 (1989): 281–292.

36. A. Belkaoui, *Behavioral Accounting* (Westport, Conn.: Quorum Books, 1989).

37. A. Belkaoui, *Judgment in International Accounting* (Westport, Conn.: Quorum Books, 1990).

38. European Federation of Financial Analysts Societies, *Report of the Permanent Commission on Standardization* (Oslo, 1967), p. 11. See also Dennis Weaver, *Investment Analysis* (New York: Longman, 1971).

39. S. J. Gray, "The Impact of International Accounting Differences from a Security-Analysis Perspective: Some European Evidence," *Journal of Accounting Research,* Spring 1980, pp. 69–76.

40. Ibid., pp. 72–73.

41. F.D.S. Choi, H. Hino, S. K. Min, S. O. Nam, J. Ujiie, and A. I. Stonehill, "Analyzing Foreign Financial Statements: The Use and Misuse of International Ratio Analysis," *Journal of International Business Studies,* Spring/Summer 1983, pp. 113–131.

42. Ibid., p. 121.

43. Ibid., p. 123.

44. Ibid., p. 125.

45. Mahmond Ezzamel and Cecilio Mar-Molinero, "The Distributional Properties of Financial Ratios in U.K. Manufacturing Companies," *Journal of Business Finance and Accounting,* Spring 1990, pp. 1–32.

46. Foster, *Financial Statement Analysis,* p. 262.

47. P. Moizer and J. Arnold, "A Survey of the Methods Used by U.K. Investment Analysts to Appraise Investment in Ordinary Shares," Working paper (Manchester, England: University of Manchester, 1982).

48. H. Schreuder and J. Klavassen, "Confidential Revenue and Profit Forecasts by Management and Financial Analysts: Evidence from the Netherlands," *The Accounting Review,* January 1984, pp. 64–77.

49. R. Marris, *The Economic Theory of Managerial Capitalism* (New York: Macmillan, 1964).

50. Michael Gort, "An Economic Disturbance Theory of Mergers," *Quarterly Journal of Economics,* November 1969, pp. 624–643.

51. M. D. Bonford, "Changes in the Evaluation of Equities," *The Investment Analyst,* December 1968, pp. 62–75.

52. J. Tzoannos and J. M. Samuels, "Mergers and Takeovers: The Financial Characteristics of Companies Involved," *Journal of Business Finance,* July 1972, pp. 5–16.

53. R. J. Chambers, "Finance Information and the Securities Market," *Abacus,* September 1965, pp. 4–30.

54. R. A. Taussig and S. L. Hayes III, "Cash Takeovers and Accounting Valuation," *The Accounting Review,* January 1968, pp. 68–72.

55. J. Vance, "Is Your Company a Takeover Target?" *Harvard Business Review,* May–June 1969, pp. 93–102.

56. R. J. Monroe and M. A. Sinkowitz, "Investment Characteristics of Conglomerate Targets: A Discriminant Analysis," *Southern Journal of Business,* November 1971, pp. 59–81.

57. A. Single, "Takeovers, Economic Natural Selection, and the Theory of the Firm: Evidence from the Post-War United Kingdom Experience," *The Economic Journal,* September 1975, pp. 497–515.

58. D. L. Stevens, "Financial Characteristics of Merged Firms: A Multivariate Analysis," *Journal of Financial and Quantitative Analysis,* March 1973, pp. 149–158.

59. J. K. Baker, T. O. Miller, and B. J. Ramsberger, "A Typology of Merger Motives," *Akron Business and Economic Review*, Winter 1981, pp. 24–25.

60. K. Schipper and A. Smith, "Effects of Recontracting on Shareholder Wealth: The Case of Voluntary Spin-Offs," *Journal of Financial Economics*, December 1983, pp. 437–467.

61. R. P. Boisjoly and T. M. Corsi, "A Profile of Motor Carrier Acquisitions, 1976 to 1978," *Akron Business and Economic Review*, Summer 1982, pp. 30–35.

62. R. S. Harris, J. F. Stewart, D. K. Guilkey, and W. T. Carleton, "Characteristics of Acquired Firms: Fixed and Random Coefficients Profit Analyses," *Southern Economic Journal*, July 1982, pp. 164–184.

63. W. P. Rege, "Accounting Ratios to Locate Takeover Targets," *Journal of Business Finance and Accounting*, Autumn 1984, pp. 302–311.

64. J. K. Dietrich and E. Sorensen, "An Application of Logit Analysis to Prediction of Merger Targets," *Journal of Business Research*, September 1984, pp. 393–402.

65. K. Palepu, "Predicting Takeover Targets: A Methodological and Empirical Analysis," Working Paper (Cambridge, Mass.: Harvard University, 1985).

66. G. Meeks, *Disappointing Marriage: A Study of the Gains from Mergers* (Cambridge: Cambridge University Press, 1977).

67. D. C. Mueller, "A Cross-National Comparison of the Results," in *The Determinants and Effects of Mergers,* ed. D. C. Mueller (Cambridge, Mass.: Oegeschlager, Gann & Hain, 1980).

68. Paul Barnes, "The Prediction of Takeover Targets in the U.K. by Means of Multiple Discriminant Analysis," *Journal of Business Finance and Accounting*, Spring 1990, pp. 73–84.

69. Ahmed Belkaoui, "Financial Ratios as Predictors of Canadian Takeovers," *Journal of Business Finance and Accounting* 5, no. 1 (1978): 93–101.

70. Moody's Investor Service, *Moody's Bond Record* (New York, December 1984).

71. Standard & Poor's, *Credit Overview: Corporate and International Ratings* (New York, 1984).

72. A. Belkaoui, *Industrial Bonds and the Rating Process* (Westport, Conn.: Quorum Books, 1983), p. 90.

73. E. I. Altman, "Financial Ratios, Discriminant Analysis, and the Prediction of Corporate Bankruptcy," *The Journal of Finance*, September 1968, pp. 589–609.

74. E. I. Altman, *Corporate Financial Distress* (New York: Wiley, 1983).

75. E. I. Altman, R. G. Halderman, and P. Narayanan, "Zeta Analysis: A New Model to Identify Bankruptcy Risk of Corporations," *Journal of Banking and Finance*, June 1977, pp. 29–54.

76. J. W. Wilcox, "A Prediction of Business Failure Using Accounting Data," *Empirical Research in Accounting: Selected Studies,* Supplement to *Journal of Accounting Research*, March 1973, pp. 163–179.

77. J. Vinso, "A Determination of the Risk of Ruin," *Journal of Financial and Quantitative Analysis*, March 1979, pp. 77–100.

78. C. J. Ko, "A Delineation of Corporate Appraisal Models and Classification of Bankruptcy Firms in Japan" (Thesis, New York University, 1982).

79. E. I. Altman, T. Baidya, and L. M. Riberio-Dias, "Assessing Potential Financial Problems of Firms in Brazil," *Journal of International Business Studies*, Fall 1979, pp. 9–24.

80. A. D. Castagna and Z. P. Matobesy, "The Prediction of Corporate Failure: Testing the Australian Experience," *Australian Journal of Management,* June 1981, pp. 42–52.

81. R. M. Kinglit, "The Determinants of Failure in Canadian Firms" (Paper presented at ASA Meetings of Canada, Saskatoon, Saskatchewan, May 28–30, 1980).

82. E. I. Altman and M. Lavallee, "Business Failure Classification in Canada," *Journal of Business Administration,* Summer 1981, pp. 63–78.

83. J. Bilderbeek, *Financiele Ratio Analyse* (Leiden: Stenfert-Kroese, 1977).

84. E. I. Altman, M. Margarine, M. Schlosser, and P. Vernimmen, "Statistical Credit Analysis in the Textile Industry: A French Experience," *Journal of Financial and Quantitative Analysis,* March 1974.

85. P. O. Bontemps, *La Notation du Risque de Credit* (Paris: Credit National, 1981).

86. Yves Collongues, "Ratios Financiers et Previsions des Failletes des Petites et Moyennes Entreprises," *Revue Banque,* no. 356 (March 1977): 16–25.

87. F. Mader, "Les Ratios et l'Analyse du Risque," *Analyse Financiere* 2 (1975): 18–32.

88. F. Mader, "Un Echantillon d'Entreprises en Difficulté," *Journée des Centrals de Belan,* January 1979.

89. E. I. Altman, "The Success of Business Failure Prediction Models: An International Survey," *Journal of Banking and Finance* 8 (1984): 194.

90. Ibid.

91. G. Weinrich, *Prediction of Credit Worthiness, Direction of Credit Operations by Risk Classes* (Wiesbaden, Germany, 1978).

92. P. F. Weibel, *The Value of Criteria to Judge Credit Worthiness in the Lending of Banks* (Bern/Stuttgart, 1973).

93. K. Beerman, *Possible Ways to Predict Capital Losses with Annual Financial Statements* (Dusseldorf, 1976).

94. G. Gebhardt, "Insolvency Prediction Based on Annual Financial Statements According to the Company Law—An Assessment of the Reform of Annual Statements by the Law of 1965 from the View of External Addresses," in *Bochumer Beitrage Zur Unternchmungs und Unternelmerns-Forschung,* vol. 22, ed. H. Besters et al. (Wiesbaden, 1980).

REFERENCES

Altman, E. I. *Corporate Financial Distress.* New York: Wiley, 1983.

———. "Financial Ratios, Discriminant Analysis, and the Prediction of Corporate Bankruptcy." *The Journal of Finance,* September 1968, pp. 589–609.

———. "The Success of Business Failure Prediction Models: An International Survey." *Journal of Banking and Finance* 8 (1984): 194.

Altman, E. I., T. Baidya, and L. M. Riberio-Dias. "Assessing Potential Financial Problems of Firms in Brazil." *Journal of International Business Studies,* Fall 1979, pp. 9–24.

Altman, E. I., R. G. Halderman, and P. Narayanan. "Zeta Analysis: A New Model to Identify Bankruptcy Risk of Corporations." *Journal of Banking and Finance,* June 1977, pp. 29–54.

Altman, E. I., and M. Lavallee. "Business Failure Classification in Canada." *Journal of Business Administration,* Summer 1981, pp. 63–78.

Altman, E. I., M. Margarine, M. Schlosser, and P. Vernimmen. "Statistical Credit

Analysis in the Textile Industry: A French Experience." *Journal of Financial and Quantitative Analysis*, March 1974.

Arnold, J., and P. Moizer. "A Survey of Methods Used by UK Investment Analysis to Appraise Investments in Ordinary Shares." *Accounting and Business Research*, Summer 1984, pp. 195–207.

Baker, J. K., T. O. Miller, and B. J. Ramsberger. "A Typology of Merger Motives," *Akron Business and Economic Review*, Winter 1981, pp. 24–25.

Barnes, Paul. "The Prediction of Takeover Targets in the U.K. by Means of Multiple Discriminant Analysis." *Journal of Business Finance and Accounting*, Spring 1990, pp. 73–84.

Beerman, K. *Possible Ways to Predict Capital Losses with Annual Financial Statements*. Dusseldorf, 1976.

Belkaoui, A. "Accounting and Language." *Journal of Accounting Literature* 8 (1989): 281–292.

———. *Behavioral Accounting*. Westport, Conn.: Quorum Books, 1989.

———. "Financial Ratios as Predictors of Canadian Takeovers." *Journal of Business Finance and Accounting* 5, no. 1 (1978): 93–101.

———. *Industrial Bonds and the Rating Process*. Westport, Conn.: Quorum Books, 1983.

———. "The Interprofessional Linguistic Communication of Accounting Concepts: An Experiment in Sociolinguistics." *Journal of Accounting Research*, Fall 1980, pp. 362–374.

———. *Judgment in International Accounting*. Westport, Conn.: Quorum Books, 1990.

Belkaoui, A., and A. Kahl. *Corporate Financial Disclosure in Canada*. Vancouver: Canadian Certified General Accountants, 1978, parag. no. 1.

———. "What Canadian Bank Financial Statements Don't Tell." *The Chartered Accountant Magazine*, June 1977, pp. 32–35.

Belkaoui, A., A. Kahl, and J. Peyrard. "Information Needs of Financial Analysis: An International Comparison." *Journal of International Education and Research in Accounting*, Fall 1977, pp. 19–27.

Belkaoui, Ahmed, and Philip Karpik. "A Comparison of the Financial Characteristics of Companies in the Core and Periphery Economies." Working paper. Chicago: University of Illinois at Chicago, 1990.

Bilderbeek, J. *Financiele Ratio Analyse*. Leiden: Stenfert-Kroese, 1977.

Boisjoly, R. P., and T. M. Corsi. "A Profile of Motor Carrier Acquisitions, 1976 to 1978." *Akron Business and Economic Review*, Summer 1982, pp. 30–35.

Bonford, M. D. "Changes in the Evaluation of Equities." *The Investment Analyst*, December 1968, pp. 62–75.

Bontemps, P. O. *La Notation du Risque de Credit*. Paris: Credit National, 1981.

Bougen, P. D., and J. C. Drury. "U.K. Statistical Distributions of Financial Ratios, 1975." *Journal of Business Finance and Accounting*, Spring 1980, pp. 39–47.

Bremser, W. G. "The Earnings Characteristics of Firms Reporting Discretionary Accounting Changes." *The Accounting Review*, July 1975, pp. 563–573.

Buijink, W., and M. Jegers. "Cross-Sectional Distributional Properties of Financial Ratios, Belgian Manufacturing Industries: Some Empirical Evidence." Working paper. Belgium: University of Antwerp, 1984.

Castagna, A. D., and Z. P. Matobesy. "The Prediction of Corporate Failure: Testing the Australian Experience." *Australian Journal of Management,* June 1981, pp. 42–52.

Chambers, R. J. "Finance Information and the Securities Market." *Abacus,* September 1965, pp. 4–30.

Chang, L. S., K. S. Most, and C. W. Brain. "The Utility of Annual Reports: An International Study." *Journal of International Business Studies,* Spring/Summer 1983, pp. 63–84.

Choi, F.D.S., H. Hino, S. K. Min, S. O. Nam, J. Ujiie, and A. I. Stonehill. "Analyzing Foreign Financial Statements: The Use and Misuse of International Ratio Analysis." *Journal of International Business Studies,* Spring/Summer 1983, pp. 113–131.

Choi, F.D.S., and G. G. Mueller. *International Accounting.* Englewood Cliffs, N.J.: Prentice-Hall, 1984.

Clarke, R. N. "SIC's as Delineators of Economic Markets." *Journal of Business* 1 (1989): 17–31.

Collongues, Yves. "Ratios Financiers et Previsions des Failletes des Petites et Moyennes Entreprises." *Revue Banque,* no. 356 (March 1977): 16–25.

Davidson, S., G. H. Sorter, and H. Kalle. "Measuring the Defensive Position of a Firm." *Financial Analyst Journal,* January–February 1964, pp. 13–26.

Day, J.F.S. "The Use of Annual Reports by U.K. Investment Analysts." *Accounting and Business Research,* Autumn 1986, pp. 295–307.

Deakin, E. B. "Distributions of Financial Accounting Ratios: Some Empirical Evidence." *The Accounting Review,* January 1976, pp. 90–96.

Dietrich, J. K., and E. Sorensen. "An Application of Logit Analysis to Prediction of Merger Targets." *Journal of Business Research,* September 1984, pp. 393–402.

European Federation of Financial Analysts Societies. *Report of the Permanent Commission on Standardization.* Oslo, 1967, p. 11.

Ezzamel, Mahmond, and Cecilio Mar-Molinero. "The Distributional Properties of Financial Ratios in U.K. Manufacturing Companies." *Journal of Business Finance and Accounting,* Spring 1990, pp. 1–32.

Financial Accounting Standards Board. "Foreign Currency Translation." *Statement of Financial Accounting Standards No. 52.* Stamford, Conn., December 1981.

Foster, George. *Financial Statement Analysis,* 2d ed. Englewood Cliffs, N.J.: Prentice-Hall, 1986.

Frecka, T. J., and W. S. Hopwood. "The Effects of Outliers on the Cross-Sectional Distributional Properties of Financial Ratios." *The Accounting Review,* January 1983, pp. 115–128.

Gale, A. P. "Computerized Research: An Advanced Tool." *The Journal of Accountancy,* January 1982, pp. 73–84.

Gebhardt, G. "Insolvency Prediction Based on Annual Financial Statements According to the Company Law—An Assessment of the Reform of Annual Statements by the Law of 1965 from the View of External Addresses." In *Bochumer Beitrage Zur Unternchmungs und Unternelmerns-Forschung.* Vol. 22. Edited by H. Besters et al. Wiesbaden, 1980.

Gort, Michael. "An Economic Disturbance Theory of Mergers." *Quarterly Journal of Economics,* November 1969, pp. 624–643.

Gray, S. J. "The Impact of International Accounting Differences from a Security-Analysis

Perspective: Some European Evidence." *Journal of Accounting Research,* Spring 1980, pp. 69–76.

Harris, R. S., J. F. Stewart, D. K. Guilkey, and W. T. Carleton. "Characteristics of Acquired Firms: Fixed and Random Coefficients Profit Analyses." *Southern Economic Journal,* July 1982, pp. 164–184.

Kahl, Alfred, and Ahmed Belkaoui. "Bank Annual Report Disclosure Adequacy," Summer 1981, pp. 196–198.

Kinglit, R. M. "The Determinants of Failure in Canadian Firms." Paper presented at ASA Meetings of Canada, Saskatoon, Saskatchewan, May 28–30, 1980, 23–41.

Ko, C. J. "A Delineation of Corporate Appraisal Models and Classification of Bankruptcy Firms in Japan." Thesis, New York University, 1982.

Lemke, K. W. "The Evaluation of Liquidity: An Analytical Study." *Journal of Accounting Research,* Spring 1970, pp. 47–77.

Levy, H., and M. Sarnat. "International Diversification of Investment Portfolios." *American Economic Review,* September 1970, pp. 66–82.

Lilian, Steven, Martin Mellman, and Victor Pastena. "Accounting Changes: Successful vs. Unsuccessful Firms." *The Accounting Review,* October 1988, pp. 642–656.

"Linguistic Relativity in Accounting." *Accounting Organizations and Society,* October 1978, pp. 97–104.

Mader, F. "Les Ratios et l'Analyse du Risque." *Analyse Financiere* 2 (1975): 18–32.

———. "Un Echantillon d'Entreprises en Difficulté." *Journée des Centrals de Belan,* January 1979.

Magee, R. P. "Industry-Wide Commonalities in Earnings." *Journal of Accounting Research,* Autumn 1974, pp. 270–287.

Marris, R. *The Economic Theory of Managerial Capitalism.* New York: Macmillan, 1964.

McLeay, Stuart J. "International Financial Analysis." In *Issues in Multinational Accounting.* Edited by C. Nobes and R. Parker. Oxford: Philip Allan, 1988.

Meeks, G. *Disappointing Marriage: A Study of the Gains from Mergers.* Cambridge: Cambridge University Press, 1977.

Moizer, P., and J. Arnold. "A Survey of the Methods Used by U.K. Investment Analysts to Appraise Investment in Ordinary Shares." Working paper. Manchester, England: University of Manchester, 1982.

Monroe, R. J., and M. A. Sinkowitz. "Investment Characteristics of Conglomerate Targets: A Discriminant Analysis." *Southern Journal of Business,* November 1971, pp. 59–81.

Monti-Belkaoui, J., and A. Belkaoui. "Bilingualism and the Perception of Professional Concepts." *Journal of Psycholinguistic Research* 12 (1983): 111–127.

Moody's Investor Service. *Moody's Bond Record.* New York, December 1984.

Mueller, D. C. "A Cross-National Comparison of the Results." In *The Determinants and Effects of Mergers.* Edited by D. C. Mueller. Cambridge, Mass.: Oegeschlager, Gann & Hain, 1980.

Palepu, K. "Predicting Takeover Targets: A Methodological and Empirical Analysis." Working paper. Cambridge, Mass.: Harvard University, 1985.

Rege, W. P. "Accounting Ratios to Locate Takeover Targets." *Journal of Business Finance and Accounting,* Autumn 1984, pp. 302–311.

Schipper, K., and A. Smith. "Effects of Recontracting on Shareholder Wealth: The Case of Voluntary Spin-Offs.'' *Journal of Financial Economics,* December 1983, pp. 437–467.

Schreuder, H., and J. Klavassen. ''Confidential Revenue and Profit Forecasts by Management and Financial Analysts: Evidence from the Netherlands.'' *The Accounting Review,* January 1984, pp. 64–77.

Schwartz, K. B. ''Accounting Changes by Corporations Facing Possible Insolvency.'' *Journal of Accounting, Auditing and Finance,* Fall 1982, pp. 32–34.

Single, A. ''Takeovers, Economic Natural Selection, and the Theory of the Firm: Evidence from the Post-War United Kingdom Experience.'' *The Economic Journal,* September 1975, pp. 497–515.

Slipkowski, John N. ''The Volvo Way of Financial Reporting.'' *Management Accounting,* October 1988, p. 23.

Smith, David B., and Susan Pourciau. ''A Comparison of the Financial Characteristics of December and Non-December Year-End Comparisons.'' *Journal of Accounting and Economics,* December 1988, pp. 335–366.

Standard & Poor's. *Credit Overview: Corporate and International Ratings.* New York, 1984.

———. *Credit Overview: Industrial Ratings.* New York, 1983.

Stevens, D. L. ''Financial Characteristics of Merged Firms: A Multivariate Analysis.'' *Journal of Financial and Quantitative Analysis,* March 1973, pp. 149–158.

Taussig, R. A., and S. L. Hayes III. ''Cash Takeovers and Accounting Valuation.'' *The Accounting Review,* January 1968, pp. 68–72.

Tzoannos, J., and J. M. Samuels. ''Mergers and Takeovers: The Financial Characteristics of Companies Involved.'' *Journal of Business Finance,* Fall 1972, pp. 5–16.

Vance, J. ''Is Your Company a Takeover Target?'' *Harvard Business Review,* May–June 1969, pp. 93–102.

Vinso, J. ''A Determination of the Risk of Ruin.'' *Journal of Financial and Quantitative Analysis,* March 1979, pp. 77–100.

Walter, J. E. ''Determination of Technical Solvency.'' *Journal of Business,* January 1957, pp. 30–34.

Weaver, Dennis. *Investment Analysis.* New York: Longman, 1971.

Weibel, P. F. *The Value of Criteria to Judge Credit Worthiness in the Lending of Banks.* Bern/Stuttgart: 1973.

Weinrich, G. *Prediction of Credit Worthiness, Direction of Credit Operations by Risk Classes.* Wiesbaden: 1978.

Wilcox, J. W. ''A Prediction of Business Failure Using Accounting Data.'' *Empirical Research in Accounting: Selected Studies.* Supplement to *Journal of Accounting Research,* March 1973, pp. 163–179.

8

Capital Budgeting for the Multinational Corporation

Capital budgeting involves a current outlay or series of outlays of cash resources in return for anticipated benefits to be received beyond one year in the future. The capital budgeting decision has two distinguishing characteristics: anticipated cash benefits and a degree of risk associated with the realization of the benefits. Ideally, a firm with a profit maximization motive will seek an investment that will generate large benefits in a short period and with a minimum of risk. Investments with potentially large benefits, however, are usually possible only with high risk and may require more time than investments with lower benefits.

Given these less-than-ideal relationships between huge dimensions of a capital budgeting decision, managements would desire a project that will meet their objectives. Although firms may choose various objective functions, the most useful one for evaluating capital budgeting decisions is the stockholders' wealth maximization model (SWMM).[1] Despite the fact that it represents a normative model, the SWMM provides a generally acceptable and meaningful criterion for the evaluation of capital budgeting proposals: maximization of owners' wealth. There are many similarities among capital domestic companies. There are, however, specific problems that may complicate capital budgeting for the multinational corporation. This section examines the similarities of and the problems encountered by multinational corporations in analyzing the financial benefits and costs of a potential investment.

UNIQUE PROBLEMS IN MULTINATIONAL CAPITAL BUDGETING

Foreign capital investment faces unique risks that can create negative effects on value. Among these risks, the following are generally cited:

1. The need to distinguish between parent company and project cash flows to avoid a distortion of the value of the project to the firm
2. The risk of adverse exchange rate movements that can directly affect the value of the local cash flows and indirectly affect the competitive position of the foreign subsidiary
3. The risk of unforseen change in inflation rates that can also affect the local cash flows as well as the competitive position of the foreign subsidiary
4. The risk of fund blockage, exchange controls expropriation, and various forms of foreign currency controls that can affect the remittance of funds to the parent company.
5. The risks of changes in the tax laws and various environmental and institutional factors that can also affect the remittance of funds to the parent company

A risk analysis is therefore called for to evaluate the impact of these risks against the rewards of a given investment. In addition, the forecast of cash flows is subject to the same risks and needs to be included in the international risk analysis. The following questions need to be addressed:

• What level of confidence is present in the various elements of the cash flow forecast?
• For the elements involving the greatest degree of uncertainty, what will be the result of a large forecasting error?
• How sensitive is the value of the investment to the foreseeable risks?[2]

DETERMINING THE PROJECT CASH FLOWS

There are material differences between the project cash flows and the cash flows back to the parent firm because of various constraints such as tax regulations and exchange controls. One opinion on project cash flows states that "to the extent that the corporation views itself as a true multinational, the effects of restrictions on repatriation may not be severe."[3] If this position is adopted, all elements of return on overseas investment must be considered project cash flows. P. O. Graddis provided the following list of elements of projected return from an overseas industrial investment:

1. All income, operating and nonoperating, from the overseas operating unit, based on its demonstrated capacity to supply existing markets with its present management and excluding any impact of the merger of resources with those of the investing company
2. Additional operating income of the overseas unit resulting from the merger of its own capabilities with those of the investing corporation
3. Additional income from increased export sales resulting from the proposed investment action, including (a) additional export income at each U.S. operating unit that manufactures products related to those that will be produced overseas and (b) additional earnings from new export activity at the overseas operating unit resulting from its increased capabilities to sell beyond the boundaries of its traditional national markets
4. Additional income from increased licensing opportunities shown both in the books of the affected U.S. units and the books of the overseas unit

5. Additional income from importing technology, product design, or hardware from the overseas operating unit to U.S. operating units

6. Income presently accruing from the investment but seriously and genuinely threatened by economic, political, or social change in an overseas region.[4]

A second position, derived from economic theory, is that the value of a project is determined by the net present value of future cash flows back to the investor. Therefore, the project cash flows that are or can be repatriated are included "since only accessible funds can be used to pay dividends and interest, amortize the firm's debt, and be reinvested."[5] In spite of the strong theoretical argument in favor of analyzing foreign projects from the viewpoint of the parent company, empirical evidence from surveys of multinationals shows that firms are using project flows and rates of return as well as parent flows and rates of return.[6] In fact, a more recent survey shows that multinationals were almost evenly split among those that loaded at cash flow solely from the parent's perspective, solely form the subsidiaries' perspective, and from both perspectives.[7] Those who viewed cash flow from the point of view of the subsidiary felt that the subsidiaries were separate businesses and should be viewed as such. Those who took the parent company's view argued that the investment was ultimately made from the parent company's stockholders. Finally, those who adopted both perspectives considered it the safest approach because it provides two ways of making a final decision. One of the respondent treasurers put it as follows: "The project must first be evaluated on its chances of success locally. It must be profitable from the subsidiary's point of view. Then you step back and look at it from the parent's point of view. What cash flows are available to be remitted or otherwise used in another country? What's going to come back to the parent is the real issue. The project has to meet both tests to be acceptable."[8]

What appears from the above discussion is that the use of the parent company's view is compatible with the traditional view of net present value in capital budgeting, whereas the use of the project's view leads to a closer approximation of the effect on consolidated earnings per share.[9]

ILLUSTRATION OF MULTINATIONAL CAPITAL BUDGETING FROM BOTH PERSPECTIVES

To illustrate the differences between the subsidiary perspective and the parent company perspective in multinational capital budgeting, consider the example of a Jordanian subsidiary and a U.S. based multinational corporation considering the decision to invest in new equipment. The following information is provided:

1. The cost of investment is JD39,100. The exchange rate was $2/JD.

2. The cash flows for an estimated useful life of six years are, respectively, JD20,000, JD14,000, JD10,000, JD6,000, JD5,000, and JD4,000.

3. The required rate of return is 10 percent.

4. The Jordanian government does not tax the earnings of the subsidiary but requires a withholding tax of 10 percent on funds remitted to the parent company.

5. The U.S. tax rate on foreign earnings of the subsidiary is 10 percent.

6. The exchange rate of the Jordanian dinar is estimated to be $8.00 at the end of years one and two, $1.80 at the end of years three and four, and $1.50 at the end of years five and six.

The capital budgeting from the project or subsidiary perspective is shown in Exhibit 8.1. The cumulative net present value (NPV) is JD7, 633; therefore, the project is acceptable from the subsidiary's point of view. The capital budgeting from the parent's perspective is shown in Exhibit 8.2. The project appears profitable from the subsidiary's perspective and unprofitable from the parent's perspective.

COST OF CAPITAL FOR THE MULTINATIONAL FIRM

In both the internal rate-of-return method and the net present value method, a cost of capital, or "hurdle rate," is needed. The two rules of thumb are as follows:

1. The internal rate of return must be superior to the hurdle to be acceptable.

2. The present value, obtained by discounting cash flows at the hurdle rate, must be positive for a project to be acceptable.

For a multinational corporation, the overall cost of capital is the sum of the costs of each financing source, weighted by the proportion of that financing source in the firm's total capital structure. The weighted average cost of capital is therefore:

$$K = \frac{E}{V} K_e + \frac{D}{V} K_d (1 - t)$$

where:

Exhibit 8.1
Capital Budgeting: Subsidiary's Perspective

	Year 1	Year 2	Year 3	Year 4	Year 5	Year 6
Cost of Investment						
JD 39,100						
Cash Flows	JD20,000	JD14,000	JD10,000	JD 6,000	JD 5,000	JD 4,000
Discount Factor (10%)	0.909	0.826	0.753	0.683	0.621	0.564
PV of Cash Flows	JD18,180	JD11,564	JD 7,530	JD 4,098	JD 3,105	JD 2,256
Cumulative NPV	-JD 20,920	-JD9,356	-JD1,826	JD 2,272	JD 5,377	JD 7,633

Exhibit 8.2
Capital Budgeting: Parent Company's Perspective

	Year 1	Year 2	Year 3	Year 4	Year 5	Year 6
Cost of the Investment						
$78,2000						
Cash Flows	JD20,000	JD14,000	JD10,000	JD 6,000	JD 5,000	JD 4,000
Withholding Tax (10%)	JD 2,000	JD 1,400	JD 1,000	JD 600	JD 500	JD 400
Funds Remitted	JD18,000	JD12,600	JD 9,000	JD 5,400	JD 4,500	JD 3,600
Exchange Rate	$2	$2	$1.8	$1.8	$1.5	$1.5
Funds to be Received	$36,000	$25,200	$16,200	$ 9,720	$ 6,750	$ 5,400
U.S. Taxes Paid (25%)	$ 9,000	$ 6,300	$ 4,050	$ 2,430	$1,687.5	$1,350
After Tax Funds	$27,000	$18,900	$12,150	$ 7,290	$5,062.5	$4,050
Discount Factor	0.909	0.826	0.753	0.683	0.621	0.564
PV of Cash Flows	$24,543	$15,611.4	$9,148.95	$4,979.07	$3,143.81	$2,284.2
Cumulative NPV	-$53,657	-$38,045.6	-$28896.65	-$23917.58	-$20773.77	-$18489.57

K = weighted average cost of capital
K_d = cost of debt
K_e = cost of equity
t   = tax rate
D = value of the firm's debt
E = value of the firm's equity
V = D + E = total value of the firm[9]

The cost of capital of a multinational corporation is assumed to be affected by a host of factors including (a) size of the firm, (b) access to international capital markets, (c) international diversification, (d) tax concession, (e) exchange rate risk, and (f) country risk.[10] The larger the firm, the greater its access to international capital markets; the greater its international diversification, the more it capitalizes on tax concessions; the lower its exchange rate exposure, the lower the country risk and the lower the cost of capital to the multinational corporation.

PROBLEMS ENCOUNTERED BY MULTINATIONALS

Besides the problem of choosing either parent company or project flows, multinationals' capital budgeting analyses are complicated by various problems.

Foreign Tax Regulations

Because only after tax cash flows are relevant, the amount of foreign income tax must be determined before conducting the capital budgeting analyses. The subject of international taxation, covered later, is complex. Not only are cash flows treated after tax, but also the project cost of capital must be adjusted to reflect the impact of taxes.

Political and Economic Risk

Multinational companies face the risks created by political, exchange, and economic changes. The appendix to this chapter covers some of the techniques used to manage political and economic risks. In a capital budgeting context, various ways may be used to account for political risks. One is to adjust each year's cash flows by the cost of an exchange risk adjustment.[11] Other ways include shortening the minimum payback period, raising the discount rate or required rate of return without adjusting cash flows, and adjusting cash flows and raising the discount rate.[12] A consensus seems to suggest that multinationals should use either the risk adjusted discount rate or the certainty-equivalent approach to adjust proper estimates for political risk.

Risk Adjusted Discount Rate Method

One of the techniques for incorporating risk in the evaluation process is the risk adjusted discount rate, which involves manipulating the discount rate applied to the cash flows to reflect the amount of risk inherent in a project. The higher the risk associated with a project, the higher the discount rate applied to the cash flows. If a given project is perceived to be twice as risky as most projects acceptable to the firm and the cost of capital is 12 percent, the correct risk adjusted discount rate is 24 percent.

Certainty-Equivalent Method

Another technique for incorporating risk in the evaluation process is the certainty-equivalent method, which involves adjusting the future cash flows so that a project can be evaluated on a riskless basis. The adjustment is formulated as follows:

$$NPV = \sum_{t=0}^{n} \frac{\alpha_t \, CF_t}{(1 + R_F)^t} - I_0$$

where

α_t = Risk coefficient applied to the cash flow of period t (CF_t)
I_0 = initial cost of the project
R_F = risk free rate

As this formula shows, the method multiplies the future cash flows by certainty equivalents to obtain a riskless cash flow. Note also that the discount rate used is R_F, which is a risk free rate of interest.

To illustrate the certainty-equivalent method, assume an investment with the following characteristics:

I_0 = initial cost = $30,000
CF_1 = cash flow, year 1 = $10,000
CF_2 = cash flow, year 2 = $20,000
CF_3 = cash flow, year 3 = $30,000
α_1 = certainty equivalent, year 1 = 0.9
α_2 = certainty equivalent, year 2 = 0.8
α_3 = certainty equivalent, year 3 = 0.6

The NPV of the investment using a risk free discount rate of 6 percent is computed as follows:

Period	Cash Flow (CF_1)	Risk Coefficient (α_t)	Certainty Equivalent	Risk Free Rate (R_F)	Present Value
1	$10,000	0.9	$ 9,000	0.943	$ 8,487

2	20,000	0.8	16,000	0.890	14,240
3	30,000	0.6	18,000	0.840	15,120
Present value of cash flows					$37,847
Initial investment					30,000
Net present value					$ 7,847

Since the NPV is positive, the investment should be considered acceptable. The main advantage of the certainty-equivalent method is that it allows the assignment of a different risk factor to each cash flow, given that risk can be concentrated in one or more periods.

The certainty-equivalent method and the risk adjusted discount rate method are comparable methods of evaluating risk. To produce similar ranking, the following equation must hold:

$$\frac{\alpha_t\, CF_t}{(1\, +\, R_F)^t} = \frac{CF_t}{(1\, +\, R_A)^t}$$

where

α_t = risk coefficient used in the certainty-equivalent method
R_F = risk free discount rate
R_A = discount rate used in the risk adjusted discount rate method
CF_t = future cash flow

Solving for α_t yields:

$$\alpha_t = \frac{(1\, +\, R_F)^t}{(1\, +\, R_A)^t}$$

Given that R_A and R_F are constant and $R_A > R_F$, then α_t decreases over time, which means that risk increases over time. To illustrate, assume that in the previous example R_A = 15 percent. Then

$$\alpha_1 = \frac{(1\, +\, R_F)^1}{(1\, +\, R_A)^1} = \frac{(1\, +\, 0.006)^1}{(1\, +\, 0.15)^1} = 0.921$$

$$\alpha_2 = \frac{(1\, +\, R_F)^2}{(1\, +\, R_A)^2} = \frac{(1\, +\, 0.006)^2}{(1\, +\, 0.15)^2} = 0.848$$

$$\alpha_3 = \frac{(1\, +\, R_F)^3}{(1\, +\, R_A)^3} = \frac{(1\, +\, 0.06)^3}{(1\, +\, 0.15)^3} = 0.783$$

In many cases this assumption of increasing risk may not be realistic.

Expropriation

Multinational companies sometimes face the extreme result of political risk—expropriation. One way to account for expropriation is to charge a premium for political risk insurance to each year's cash flow whether or not such insurance is actually purchased. Another way, suggested by Alan Shapiro, is to examine the impact of expropriation on the project's present value to the parent company.[13] As a result, the old and new present values will equal:

$$\text{Old Present Value} = -C_o + \sum_{t=1}^{n} \frac{X_t}{(1 + k)^t}$$

$$\text{New Present Value} = C_o + \sum_{t=1}^{h-1} \frac{X_t}{(1 + k)^t} + \frac{G_h}{(1 + k)^t}$$

where

C_o = initial investment outlay
X_t = parent's expected after tax dollar cash flow from the project in year t
n   = life of the project
k   = project cost of capital
h   = year in which expropriation takes place
G_h = expected value of the net compensation provided

The compensation (G_h) is supposed to come from one of the following sources:

Direct compensation paid to the firm by the local government

Indirect compensation such as other business contracts to the firm expropriated (an example would be the management contracts received by oil companies after the Venezuelan government nationalized their properties)

Payment received from political insurance

Tax deductions received after the parent declares the expropriation as an extraordinary loss

A reduction in the amount of capital that must be repaid by the project equal to the unamortized portion of any local borrowing

Blocked Funds

Multinationals sometimes face the situation in which funds are blocked for various reasons including forms of exchange control. Again, Shapiro suggested raising the present value expression to include the impact of locked funds on the project's cash flows.[14] As a result, the old and the new present values will equal:

$$\text{Old Present Value} = -C_o + \sum_{t=1}^{n} \frac{X_t}{(1 + k)^t}$$

$$\text{New Present Value} = -C_o + \sum_{t=1}^{j=1} \frac{X_t}{(1 + k)^t} + \sum_{t=j}^{n} \frac{Y_t}{(1 + k)^t}$$

$$+ (1 - \alpha_j) \sum_{t=j}^{n} \frac{(X_t - Y_t)}{(1 + k)^t} + \alpha_j \sum_{t=j}^{n} \frac{(X_t - Y_t)}{(1 + r)^{n-t}}$$

where the symbols C_o, X_t, n, and k are as in the formulas used for expropriation. The new symbols are:

j   = year in which funds become blocked
n   = year in which exchange controls are removed
α_j = probability of exchange controls in year 1 and 0 in other years
Y_t = number of dollars that can be repatriated when exchange costs do exist

Inflation

With the high rates of inflation experienced by most countries, it is advisable to consider the rate of inflation explicitly in developing cash flow forecasts. The correct analysis can be done in either of two ways: using a money discount rate to discount money cash flows or using a real discount rate to discount real cash flows.

Uncertain Salvage Value

When the salvage value may be uncertain, Jeff Madura suggested the estimation of a break-even salvage value or break-even terminal value, the salvage value for which NPV = 0. The break-even salvage value is estimated by setting the net present value equal to zero as follows:

$$\text{NPV} = -\text{OI} + \sum_{t=1}^{n} \frac{CF_t}{(1 + r)^t} + \frac{SV_n}{(1 + z)^n}$$

$$0 = -\text{OI} + \sum_{t=1}^{n} \frac{CF_t}{(1 + r)^t} + \frac{SV_n}{(1 + z)^n}$$

$$SV_n = [\text{OI} - \sum_{t=1}^{n} \frac{CF_t}{(1 + z)^t}] (1 + z)^n$$

where

NPV = net present value
OI = original investment
CF_t = cash flow at time t
Z   = desired rate of return[15]

THE ADJUSTED PRESENT VALUE TECHNIQUE

In the evaluation of foreign projects, Donald Lessard proposed an adjusted present value technique whereby the adjusted present value is equal to the following:

1. The capital outlay
2. The remittable after tax operating cash flows
3. Depreciation tax shields
4. Tax shields due to normal borrowing
5. Financial subsidiaries or penalties
6. Tax reduction or deferral via interaffiliate transfers
7. Additional remittances via interaffiliate transfers[16]

This is expressed as follows:

$$APV = -I + \sum_{t=1}^{T} \frac{\overline{CF}_t\,(1 - \tau)}{(1 + \rho_1)^t} + \sum_{t=1}^{T} \frac{DEP_t(\tau)}{(1 + \rho_2)^t} + \sum_{t=1}^{T} \frac{INT_t(\tau)}{(1 + \rho_3)^t}$$
$$+ \sum_{t=1}^{T} \frac{\Delta INTt}{(1 + \rho_4)^t} + \sum_{t=1}^{T} \frac{TR_t}{(1 + \rho_5)^t} + \sum_{t=1}^{T} \frac{REM_t}{(1 + \rho_6)^t}$$

where

APV = adjusted present value
CF = cash flows
DEP = depreciation
INT = interest
TR = tax reduction or deferral
REM = additional remittance
ρ_i = discount rates

Maurice Levi expanded Lessard's formulation as follows:

$$APV = -S_0 K_0 + S_0 AF_0 + \sum_{t=1}^{T} \frac{(S_i^* CF_i^* - LS_i^*)\,(1 - r)}{(1 + DR_e)^t} + \sum_{t=1}^{T} \frac{DA_t \tau}{(1 + DR_a)^t}$$
$$+ \sum_{t=1}^{T} \frac{r_g BC_0 \tau}{(1 + DR_b)^t} + S_0 \left[CL_0 - \sum_{t=1}^{r} \frac{LR_t}{(1 + DR_c)^t} \right] + \sum_{t=1}^{r} \frac{TD_i^*}{(1 + DR_d)^t}$$
$$+ \sum_{t=1}^{r} \frac{LR_t}{(1 + DR_c)}$$

where

S_0 = spot exchange rate, period zero
S_i^* = expected spot rate, period t
K_0 = capital cost of project in foreign currency units
AF_0 = restricted funds activated by project
CF_i^* = expectable remittable cash flow in foreign currency
LS_i^* = profit from lost sales, in dollars
τ = higher of U.S. and foreign corporate tax rates
T = life of the project
DA_t = depreciation allowances in dollar units
BC_0 = contribution of project to borrowing capacity in dollars
CL_0 = face value of concessionary loan in foreign currency
LR_t = loan repayments on concessionary loan in foreign currency
TD_i^* = expected tax savings from deferrals, intersubsidiary transfer pricing
RF_i^* = expected illegal repatriation of income
DR_e = discount rate for cash flows, assuming all equity financed
DR_a = discount for depreciation allowances
DR_b = discount rate for tax saving on interest deduction from contribution to borrowing
    capacity
DR_c = discount rate for saving on concessionary interest rate
DR_d = discount rate for saving via intersubsidiary transfers
DR_f = discount rate for illegally repatriated project flows
r_g = market borrowing at home[17]

The terms are explained as follows:

a. $-S_0K_0$ is the capital cost of the project computed in dollars at S_0.

b. S_0AF_0 is the blocked funds activated by the project converted in dollars at S_0.

c. $\sum_{t=1}^{T} \dfrac{(S_i^*CF_i^* - LS_i^*)(1 - \tau)}{(1 + DR_e)^t}$

is the remittable after tax operating cash flows.

d. $\sum_{t=1}^{T} \dfrac{DA_t\tau}{(1 + DR_a)^t}$

is the depreciation tax shield.

e. $\sum_{t=1}^{T} \dfrac{r_gBC_0\tau}{(1 + DR_b)^t}$

is the tax shield due to normal borrowing.

f. $S_0\left[CL_0 - \sum_{t=1}^{T} \dfrac{LR_t}{(1 + DR_c)^t}\right]$

is the financial subsidy or penalty.

g. $\sum_{t=1}^{T} \dfrac{TD_i^*}{(1 + DR_d)^t}$

is the tax reduction or deferral via interaffiliate transfers.

h. $\sum_{t=1}^{T} = \dfrac{LR_t}{(1 + DR_c)}$

is the additional remittance via interaffiliate transfers.

CAPITAL BUDGETING IN THE DEVELOPING COUNTRIES

Nature of Cost-Benefit Analysis

Cost-benefit analysis should be used for capital budgeting in the developing countries. *Cost-benefit analysis* is a method used to assess the desirability of projects when it is necessary to take both a long and a wide view of the impact of a proposed project on the general welfare of a society. It calls for an enumeration and evaluation of all of the relevant costs and benefits the project may generate and for choosing the alternatives that maximize the present value of all benefits less costs, subject to specified constraints and given specific objectives. Cost-benefit analysis is very useful when all of the economic impacts of a project, indirect as well as direct effects, have to be considered. It is a favorite method of analysis by governmental agencies for assessing the desirability of particular program expenditures or policy changes. In fact, it has been formally adopted into U.S. federal government budgetary procedures under the Planning-Programming-Budgeting System. It acts as a structure for a general theory of government resource allocation. Above all, it is a decision technique whose aims are first to take all effects into consideration and second to maximize the present value of all benefits less that of all costs, subject to specified constraints. This brings into focus the major considerations of cost-benefit analysis.

1. What are the objectives and constraints to be considered?
2. Which costs and benefits are to be included?
3. How are the costs and benefits to be valued?
4. What are the investment criteria to be used?
5. Which discount rate should be used?

Objectives and Relevant Constraints

The main objective of cost-benefit analysis is to determine whether or not a particular expenditure is economically and socially justifiable. The basic criteria used in cost-benefit analysis is an efficiency criterion. One such efficiency criterion is Pareto optimality. A program is said to be "Pareto efficient" if at least one person is made better off and no one is made worse off. This criterion is too strong and too impractical for cost-benefit analysis, however, given that few programs are likely to leave some individual better off and no one worse off. A weaker notion of efficiency, known as the "Kaldor-Hides criterion," is generally used for cost-benefit analysis. Under this criterion, also known as the "potential Pareto improvement criterion," a program is acceptable if it is pareto optimal or if it could redistribute the net benefits to everyone in the community so that everyone is at least as well off as before the initiation of the program. Basically, a program is efficient and should be undertaken if its total discounted societal benefits exceed the total discounted costs.

Besides the objectives of cost-benefit analysis, which are basically intended to maximize society's wealth, it is important to recognize some of the constraints. Otto Eckstein provided a helpful classification of constraints:

1. *Physical constraints*: The program alternatives considered may be constrained by the state of technology and more generally by the production function, which relates the physical inputs and outputs of a project.

2. *Logical constraints*: The program alternatives considered must be done within the framework of the law. Examples of legal constraints include property rights, time needed for public inquiries, regulated pricing, the right of eminent domain, and limits to the activities of public agencies.

3. *Administrative constraints*: Each of the alternative programs requires the availability and the hiring of individuals with the right administrative skills.

4. *Distributional constraints*: Any program is bound to generate gainers and losers. The unfavorable effects on income distribution may be alleviated by expressing the objective cost-benefit analysis as either (a) maximizing the excess of total benefits over total costs subject to constraints on the benefits less costs of particular groups or (b) maximizing the net gain (or minimizing the net loss) to a particular group subject to a constraint relating to total benefits and costs.

5. *Political constraints*: Political considerations may act as constraints, shifting the decision from what is best to what is possible. Regional differences and presence of various competing interest groups are examples of actors bound to create political constraints on the choice of the best program.

6. *Budgetary constraints*: Capital rationing and evaluating may act as constraints, shifting the objective function from maximizing to suboptimizing of net benefit given a target budget.

7. *Social and religious constraints*: Social and religious taboos are bound to act as constraints, shifting the decision from what is best to what is acceptable.[18]

Enumeration of Costs and Benefits

Enumeration of costs and benefits is important in determining which of the costs and benefits of a particular project should be included in a cost-benefit analysis.

Benefits of a project are either direct or indirect. *Primary* or *direct benefits* of a project "are those benefits which accrue directly to the users of the service provided by the project." They consist of the value of foods or services that result from conditions within the project as compared to conditions outside of the project. *Secondary* or *indirect benefits* of a project are the benefits accruing to those other than the users of the service provided by the project. They are of two types: (1) real or technological benefits or (2) pecuniary benefits.[19] *Real* or *technological benefits* are those benefits resulting from changes in total production possibilities and consumption opportunities. For example, if a dam creates a reduction in flooding the more pleasant scenery, these benefits are real benefits. *Pecuniary benefits* are those benefits that alter the distribution of total income without changing its volume. They generally take the form of lower input cost, increased volumes of business, or changes in the land values. Only direct real benefits should be included; pecuniary benefits should be excluded in the enumeration of the benefits of a project. Other benefits that are of an intangible nature and difficult to identify should be also considered. Costs of a project are also either direct or indirect. *Direct* or *primary costs* of a project are costs incurred directly by the users of the service provided by the project. They include the capital costs, operating and maintenance costs, and personnel expenses required by the project. *Indirect* or *secondary costs* are incurred by those other than the users of the service provided by the project. They may also be of two types: (1) real or technological costs and (2) pecuniary costs. Again, only the real secondary cost should be counted in a cost-benefit analysis.

Briefly, in enumerating the costs and benefits of a project, the analyst must be careful to distinguish their allocative effects from their pecuniary or distributional effects. In fact, the confusion of pecuniary and allocative effects constitutes a primary defect in many analyses of the efficiency of public projects. The only effects that should be taken into account in enumerating the costs and benefits of a public project are the real or technological externalities, that is, those that affect total opportunities for production and consumption, as opposed to pecuniary externalities, which do not affect total production or consumption.

Valuation of Costs and Benefits

In general, benefits should measure the value of the additional goods or services produced or the value of cost savings in the production of goods or services, and costs should measure the value of real resources displaced from other uses.

Assuming a competitive economy, benefits and costs will be valued on the basis of the observable market prices of the outputs and inputs of the program. More precisely, the benefits will be valued on either the market price of the output of the program or on the amounts users are willing to pay if charged (that is, the consumers' surplus, which is the difference between the aggregate willingness to pay and the costs of the projects).

When market prices do not accurately reflect the value of the market transactions to society as a result of externalities, the shadow prices, as adjusted, or input prices may be used. The general principle for estimating shadow prices for the output of public projects is to simulate what users would be willing to pay if they were charged as if the goods were sold in perfectly competitive markets.

Investment Criteria

Cost-benefit analysis is a method used to evaluate long-term projects. As such, the benefits and costs of each project have to be discounted to be comparable at time 0 when evaluation and decision on the projects have to be made. There is a need to rely on some form of discounting in the choice of investment criteria. There are exactly three possible investment or decision criteria: net present value, benefit-cost ratio, and internal rate of return.

Under the net present value, the present value of a project is obtained by discounting the net excess of benefits (B_t) over the cost (C_t) for each year during the life of the project back to the present time using a social discount rate. More explicitly:

$$V = \sum_{t=1}^{\alpha} \frac{B_t - C_t}{(1 + r)^t}$$

where

V = the value of the project
B_t = benefit in year t
C_t = cost in year t
r = social discount rate
α = life of the project

A project is found acceptable if the present value V is positive. If there are binding constraints on a project (for example, budget appropriation, foreign exchange, private investment opportunity foregone), the following model proposed by George Steiner would be more appropriate.[20]

$$V = \sum_{t=1}^{\alpha} \frac{B_t - C_t}{(1 + r)^t} - \sum_{j=1}^{n} p_j k_j$$

where

p_j = shadow price of a binding constraint
k_j = number of units of a constrained resource

Under the benefit-cost ratio, the decision criterion is expressed in terms of the ratio of the present value of benefits to the present value of costs (both discounted at the social discount rate). More explicitly, the benefit-cost ratio is:

$$\frac{\displaystyle\sum_{t=1}^{\alpha} \frac{b_t}{(1 + r)^t}}{\displaystyle\sum_{t=1}^{\alpha} \frac{C_t}{(1 + r)^t}}$$

All projects that are not mutually exclusive with a benefit-cost ratio in excess of 1 are acceptable.

Under the internal rate of return, the decision criterion is expressed in terms of the internal rate of return, that is, the discount rate will equate the net benefits over the life of the project with the original cost. In other words, r is the rate of interest for which

$$\sum_{t=1}^{\alpha} \frac{b_t}{(1 + r)^t} - \sum_{t=1}^{\alpha} \frac{C_t}{(1 + r)^t} = 0$$

All projects in which the internal rate of return exceeds the closer social discount rate are deemed acceptable.

Choice of a Discount Rate

The choice of a discount rate is important for at least two reasons. A high rate will lead the firm or the government away from the undertaking of the project, and a low rate may make the project more acceptable from a return point of view. Furthermore, a low discount rate tends to favor projects yielding net benefits further into the future relative to projects yielding more current net benefits. Choosing the appropriate interest rate becomes, therefore, an important policy question. There are several possible alternative rates.

Given that the discount rate allows the allocation of resources between the public and private sectors, it should be chosen so that it indicates when resources should be transferred from one sector to another. This means that the discount rate should represent the opportunity cost of funds withdrawn from the private sector to be used in the public sector. As William Baumol stated, "The correct discount rate for the evaluation of a government project is the percentage rate of return that the resources utilized would otherwise provide in the private sector."[21]

These considerations enter in the choice of the marginal productivity of capital as a discount rate in private investment: (1) an effort to minimize governmental activity, (2) a concern for efficiency, and (3) a belief that the source of funds for government investment in the private sector or that government investment will displace private investment that would otherwise be made.

Social time preference expresses a concern for future generations in that the welfare of the future generations will be increased if investments are made now. It follows that the discount rate should be the *social rate of time preference,* that is, the compensation required to induce consumers to refrain from consumption and save. One study committee argued that the federal government should use the "administration's social rate of time discount" to be established by the president in consultation with his advisors, such as the Council of Economic Advisors.[22] The strongest argument for the social rate of time preference was made by A. C. Pigou, who suggested that individuals were shortsighted about the future ("defective telescopic faculty") and that the welfare of future generations would require governmental intervention.[23]

Advantages and Limitations

There are thousands of cost-benefit analyses of government and not-for-profit projects. The popularity of the method is a witness to some of its advantages. There are also some limitations well recognized in the literature. Among the advantages of cost-benefit analysis, we may cite the following:

1. It is most effective in dealing with cases of intermediate social goods.[24]
2. It establishes a framework for a reasonably consistent evaluation of alternative projects, especially when the choice set is narrow in that the projects are not only similar but generate the same volume of externalities.
3. It allows one to ascertain the decision most advantageous in terms of the objectives accepted.

Among its limitations, we may cite the following:

1. There are limitations within which social objectives can be measured in money terms. An example of a nonefficiency objective that is not measurable in dollar terms is an equitable distribution of income.
2. Cost-benefit analysis falls under what is known as partial equilibrium analysis. It is useful in evaluating only projects that have negligible impact outside the immediately affected areas of the economy.
3. There are obvious problems of enumeration and evaluation of the costs and benefits of particular projects. A committee of the House of Representatives, pointing to the difficulty inherent in estimating the direct effects of a policy and assigning dollar terms to them, argued that such estimates are seldom accurate.[25] Similarly, Michael Baram argued that "monetaretization of environmental and health amenities constitutes an inappropriate treatment of factors that transcend economies."[26]

CONCLUSION

Capital budgeting for multinational corporations relies on the same evaluation techniques as for domestic operations. There are, however, new adjustments to be made to account for (a) project cash flows, (b) foreign tax regulations, (c) political and economic risks, (d) expropriation, (e) blocked funds, (f) inflation, and (g) the determination of the cost of capital. Capital budgeting in the developing countries requires the use of cost-benefit analysis. These issues and their corresponding solutions are examined in this chapter.

NOTES

1. Ahmed Belkaoui, *Conceptual Foundations of Management Accounting* (Reading, Mass.: Addison-Wesley, 1980), pp. 58–60.

2. Michael R. Czinkota, Rietra Rivoli, and Illslea A. Ronkainen, *International Business* (Chicago: Dryden Press, 1989), p. 529.

3. Rita M. Rodriguez and E. Eugene Carter, *International Financial Management* (Englewood Cliffs, N.J.: Prentice-Hall, 1979), p. 34.

4. Paul O. Graddis, "Analyzing Overseas Investments," *Harvard Business Review,* May–June 1966, p. 119.

5. A. C. Shapiro, "Capital Budgeting and Long-Term Financing," *Financial Management,* Spring 1978, p. 8.

6. U. B. Bavishi, "Capital Budgeting Practices of Multinationals," *Management Accounting,* August 1981, pp. 32–35.

7. Charles M. Newman II and I. James Czechowicz, *International Risk Management* (Morristown, N.J.: Financial Executives Research Foundation [FERF], 1983), p. 88.

8. Ibid., p. 89.

9. The weighted cost of capital concept can be extended to include debt denominated in foreign currencies, debt issued by foreign subsidiaries, and retained earnings of foreign subsidiaries.

10. Jeff Madura, *International Financial Management* (St. Paul, Minn.: West, 1989), p. 470.

11. Arthur Stonehill and Lessard Nathanson, "Capital Budgeting Techniques and the Multinational Corporation," *Journal of International Business Studies,* Spring 1975, p. 67.

12. Newman and Czechowicz, *International Risk Management,* p. 93.

13. Alan C. Shapiro, "Capital Budgeting for the Multinational Corporation," *Financial Management,* Spring 1978, p. 10.

14. Ibid., p. 11.

15. Madura, *International Financial Management,* p. 457.

16. Donald R. Lessard, "Evaluating Foreign Projects: An Adjusted Present Value Approach," in *International Financial Management: Theory and Application,* ed. Donald R. Lessard (Boston: Warren, Gorham and Lamont, 1979), pp. 578–592.

17. Maurice Levi, *International Finance* (New York: McGraw-Hill, 1983), p. 393.

18. Otto Eckstein, "A Survey of the Theory of Public Expenditure Criteria," in *Public Finances: Need, Sources, and Utilization,* ed. James M. Buchanan (Princeton, N.J.: Princeton University Press, 1961).

19. R. N. McKean, *Efficiency in Government Through Systems Analysis* (New York: Wiley, 1958), chap. 8.

20. George A. Steiner, "Problems in Implementing Program Budgeting," in *Program Budgeting,* ed. David Norick (Cambridge, Mass.: Harvard University Press, 1965).

21. William J. Baumol, "On the Discount Rate for Public Projects," in *Public Expenditures and Policy Analysis,* ed. Robert Haveman and Julius Margolis (Chicago: Markham, 1970), p. 274.

22. U.S. Bureau of the Budget, *Standards and Criteria for Formulating and Evaluating Federal Water Resources Development* (Washington, D.C.: U.S. Government Printing Office, 1961), p. 67.

23. A. C. Pigou, *The Economics of Welfare,* 4th ed. (London: Macmillan, 1932).

24. R. A. Musgrave, *Fiscal Systems* (New Haven: Yale University Press, 1969), pp. 797–806.

25. U.S. House of Representatives, Committee on Interstate and Foreign Commerce, Subcommittee on Oversight and Investigation, *Federal Regulation and Regulatory Reform* (94th Cong., 2d sess., 1976, Chapter 15, Subcommittee Print).

26. Michael S. Baram, "Cost-Benefit Analysis: An Inadequate Basis for Health, Safety, and Environmental Regulatory Decision Making," *Ecology Law Quarterly* 8 (1980): 475–531.

REFERENCES

Baram, Michael S. "Cost-Benefit Analysis: An Inadequate Basis for Health, Safety, and Environmental Regulatory Decision Making." *Ecology Law Quarterly* 8 (1980): 475–531.

Baumol, William J. "On the Discount Rate for Public Projects." In *Public Expenditures and Policy Analysis.* Edited by Robert Haveman and Julius Margolis. Chicago: Markham, 1970.

Bavishi, U. B. "Capital Budgeting Practices of Multinationals." *Management Accounting,* August 1981, pp. 32–35.

Belkaoui, Ahmed. *Conceptual Foundations of Management Accounting.* Reading, Mass.: Addison-Wesley, 1980.

Czinkota, Michael R., Rietra Rivoli, and Illslea A. Ronkainen. *International Business.* Chicago: Dryden Press, 1989.

Eckstein, Otto. "A Survey of the Theory of Public Expenditure Criteria." In *Public Finances: Need, Sources and Utilization.* Edited by James M. Buchanan. Princeton, N.J.: Princeton University Press, 1961.

Graddis, Paul O. "Analyzing Overseas Investments." *Harvard Business Review,* May–June 1966, pp. 118–130.

Lessard, Donald R. "Evaluating Foreign Projects: An Adjusted Present Value Approach." In *International Financial Management: Theory and Application.* Edited by Donald R. Lessard. Boston: Warren, Gorham and Lamont, 1979, pp. 578–592.

Levi, Maurice. *International Finance.* New York: McGraw-Hill, 1983.

Madura, Jeff. *International Financial Management.* St. Paul, Minn.: West, 1989.

McKean, R. N. *Efficiency in Government Through Systems Analysis.* New York: Wiley, 1958, chap. 8.

Musgrave, R. A. *Fiscal Systems.* New Haven: Yale University Press, 1969.

Newman, Charles M., II, and I. James Czechowicz. *International Risk Management.* Morristown, N.J.: Financial Executives Research Foundation (FERF), 1983.

Pigou, A. C. *The Economics of Welfare.* 4th ed. London: Macmillan, 1932.

Rodriguez, Rita M., and E. Eugene Carter. *International Financial Management.* Englewood Cliffs, N.J.: Prentice-Hall, 1979.

Shapiro, A. C. "Capital Budgeting and Long-Term Financing." *Financial Management,* Spring 1978, pp. 5–25.

————. "Capital Budgeting for the Multinational Corporation." *Financial Management*, Spring 1978, pp. 6–15.

Steiner, George A. "Problems in Implementing Program Budgeting." In *Program Budgeting*. Edited by David Norick. Cambridge, Mass.: Harvard University Press, 1965.

Stonehill, Arthur, and Lessard Nathanson. "Capital Budgeting Techniques and the Multinational Corporation." *Journal of International Business Studies*, Spring 1975, pp. 63–72.

U.S. Bureau of the Budget. *Standards and Criteria for Formulating and Evaluating Federal Water Resources Development*. Washington, D.C.: U.S. Government Printing Office, 1961.

U.S. House of Representatives, Committee on Interstate and Foreign Commerce, Subcommittee on Oversight and Investigation. *Federal Regulation and Regulatory Reform*. 94th Cong., 2d sess., 1976, Chapter 15, Subcommittee Print.

Appendix 8.A

Managing Political Risk

Because of the political risk elements in most international operations and investments there is a strong need for a systematic evaluation of political risks.[1] Accordingly, in this appendix, the nature of political risk, the ways of forecasting it, and the accounting role in managing political risk are examined.

NATURE OF POLITICAL RISK

Political risk is not necessarily limited to unfavorable conditions encountered by multinationals in most developing countries. It can easily be encountered in industrialized countries including the United States. In general, it refers to the potential economic losses resulting from some forms of most government influences that may either limit the multinational activities of a firm or eliminate (through takeover, for example) these same activities. Various operational definitions of political risks have been proposed. Stephan Robock and Kenneth Simmonds maintained that political risk in international business exists "(1) when discontinuities occur in the business environment, (2) when they are difficult to anticipate, and (3) when they result from political change."[2]

They also made a distinction between macropolitical risks when politically motivated environmental changes affect all foreign firms and micropolitical risks when the changes affect only selected foreign firms or industries or foreign firms with specific characteristics. Fred Greene defined *political risk* as "that uncertainty stemming from unanticipated and unexpected acts of governments or other organizations which may cause loss to the business firm."[3] Political risk is manifest through a climate of uncertainty dominated by a probable loss to the business enterprise. It may arise from different sources. S. N. Root noted that a wide spectrum of political risks may be generated "by the attitudes, policies and overt behavior of those governments and other local power centers such as rival political parties, labor unions, and nationalistic groups."[4] A study prepared for the Financial Executives Research Foundation identified instead the following twelve political risk factors: radical change in government composition or policy, expropriation, nationalization, attitude of opposition groups, probability of opposition-group takeover, attitude toward foreign investment, quality of government management, ownership requirements, antiprivate-sector influence, labor instability, relationship with the company's home government, and relationship with neighboring countries.[5] Political risk may lead to various possible outcomes, namely, expropriation/nationalization, compulsory local equity participation, operational restrictions, discrimination, price controls, blockage of remittances, and breach of government contracts. Given the negative impacts of the outcomes of political risk on foreign operations, especially in the extreme cases in which a government takes over a business activity through confiscation and expropriation, there is a strong need to be able to forecast political risk.

HOW TO FORECAST POLITICAL RISKS

It would not be surprising to learn that various proposals have been made about how to forecast political risks. Robock and Simmonds suggested an evaluation of the vulnerability of a company to political risk by an analysis of its operations, with the following questions in mind:

1. Are periodic external inputs of new technology required?
2. Will the project be competing strongly with local nationals who are in, or trying to enter, the same field?
3. Is the operation dependent on natural resources, particularly minerals or oil?
4. Does the investment put pressure on balance of payments?
5. Does the enterprise have a strong monopoly position in the local market?
6. Is the product socially essential and acceptable?[6]

Robert Stobaugh noticed that a number of U.S.-based multinational enterprises had developed scales to rate countries on the basis of their investment climates.[7] An *Argus Capital Market Report* offered for country risk analysis a laundry list of economic indicators to "educate the decision-maker and force him to think in terms of the relevant economic fundaments."[8] These indicators are monetary base, domestic base, foreign reserves, purchasing power parity index, currency/deposit ratio, consumer prices as a percentage change, balance of payments—goods and services as a percentage of the GNP, balance of payments—goods and services as a percentage of foreign reserves, percentage change exports/percentage change imports, exports as a percentage of the GNP, imports as a percentage of the GNP, foreign factor income payments as a percentage of the GNP, average tax rate, government deficit as a percentage of the GNP, government expenditures, real GNP as a percentage change, and real per capita GNP as a percentage change.

Shapiro offered the following common characteristics of country risk:

1. A large government deficit relative to GDP.
2. A high rate of money expansion if it is combined with a relatively fixed exchange rate.
3. High leverage combined with highly variable terms of trade.
4. Substantial government expenditures yielding low rates of return.
5. Price controls, interest rate ceilings, trade restrictions, and other government imposed barriers to the smooth adjustment of the economy to changing relative prices.
6. A citizenry that demands, and a political system that accepts, government responsibility for maintaining and expanding the nation's standard of living through public sector spending. The less stable the political system, the more important this factor is likely to be.[9]

More recently, R. J. Rummel and Donald Heenan provided a four-way classification of attempts to forecast political interference: "grand tours," "old hands," Delphi techniques, and quantitative methods.[10] A grand tour involves a visit of the potential host country by an executive or a team of people for an inspection tour and later to the home office. Superficiality and overdose of selective information have marred the grand tour technique.

The old hands technique involves acquiring area expertise from seasoned educators, diplomats, journalists, or businesspersons. Evidently, too much implicit faith is put in the judgment of these so-called experts.

The Delphi techniques may be used to survey a knowledgeable group. First, selective elements influencing the political climate are chosen. Next, experts are asked to rank these factors toward the development of an overall measure or index of political risk. Finally, countries are ranked on the basis of the index. As stated by Rummel and Heenan, the "strength of the Delphi technique rests on the posing of relevant questions. When they are defective, the entire structure crumbles."[11]

The quantitative methods technique involves developing elaborate models using multivariate analysis to either explain and describe underlying relationships affecting a nation-state or predict future political events. Two such political risk models using this technique may be identified in the literature and are examined next.

THE KNUDSEN "ECOLOGICAL APPROACH"

Harald Knudsen's model involves gathering socioeconomic data depicting the "ecological structures" or investment climate of a particular foreign environment to be used to predict political behavior in general and the national propensity to expropriate in particular.[12] The model maintains that national propensity to expropriate may be explained by "a nation frustration" factor and "scapegoat function of foreign investment." Basically, if the level of national frustration is high and at the same time the level of foreign investment presence is also high, these foreign investments become a scapegoat leading to a high propensity to expropriate.

The variables in the model are defined as follows: The *level of frustration* is expected to be the difference between the level of aspirations and the level of welfare and expectations. Also, the scapegoat of foreign investment is determined by the perceived general and special role of foreign investment.

The variables are measured as follows: First, national aspirations may be measured by six proxy variables, namely, degree of urbanization, literacy rate, number of newspapers, number of radios, degree of labor unionization, and the national endowment of national resources. Second, the welfare of people may be measured by proxy variables, namely, infant survival rate, caloric consumption, number of doctors per population size, number of hospital beds per population size, percentage of housing with piped water supply, and per capita gross national product. Third, national expectations may be measured by the percentage change in per capita gross national product and the percentage of gross national product being invested. These are surrogate measures of the underlying factors in Knudsen's model. The model's reliability may be improved by a search for more relevant measures by subjecting a bigger selection of these surrogate measures to factor analysis. Such an analysis used in a conformatory way may reduce their number to only the salient measures. But more research, especially in the management accounting field, may be needed to improve and test Knudsen's model or similar "components-based" models of predicting political risk.

THE HAENDEL-WEST-MEADOW "POLITICAL SYSTEM STABILITY INDEX"

Another components approach to the forecasting of political risk was provided by Dan Haendel, Gerald West, and Robert Meadow in an empirical, indicator-based measure of political system stability—the Political System Stability Index (PSSI)—in sixty-five developing countries.[13] It is composed of three equally weighted indexes: the Socioeconomic Index, the Governmental Process Index, and the Societal Conflict Index, which is itself derived from three sub-subindexes on public unrest, internal violence, and coercion potential. All of these indexes are derived from fifteen indirect measures of the political system's stability and adaptability. Basically, the higher the PSSI score, the greater the stability of the political system. The index was based on data from the 1961–1966 period. There is a need to test the validity of the index with more recent data before using it as a forecasting tool. In any case, the model demonstrates again the feasibility of a components approach to the study of political risk. As stated by Haendel: "The Political System Stability Index (PSSI) derives its importance from the role the political system plays in establishing power relationship and norms for resolving conflicts in society. It assumes that the degree of political stability in a country may indicate the society's capacity to cope with new demands."[14]

COPING WITH POLITICAL RISK

Forecasting political risk is not enough; the problem is how to cope and live with it or to minimize it. Various techniques have been proposed for minimizing political risk. D. K. Eiteman and A. I. Stonehill suggested the following three categories of techniques for dealing with political risk:

1. Negotiating the environment before investment by including concession agreements, adaptation to host-country goals, planned investment, and investment guarantees.

2. Implementing specific operating strategies after the investment decision in production, logistics, marketing, finance, organization, and personnel. For example, local zoning, a safe location of facilities, and control of transportation and of patents and processes are examples of operating strategies in production and logistics that may reduce the likelihood of political interference or expropriation.

3. Resorting to specific compensation strategies after expropriation, including rational negotiation, application of power tactics to bargaining, legal remedies, use of the International Centre for Settlement of Investment Disputes, and surrenders in the interest of seeking salvage.[15]

Another way of coping with political risk is to negotiate a tight investment agreement that spells out specific rights and responsibilities of both the foreign firm and the host government. Eiteman and Stonehill suggested that the investment agreement spell out, among other things, the following policies on financial and managerial issues:

- The basis on which fund flows, such as dividends, management fees, royalties, patent fees, and loan repayments, may be remitted.
- The basis for setting any applicable transfer prices.
- The right to export to third-country makers.
- Obligations to build, or fund, social and economic overhead projects, such as schools, hospitals, and retirement systems.
- Methods of taxation, including the rate, the type of taxation, and how the rate base is determined.
- Access to host country capital markets, particularly for long-term borrowing.
- Permission for 100% foreign ownership versus required local ownership (joint venture) participation.
- Price controls, if any, applicable to sales in the host country markets.
- Requirements for local sourcing versus import of raw materials and components.
- Permission to use expatriate managerial and technical personnel.
- Provision for arbitration of disputes.[16]

Haendel classified, appropriately, the traditional tools of risk management into five general categories:

1. Avoidance, whereby the risk manager may recommend not investing or diversifying or else imposing a ceiling on the exposure a firm allows a country.
2. Transfer, whereby the risk manager may recommend including local individuals as either investors or managers.
3. Diversification and loss prevention, whereby the risk manager may recommend diversifying to reduce the reliance on a production facility or natural resource supply in one given country.
4. Insurance, whereby the risk manager may recommend that the firm secure insurance against political risk as a way of shielding the firm's assets from unexpected losses. This may even include self-insurance in the form of a separate fund.
5. Retention, whereby the risk manager may recommend that not all political risks can be avoided, transferred, diversified, or insured against. In such a case the firm should include political risk analysis in its decision-making process.[17]

The question remains to know what the multinationals actually do to cope with political risk. A study prepared for the Financial Executives Research Foundation surveyed multinationals and found a number of techniques that could be used both before the investment and when operating overseas.[18] The techniques found to be most useful by the participant firm in their preinvestment negotiations with local governments are using local nationals, securing prior agreements on the remittance of funds or other fees and on control of the company, and looking into joint ventures with local business. The techniques found to be most useful by the participant firms once the investment had been made and the firms were committed are maximizing the use of local debt and local funding, adapting to changing governmental priorities, sourcing locally to stimulate the economy and to reduce dependence on imports, and increasing exports. Besides using those techniques the respondent firms admitted to insuring against the losses that may be caused by expropriation/confiscation, nationalization, foreign exchange inconvertibility, war, revolution or insurrection damages, kidnapping and ransom, long-term currency losses, and even inflation. The insurance was provided by the Overseas Private Investment Corporation (OPIC), a credit insurance program administered by the Export/Import Bank of the U.S. (Eximbank) jointly with Foreign Credit Insurance Association (FCIA), and private political risk insurance organizations like the American International Group (AIG) and Lloyds of London.

NOTES

1. Stephan H. Robock and Kenneth Simmonds, *International Business and Multinational Enterprises* (Homewood, Ill.: Irwin, 1973).

2. Ibid., p. 356.

3. Fred Greene, "The Management of Political Risk," *Best's Review*, July 1974, p. 15.

4. S. N. Root, "U.S. Business Abroad," p. 73.

5. Charles M. Newman II and I. James Czechowicz, *International Risk Management* (Morristown, N.J.: FERF, 1983), pp. 15–16.

6. Robock and Simmonds, *International Business and Multinational Enterprises,* p. 371.

7. Robert Stobaugh, Jr., "How to Analyze Foreign Investment Climates," *Harvard Business Review,* September–October 1969, pp. 101–102.

8. "A Primer on Country Risk," *Argus Capital Market Report,* June 4, 1975, pp. 15–25.

9. Alan C. Shapiro, "Currency Risk and Country Risk in International Banking," *The Journal of Finance,* July 1985, p. 891.

10. R. J. Rummel and David A. Heenan, "How Multinationals Analyze Political Risk," *Harvard Business Review,* January–February 1978, pp. 67–76.

11. Ibid., p. 70.

12. Harald Knudsen, "Explaining the National Propensity to Expropriate: An Ecological Approach," *Journal of International Business Studies,* Spring 1974, pp. 51–71.

13. Dan Haendel and Gerald T. West, with Robert G. Meadow, *Overseas Investment and Political Risk,* Monograph Series, no. 21 (Philadelphia: Foreign Policy Research Institute, 1957).

14. Dan Haendel, *Foreign Investments and the Management of Political Risk* (Boulder, Colo.: Westview Press, 1979), pp. 106–107.

15. D. K. Eiteman and A. I. Stonehill, *Multinational Business Finance* (Reading, Mass.: Addison-Wesley, 1989), pp. 203–223.

16. Eiteman and Stonehill, *Multinational Business Finance,* p. 503.

17. Haendel, *Foreign Investments,* pp. 139–146.

18. Newman and Czechowicz, *International Risk Management,* p. 81.

9

Pricing Strategies for International Operations

Pricing for international operations is definitely a more complex phenomena than it is for monastic operations since various new factors have to be accounted for in the final decision if the multinational corporation is aiming at a maximization of the total return of the firm. Similarly, transfer pricing in the multinational firm involves various considerations that need to be accounted for and can be used as a mechanism for the firm to achieve various outcomes that are beneficial to the total profit of the firm. Both product pricing and transfer pricing techniques are presented below along with their international ramifications.

PRODUCT PRICING IN GENERAL

Pricing decisions in most firms are preceded by and depend on pricing policies, which indicate the main factors to be considered in pricing decisions. Pricing policies must be congruent with the overall goals of the organization, such as profit maximization, achieving a target rate of return on investment, or reaching a target market share. When these goals and the corresponding pricing policies are determined, management can proceed with pricing decisions. It is useful to make a distinction between the economist's and the accountant's approaches.

Economist's Approach

The economist reasons on the basis of a nonlinear total revenue and cost function and assumes the existence of a profit maximizing sales volume whereby marginal costs equal marginal revenues. Hence the optimal selling price for the economist would be the price necessary to reach the optimal sales volume. To illustrate the computation of such a price, assume the following example:

Demand function: $x = 22 - 10p$.

Total cost function: $y = 3.2 + 0.2x + 0.1x^2$

Solving the demand function for p yields the price function as follows:

Price function: $p = 2.2 - 0.1x$

The total revenue, marginal cost, and marginal revenue can be computed as follows:

Total revenue function: $R = 2.2x - 0.1x^2$

Marginal cost $= MC = \dfrac{dy}{dX} = 0.2 + 0.2x$

Marginal revenue $= MR = \dfrac{dr}{dX} = 2.2 - 0.2x$

Setting the marginal cost equal to the marginal revenue and solving for x yields the optimal sales volume:

$MR = MC = 0.2 + 0.2x = 2.2 - 0.2x$, where $x = 5$

Finally, solving the price function on the basis of the optimal sales volume yields the optimal sales price, as follows:

$p = \$2.2 - 0.1(5) = \$1.7$

Accountant's Approaches

The accountant's approaches can be based on either a target rate of return on investment or a cost-plus approach.

Product Pricing Based on Target Rate of Return on Investment: Firms generally set a target rate of return on investment computed as follows:

Return on investment (ROI) $= \dfrac{\text{Income}}{\text{Total investment}}$

Assuming p = price, Q = sales volume, v = variable cost, F = total fixed cost, t = tax rate, and C = investment, the rate of return on investment can be computed as follows:

$ROI = \dfrac{[Q(p - v) - F](1 - t)}{C}$

Solving for p yields:

$$p = \frac{\dfrac{ROI \times C}{(1 - t)} + F}{\varphi} + \upsilon$$

Assume that Fabiani Ltd. has a target rate of return on investment of 20 percent, a capital investment of $300,000, a tax rate of 40 percent, a total fixed cost of $300,000, expected sales volume of 40,000 units, and a unit variable cost of $100. The selling price can be determined as follows:

$$p = \frac{\dfrac{20\% \times 300,000}{(1 - 0.4)} + 300,000}{40,000} + 100 = 110$$

Cost Based Approaches: The cost-plus pricing methods can be determined on the basis of either the full cost or the incremental cost. The markup will vary between the two methods as follows:

Full cost markup = Target profit/Estimated full costs

Incremental cost markup $= \dfrac{\text{Target profit } + \text{ Estimated unallocated fixed costs}}{\text{Estimated incremental costs}}$

Assume that Fabiani Ltd. is instead using an accounting product pricing method. The target profit before tax is estimated to be $500,000, the fixed cost to be $15,000,000, and the total production to be 1,000,000 units. The markup for Fabiani Ltd. will be either:

Full cost markup = $500,000/$5,000,000 + $15,000,000 = $0.025

or

Incremental cost markup = $5,000,000 + $15,000,000/$5,000,000 = $3.1

If we also assume that Fabiani Ltd. has an incremental cost per unit of $5 and a fixed cost per unit of $15, the selling price would be as follows:

Full cost markup method: (1 + 0.025) ($15.00 + $5.00) = $20.50

Incremental cost markup method: (1 + 3.1)($5.00) + $20.50

The cost-plus methods are generally favored by corporations, because they provide a practical benchmark in pricing decisions.

The cost-based approaches to pricing are useful if the firm is to remain in operation in the long run, given that the approach allows a recovery of all costs, and secure an adequate return on investments in the form of the markup. There are, however, some limitations to the use of cost based pricing.

1. First, the cost based approaches ignore the type of market demand facing the firm.
2. Second, the cost based approaches computed the markup for a given target volume and target profit. Different target volumes and target profits require a different markup.
3. The cost based approaches to pricing relied on the unit costs (unit variable cost and unit fixed cost) in the determination of the price, by adding a markup to the per-unit cost of the product. The unit fixed cost is affected by the choice of volume of production. It is high when the volume is low and low when the volume is high. Therefore if prices are based on per-unit cost of the product, they will be set higher when the volume is low and low when the volume is high.
4. In the analysis of special contracts, the use of a cost based pricing can lead to incorrect decisions.

Time and Materials Pricing: Small service oriented firms use an alternative approach to the cost-plus formula, given as time and materials pricing. The approach consists of deriving two pricing rates: one based on direct labor time and one based on direct materials used. The rest includes allowance for other indirect costs, selling and administrative, and one for a desired profit. The two rates are derived as follows:

a. The time rate is computed as the sum of (1) the direct labor cost of the worker, including salaries and fringe benefits; (2) a pro rata allowance for the indirect costs and selling and administrative expenses of the unit; and (3) a provision for a desired profit per hour of the worker's time.
b. The materials loading charge to be added to the invoice price of the materials used on the job includes the costs of ordering, handling and carrying materials in stock, plus a provision for a desired profit on materials.

To illustrate the use of time and materials pricing, assume that a TV repair shop incurred the following expenses for its employees involved in repairs:

1. Shop supervision	$ 10,000
2. Supplies	3,000
3. Depreciation	2,000
4. Selling and administrative expenses	5,000
Total	$ 20,000

The employees worked 20,000 hours per year. The owner planned a profit of $6 per hour of employee's time. The employee is paid an average of $10 an hour including fringe benefits.

The shop incurred the following expenses for its employees involved in handling materials:

1. Wages and fringe benefits	$10,000
2. Property taxes	2,000
3. Utilities	5,000
4. Insurance	2,000
5. Miscellaneous	8,000
Total	$30,000

The invoice cost of materials for the year was $100,000. The owner planned for a profit of 6 percent of the invoice cost of materials used. The time rate and the materials loading charge are computed as follows:

1. Time rate:

a. Direct labor cost per hour	$ 6
b. Prorated allowance of indirect costs ($200,000/20,000 hours)	1
c. Provision for profit per hour	10
Total time rate per hour of service	$17

2. Materials loading charge:

   a. Material servicing costs ($25,000/$75,00): 30 percent of invoice

   b. Provision for profit on materials: 10 percent of invoice

   c. Materials loading charge: 40 percent of invoice

Therefore if our employee completed a repair job in three hours using $30 in materials, the price would be as follows:

1. Labor cost: 3 hours × 17		$51
2. Materials used		
a. Invoice cost	$30	
b. Materials loading charge (40% × 30%)	$12	$42
3. Total price of the repair job		$93

Pricing Under the Robinson-Patman Act

The Robinson-Patman Act of 1936 prohibits certain kinds of price discrimination. Its purpose is:

To make it unlawful for any person engaged in commerce to discriminate in price or terms of sale between purchasers of commodities of like grade and quality; to prohibit the payment of brokerage or commission under certain conditions, to suppress pseudo advertising allowances; to provide a presumptive measure of damages in certain cases; and to protect the independent merchant, the public whom he serves; and the manufacturer from whom he buys, from exploitation by unfair competitors.[1]

The legislation, however, does not prohibit price discrimination when it is justified by differences in costs of manufacturing, sales, or delivery. The act states "that nothing herein contained shall prevent differentials which make only due allowances for differences in cost of manufacture, sale, or delivery resulting from the differing methods or quantities in which such commodities are to such purchasers sold or delivered."[2] Because the act rests on the interpretation of cost, Wright Patman defined cost as including all costs of manufacture and sale, excluding the return on invested capital by including a prorated share of all overhead costs. The courts and the Federal Trade Commission base their decisions accordingly—on the full cost rather than on the direct or differential cost.

PRODUCT PRICING INTERNATIONALLY

In an international context the pricing decision is complicated by a myriad of new factors. Some of these factors include the following:

First, multinational companies may be faced with different pricing policies needed to maximize the total profit. Examples of these strategies include (a) *presentation pricing,* which is equivalent to lowering prices to penetrate a market or gain a dominant position; (b) *market skimming,* which is equivalent to setting a specific high price to target one clientele willing to pay the high price; (c) *market holding,* which is equivalent to adapting prices to local conditions to hold a certain market share.

Second, multinational companies' unique costs such as transportation, duty, and distributor margin force them to increase their prices. This price escalation is a good explanation for the disparity in the prices charged for the same product by the company in two different countries. Two options are available to multinational corporations for dealing with price escalation as follows:

One option is to search the international manufacturing system of the company to identify a potential lower-cost source of merchandise. This source could include local manufacture but, alternatively, could improve sourcing to other points in the world to take advantage of lower freights and duty charges. The second weapon available is a thorough audit of the distribution structure in the target markets. In some cases distribution channels include intermediaries who perform no real function or make no contribution to the total marketing program and who therefore unnecessarily add to the price of the product in the marketplace. When this situation exists, a rationalization of the distribution structure by selecting new intermediaries, assigning new responsibilities to old intermediaries, or by establishing direct marketing operations can substantially reduce the total markups required to accomplish distribution programs in the target market.[3]

Third, multinational companies face fluctuating exchange and inflation rates that can undermine their most careful and elaborate pricing policies. They need to deal with those exchange and inflation gains and losses in their pricing policies by either (a) passing the increase in price to customers or (b) cutting expenses to be able to maintain the price at its present level and (c) negotiating to bill in a strong currency.

Fourth, multinational companies that need to convince their clientele of their new pricing strategy rely on (a) timing their price changes, (b) making a number of price changes rather than a sudden materials change, (c) using various discounts and credit, and (d) bundling and unbundling the product.

Fifth, dumping as defined by Congress is equivalent to unfair trade practices—unfair price cutting having for its objective the injury, destruction, or prevention of the establishment of American industry. The General Agreement on Tariffs and Trade (GATT) refers to dumping as the difference between the normal domestic price and the export price. Each country has its own international dumping regulations as an attempt to either protect the local industry or limit foreign competition. Dumping has been categorized as (a) *sporadic dumping*, when the company wants to dispose of excess or distressed inventories; (b) *predatory dumping*, when the company decreases its prices to get rid of the competition and acquire a monopoly position; (c) *persistent dumping*, when the company consistently lowers the price in one market identified as being different in terms of overhead costs and demand characteristics; and (d) *Reverse dumping*, when the company increases its price because the foreign demand is less elastic and the foreign market can tolerate higher prices.[4] Dumping can be avoided by differentiating the exported item from the item being sold in the home market or by moving the manufacturing of the product in the foreign country.

TRANSFER PRICING

Nature of Transfer Pricing

Transfer pricing is a major issue confronting decentralized organizations that expect division managers to operate their divisions as a semiautonomous business. These organizations face the problem of what price to charge for goods and services sold by one organizational unit to another in the same company. This situation prevails within vertically integrated organizations, where transactions often occur between divisions; the revenue of the supplying unit becomes the cost of the purchasing unit. These intracompany charges ultimately will be reflected in the profit and loss statements of the respective divisions. Since divisional performance is evaluated by a profit based criterion such as ROI or residual income, the profit center managers will attempt to maximize their own center's profit. A conflict occurs when improved divisional performance is achieved at the expense of overall company profits.

In theory, to optimize an organization's profits, the transfer price should be selected so that it motivates and guides managers to choose their inputs and outputs in coordination with the other subunits. Ideally, any intracompany pricing method should be consistent with the goals of maximizing both company and divisional profits: Transfer pricing should insure goal congruence between units.

Because of the potential conflicts that can arise in transfer price determination, three primary objectives can be used to establish a proper transfer price.

1. To assist top management in evaluating and guiding divisional performance by providing adequate information on divisional revenues and expenses
2. To help the division manager in running the division
3. To insure divisional autonomy and allow each profit center to act as an independent agent

In theory, the design of a transfer pricing scheme ultimately must point each division manager toward top management's goals. The scheme must reward divisional external economies and prevent and penalize diseconomies. Furthermore, a firm's transfer pricing divisions must acknowledge domestic and foreign legal and tax requirements, as well as antitrust and financial reporting constraints.

Developing a set of transfer pricing rules that can integrate the complex dimensions of an organization, insure divisional autonomy, and at the same time achieve overall corporate goals is a very difficult task. Consequently, a transfer pricing system must be developed with an awareness of these difficulties.

The main positive characteristics of a transfer pricing system include insuring goal congruence, being fair to all concerned parties, and minimizing conflicts between divisions. Some corporations set guidelines to insure an effective pricing system.

A *transfer price* is the price agreed upon between two divisions, a selling division I and a buying division II, for a product or service A supplied by the selling to the buying division. The buying division uses the product or service for further processing toward a final product B. Product A is termed an *intermediate product* and product B may be either another intermediate product if it is sold to another division or a final product of the firm if it is sold to an external market. In most situations the buying division II may have the option of buying the product A from an external market for product A rather than internally from division I, and the selling division may have the option of selling outside. If the firm is perfectly decentralized, the option of buying and selling outside is available to both divisions.

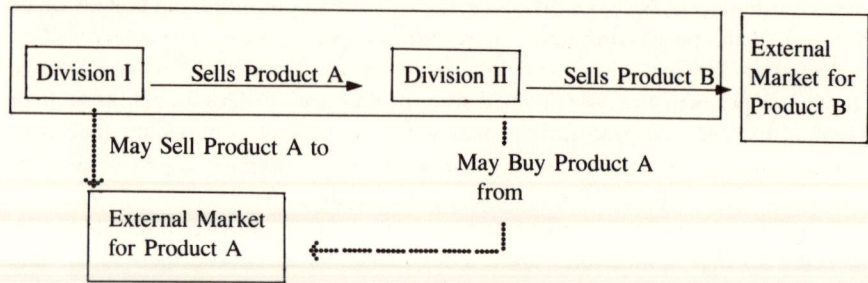

Three fundamental transfer pricing methods are used:

1. Market based transfer price
2. Cost based transfer prices
3. Negotiated prices

Example of Transfer Pricing

Backwoods Lumber is a decentralized company with three divisions operating as profit centers:

1. The Raw Lumber Division manages the cutting of raw lumber from a large forest owned by the company.
2. The Transportation Division is in charge of carrying the raw lumber from the forest area to a nearby harbor city.
3. The Finished Lumber Division, located in the harbor city, is in charge of turning the raw lumber into finished lumber to be sold to outside markets. One hundred board feet of raw lumber are needed to produce ninety board feet of finished lumber.

The total annual finished lumber production of 9,000 board feet resulting from the processing of 10,000 board feet of raw lumber is sold entirely to the outside market.

The cost and price information for each of the three divisions is shown in Exhibit 9.1. Three pricing methods are considered:

Method A: Transfer price is set at 120 percent of variable costs.

Method B: Transfer price is set at 110 percent of absorption costs.

Method C: Transfer price is set at market prices.

The transfer prices per 100 board feet of finished lumber under each method are:

A. 120 percent of variable costs
   1. Raw Lumber Division to Transportation Division = 1.2($120) = $144
   2. Transportation Division to Finished Lumber Division = 1.2($144 + $21) = $198

B. 110 percent of absorption costs
   1. Raw Lumber Division to Transportation Division = 1.1($270) = $297
   2. Transportation Division to Finished Lumber Division = 1.1($2.97 + 61) = $393.80

C. Market Price
   1. Raw Lumber Division to Transportation Division = $300
   2. Transportation Division to Finished Lumber Division = $400

Exhibit 9.2 illustrates the impact of the use of each of the transfer prices on the incomes of the three divisions and on the total income of the firm. Two points are worth considering:

Exhibit 9.1
Information on Backwoods Lumber's Three Divisions

Raw Lumber Division

		Market Price
Variable Costs per 100 Feet of Raw Lumber	= $120 ◄────	per 100 Feet
Fixed Costs per 100 Feet of Raw Lumber	= $150	of Raw Lumber
Absorption Costs per 100 Feet of Raw Lumber	= $270	= $300

Transportation Division

Variable Costs per 100 Feet of Raw Lumber	= $21
Fixed Costs per 100 Feet of Raw Lumber	= $40
Absorption Costs per 100 Feet of Raw Lumber	= $61

Finished Lumber Division

Market Price per
100 Feet of Raw
Lumber Delivered
to the Finished

		Lumber Division by
Variable Costs per 100 Feet of Raw Lumber	= $140 ◄────	the Intermediate
Fixed Costs per 100 Feet of Raw Lumber	= $ 60	Market = $400
Absorption Costs per 100 Feet of Raw Lumber	= $200	

External Sale

Market Price per 100 Feet of Finished lumber
sold to External Market = $600

First, the transfer price used has no impact on the total income of the firm. The total is equal to $1,290,000 under either method.

Second, the transfer price method used has a definite impact on the operating income of each of the three divisions, fluctuating from huge losses to material profits for the Raw Lumber Division and the Transportation Division and from huge profits to huge losses for the Finished Lumber Division. What this result implies is that the divisions whose managers are compensated on the basis of divisional incomes will strive to choose the transfer price that will generate positive divisional incomes. That sets the state for divisional transfer pricing policies that may differ from one division to another and that may result in a conflict situation. Those transfer pricing policies and their implications are reviewed next.

Exhibit 9.2
Division Operating Income of Backwoods' Raw Lumber Division per 10,000 Board Feet of Lumber

	Transfer Price Set at 120% of Variable Costs	Transfer Price Set at 110% of Absorption Costs	Transfer Price Set at Market Price
1. *Raw Lumber Division*			
Revenues			
$144, $297, $300 × $10,000 Feet of Raw Lumber	$1,440,000	$2,970,000	$3,000,000
Division Variable Costs			
$120 × 10,000 Feet of Raw Lumber	1,200,000	1,200,000	1,200,000
Division Fixed Costs			
$50 × 10,000 Feet of Raw Lumber	500,000	500,000	500,000
Division Operating Income	$ (260,000)	$1,270,000	$1,300,000
2. *Transportation Division*			
Revenues			
$198, $393.8, $400 × 10,000 Feet of Raw Lumber	$1,980,000	$3,938,000	$4,000,000
Division Variable Costs			
$21 × 10,000 Feet of Raw Lumber	210,000	210,000	210,000
Division Fixed Costs			
$40 × 10,000 Feet of Raw Lumber	400,000	400,000	400,000
Transferred-in Costs			
$144, $297, $300 × 10,000 Feet of Raw Lumber	1,440,000	2,970,000	3,000,000
Division Operating Income	$ (70,000)	$ 358,000	$ 390,000

Exhibit 9.2 (continued)

	Transfer Price Set at 120% of Variable Costs	Transfer Price Set at 110% of Absorption Costs	Transfer Price Set at Market Price
3. *Finished Lumber Division*			
Revenues			
$600 × 9,000 Feet of Raw Lumber	$5,400,000	$5,400,000	$5,400,000
Division Variable Costs			
$140 × 9,000 Feet of Finished Lumber	1,269,000	1,260,000	1,260,000
Division Fixed Costs			
$60 × 9,000 Feet of Finished Lumber	540,000	540,000	540,000
Transferred-in Costs			
$198, $393.8, $400 × 10,000 of Raw Lumber	1,980,000	3,938,000	4,000,000
Division Operating Income	$1,620,000	$ (338,000)	$ (400,000)
4. Total Company Income	$,1,290,000	$1,290,000	$1,290,000

Transfer Pricing Methods

Market Price: A *market price* is the price at which the producing division would sell the product externally. In other words, the producing division charges the same price to its divisions as it would charge to outside customers in open market transactions. The market price has the advantage of providing an objective measure of value for goods or services exchanged, and it may result in the best information for use in performance evaluation of the profit centers. A transfer pricing system based on market prices requires a competitive market, minimal interdependencies of the profit centers, and the availability of dependable market quotations.

There are also serious drawbacks to using a transfer price based on market price. First, in today's regulated economy, perfectly competitive markets are very rare. In an imperfect market, one seller or buyer, by itself, can affect the market price, rendering it inapplicable as an effective price.

Second, even if the intermediate is perfect, there is no guarantee that the market price is for a product strictly comparable in terms of grade and other relevant characteristics.

Third, a situation may arise in which the market price is a distress price. Should the transfer price be the distress price, or should it be a long-run average, or "normal," market price? Both prices are defensible. On the one hand, the use of a distress price may lead managers of the supplying division to dispose of productive facilities to affect positively the short-run ROI. This may reduce the activities of the buying division, however, which would be disadvantageous to the company as a whole. On the other hand, the use of the long-run average market price may penalize the buying division by forcing it to buy at a price higher than the market price. If the objective is to preserve the spirit of decentralization and if safeguards exist to prevent the supplying division from disposing of productive facilities, the distress price should be chosen.

Finally, there may be problems if the goods or services transferred do not have a ready market price.

In spite of these limitations, the market price is considered the most effective transfer price because (1) it insures divisional autonomy, (2) it provides a good performance indication for use in performance evaluation, and (3) it creates a climate conducive to goal congruence.

Negotiated Price: A *negotiated transfer price* is the price set after bargaining between the buying and selling divisions. This system requires that these divisions deal with one another in the same way that they deal with external suppliers and buyers. Thus one basic requirement for the success of the bargaining process is the freedom of the divisions not only to bargain with one another but also to deal with external markets if unsatisfied with the internal offers. This freedom will avoid the bilateral monopoly that exists when the divisions are allowed to deal with only themselves. In fact, the negotiated transfer system works best when an intermediate market exists for the product or service transferred, providing the divisions with objective and reliable information for successful negotiations.

The literature contains several recommendations for the use of negotiated prices.[5] The writers maintain that prices negotiated in arm's-length bargaining by divisional managers help accomplish goal congruence. They view these prices as compatible with profit decentralization, insuring the division managers' freedom of action and increasing their accountability for profits. A survey conducted by R. K. Mautz indicates that about 24 percent of the participating diversified companies revealed negotiation as the basis for setting transfer prices between divisions.[6]

The negotiated transfer price system also may have a negative behavioral impact when personality conflicts arise between the bargainers; succeeding in the negotiation may become a more important goal than the company's profitability. Another drawback of the negotiated price system is that it can be time consuming. Division managers may lose an overall company perspective and direct their efforts to improve their divisional profit performance. In their attempts to obtain the best possible price, managers may find themselves in very lengthy argumentation.

When these conflicts arise, a transfer price should be set arbitrarily by a central decision of top management. This arbitrary, or imposed, price is the price believed to serve the overall company interests. But the arbitrary price contradicts the spirit of decentralization, given the possible loss of divisional autonomy. Some authors in the accounting literature have fundamental objections to negotiation. R. M. Cyert and J. G. March viewed the organization as a coalition of interests and suggested that negotiation and renegotiation of transfer pricing can be expected to create conflict among the subunits constituting the coalition.[7] Nicholas Dopuch and D. F. Drake suggested that the negotiated price implies an evaluation of the power to negotiate rather than an evaluation of performance itself.[8]

Actual Cost: A transfer price based on actual absorption cost is a price based on the historical full cost of the product or service exchanged. It has the obvious advantage of being measurable, verifiable, and readily available.

When the actual costs are accepted for the determination of transfer prices, the problem remains of motivating the selling division to sell internally at a price other than the market price. One way of motivating the selling division is to set the transfer price at full actual cost plus some markup as a way of approximating the market price. The resulting synthetic market price may be better than the actual market price when the product existing in the intermediate market differs in terms of quality, grade, and other relevant characteristics from the product transferred.

The full-cost-plus or synthetic market price has been found to be the most popular approach under the following conditions: (1) an absence of competitive prices, (2) the presence of an interest in saving the cost of negotiating prices, and (3) the presence of a need to implement a policy of pricing the final product.[9]

There are several limitations inherent in the implementation of a transfer pricing model based on actual cost:

1. A transfer price based on actual cost is actually based on absorption cost in that it includes all direct and indirect expenses (variable and allocated joint and fixed costs). As a result, this type of transfer price may transfer the inefficiencies of the selling division to the buying division, making it unwise to use divisional profit for divisional performance evaluation.
2. A transfer price based on actual cost may lessen the selling division's incentive to control costs.
3. Martin Shubik noted that cost-plus pricing of transfer goods can impede the search for technological progress by the manufacturing division.[10]

Standard Cost: We have seen that a transfer price based on actual cost can reinforce the inefficiencies of the selling division and lessen its motivation to control costs. A transfer price based on standard cost can correct for these problems. It reflects a normative portion by expressing what costs would be under certain circumstances. As a result, a transfer price based on standard cost eliminates the inefficiencies of the selling division; when compared with actual cost, it may create an incentive to control costs.

Marginal or Variable Cost: A company using a transfer price based on either the full actual cost or the full standard cost may face at least two situations:

1. The full actual cost and full standard cost may be higher than the market price.
2. The full actual cost and the full standard cost include both direct and indirect costs (variable and fixed).

The indirect costs can result from arbitrary allocation procedures. The fixed costs can be committed costs that are incurred whether the selling division operates at full or at less-than-full capacity. Thus the buying division may feel that either the indirect costs or the fixed costs should not be included in the determination of the transfer price. When this situation arises, it may be more motivating and important to maintain the spirit of decentralization and resort to a transfer price based on partial cost, which charges only a portion of the full actual or, preferably, full standard cost. Conceptually, this partial cost includes values between full cost and zero cost and refers to either the marginal cost or the variable cost.

The *marginal cost* is the incremental cost of producing additional units. In general, the buying division will be willing to buy as long as the marginal revenue is superior to the marginal cost. Although conceptually appealing, a transfer price based on marginal cost requires available information on all production levels. Because such figures are not always available, a surrogate for the marginal cost may have to be used—the variable cost.

The variable cost or the variable cost plus a lump sum can be used either a as surrogate for marginal cost or as a way of encouraging the use of some facilities' services. First, the variable cost can be used when marginal cost cannot easily be computed because of the absence of adequate information. Second, the use of the variable cost can encourage divisions to use the services of facilities with excess capacity until it becomes more profitable or advantageous to the selling division to switch to a full cost (actual or standard).

Dual Price: From the preceding discussion of transfer pricing alternatives, it can be seen that (1) the best motivation transfer price for the selling division is the market price, and (2) the most acceptable price for the buying division is the variable cost.

One way of meeting both of these optimal situations is to use a dual transfer price rather than a single transfer price. The dual price system allows the selling division to sell either at a market price or at a synthetic market price, hence creating a profit and motivating the selling division to sell. This system allows the buying division to buy inside the company at variable cost, which prevents the selling division from having excess capacity when the buying division buys outside at market prices equal to or lower than the variable cost. In short, the dual price system motivates both the buying and selling divisions to operate in the best interests of the company as a whole. One possible drawback of this system is the possibility that the division may no longer be motivated to control costs.

General Guideline for Computing Transfer Prices

The various methods discussed in the preceding sections illustrate the general infeasibility of one given method for all circumstances. There is, however, a general guideline that can be used as a benchmark in setting a transfer price. The guideline can be expressed as follows:

a. The minimum transfer price is: the additional outlay cost per unit incurred to the point of transfer (these costs may sometimes be approximated by the variable costs) *plus*

b. The opportunity costs per unit to the firm as a whole (contribution margin per unit on outside sales)

With this guideline, the transfer price would be equal to the variable costs in those cases in which no alternative uses of the resources existed and to the market price in the case of a strong external market for the product.

To illustrate the use of the guideline, assume that a multidivisional electronic company has a monitor division aimed at the external market. The monitor requires $400 in variable costs and sells for $700. The monitor division has a production capacity of 4,000 monitors. Another division, the computer division, needs a different monitor from the one presently produced by the monitor division. It can buy the monitor from an outside supplier at a price of $650 per monitor based on an order of 4,000 monitors. The monitor division has advised, however, that it would devote all of its capacity to the production of the new monitor required by the computer division. The variable cost of the new monitor would be $300 per unit.

Applying the guideline to this data, the transfer price for the monitor division would be:

> Transfer price = $300 (variable cost of the new monitor) + $300 (the contribution margin lost to the monitor division as a result of giving up outside monitor sales: $700 selling price − $400 variable costs = $300)
>
> Transfer price = $600

The decision should be to authorize the computer division to buy the new monitor from the monitor division at $600 per unit rather than from an outside supplier at $650 per unit, given the prevailing market conditions.

Multinational Transfer Pricing

Tax Considerations: The following three criteria are used for the setting of transfer prices: goal congruence, divisional autonomy, and performance evaluation. These criteria are, however, most dominant for domestic transfer pricing. Other factors stated by executives to be important in domestic transfer pricing include the following (by order of importance):

1. Performance evaluation—to measure the results of each operating unit.
2. Managerial motivation—to provide the company with a "profit-making" orientation throughout each organizational entity.
3. Pricing driven—to better reflect "costs" and "margins" that must be received from customers.
4. Market driven—to maintain an internal competitiveness so that the company stays in balance with outside market forces.[11]

In the case of multinational transfer pricing there are other "external" conditions that may exert influence in establishing procedures and policies for a firm's transfer pricing mechanism. Factors stated by executives to be important in international transfer pricing include the following (by order of importance):

1. Overall income to the company.
2. The competitive position of subsidiaries in foreign countries
3. Performance evaluation of foreign subsidiaries.
4. Restrictions imposed by foreign countries on repatriation of profits or dividends.
5. The need to maintain adequate cash flows in foreign subsidiaries.
6. Maintaining good relationships with host governments.[12]

Although the above factors reflect the positions stated by executives, a book written on behalf of the European Center for Study and Information on Multinational Corporations, stated that "transfer price" has acquired a bad meaning because it "evokes the idea of systematic manipulation of prices in order to reduce profits artificially, cause losses, avoid taxes or duties."[13] The resulting situation may be summarized as the parent company dictating what the transfer price should be. But the complexities of the situation may transform the transfer price problem into a major hurdle. As noted by Irwin Fantl:

The first hurdle involves personal relations with foreign management: it is easier to explain the need for arbitrary pricing to a domestic executive and to discount its effects in evaluating its performance. The foreign manager starts from a basis of suspicion of the motives by the U.S. parent. Any system that would make him feel unappreciated or misunderstood can undermine the success of the foreign venture. For internal measurement purposes, transfer pricing becomes more crucial than in domestic relations.[14]

The whole situation is, in fact, created by one of the goals of multinational corporations, which is the maximization of global after tax profits. This is accomplished by minimizing the global income tax liability. Other things being the same, profits are increased by setting high transfer prices to take out profits from subsidiaries located in high-tax countries and low transfer prices to move profits to subsidiaries domiciled in low-tax countries. This arbitrary shifting of profits purely for tax avoidance is being challenged by most governments in the developing and developed countries through their enacting appropriate legislations. In the United States, the main legislation restricting the internal-pricing policies of multinational corporations is contained within the 1954 Internal Revenue Code, Section 482, and the 1977 Regulation 861.

Intercorporate Transfer Pricing, Section 482: In any case of two or more organizations, trades, or businesses (whether or not incorporated, whether or not organized in the United States, and whether or not affiliated) owned or controlled directly or indirectly by the same interests, the secretary or his delegate may distribute, apportion, or allocate gross income, deductions, credits, or allowances between or among such organizations, trades, or businesses, if he determines that such distribution, appointment, or allocation is necessary to prevent evasion of taxes or to reflect clearly the income of such organizations, trades, or businesses.[15]

The purpose of Section 482 is to place a controlled taxpayer on a tax parity with an uncontrollable taxpayer by determining according to the standards on an uncontrolled taxpayer the true taxable income from the property and business of a controlled taxpayer. The IRS is allowed to disallow an existing transfer pricing system and reallocate income to reflect the "true taxable income." The *true taxable income* is described as the income resulting if each member were acting "at arm's length" with the others. Detailed regulations were issued under the section based on the principle that transactions between related parties should take place on an arm's length basis. These regulations set forth three pricing methods to be used in determining the arm's length price, namely, in order of preference, the comparable uncontrolled price method, the resale price method, and the cost-plus method.

The comparable uncontrolled price method determined the transfer price as the basis of "uncontrolled sales" made to buyers that are not part of the same controlled group. Guidelines for what constitutes a "comparable uncontrolled price" are provided in the regulations as follows: Uncontrolled sales are considered comparable to controlled sales if the physical property and circumstances involved in the uncontrolled sales are identical to the physical property and circumstances involved in the controlled sales, or if such properties and circumstances are so nearly identical that any differences either have no effect on price, or such differences can be reflected by a reasonable number of adjustments to the price of uncontrolled sales. Some of the differences which may affect the price of property are differences in the quality of the product, terms of sale, intangible property associated with the sale, time of sales, and the level of the market and the geographic market in which the sale takes place.[16]

Uncontrolled sales are defined to include sales made by the seller to an unrelated party, to the buyer by an unrelated party, or when neither party is a member of a controlled group. If there are no comparable uncontrolled sales, the regulations prescribed the use of the resale price method.

The resale price method is applicable when the buyer does not add significant value to the product, that is, is simply a distributor. In such a case, the transfer price is equal to the resale price to unrelated parties less appropriate markup plus or minus certain adjustments. The resale price method establishes the "arm's length" price by working back from a third-party selling price. The "arm's length" price is equal to:

1. *The applicable resale price*: the price at which property purchased in the controlled sales is resold by the buyer, or ultimately resold by some late buyer, in an uncontrollable sale.

2. *Adjusted by the appropriate markup percentage*: equal to the percentage of gross profit earned by the reseller or another party on the resale of property that is both purchased and resold in an uncontrolled transaction similar to the controlled sale

3. *Property adjusted for any differences*: the functions or circumstances that have a definite and readily measurable effect on price, such as warranty or advertising contributions[17]

The cost-plus method is prescribed in those situations when both the comparable uncontrolled price and the resale-price methods are not applicable. The cost-plus price is equal to full cost (actual or standard) plus an appropriate profit percentage similar to that earned by the division or other companies in similar transactions with unrelated parties. in this case, the "arm's length" price is equal to:

1. *The cost of production*: computed in a consistent manner in accordance with sound accounting practices for allocating or appropriating costs that neither favor nor burden controlled sales in comparison with uncontrolled sales

2. *Add appropriate gross-profit percentage*: equal to the gross profit percentage earned by the seller or another party on uncontrolled sales that are most similar to the controlled sales in question

3. *Property adjusted for any difference*: differences that have a definite and readily measurable effect on price that would warrant an adjustment of price in uncontrolled transactions.[18]

Besides these three methods, the regulations prescribe the use of some "appropriate method" of pricing if it is comparable to the pricing that would be charged to an unrelated party.

Allocation of Expenses, Section 861: Section 482 is intended to allocate the proper taxable income to the parent at arm's length, and Section 861 is intended to allocate corporate expenses to the foreign source income. It allocates and apportions all of a firm's expenses, losses, and other deductions to specific sources of income (sales, royalties, dividends) and then apportions the expenses between domestic and foreign source income.

More Power to the IRS: In spite of Section 482 and Section 681, the U.S. situation is puzzling. Although foreign owned assets have tripled in the past decade to $1.8 trillion, the gross income of foreign owned companies merely doubled, and the taxes they paid hardly changed. Such was the finding of a 1986 IRS study of the returns of 36,800 foreign owned companies. The job of the IRS is very difficult given that most records of these companies are kept abroad and in different languages. The situation allowed foreign companies in 1986 to take tax deductions of $544.0 billion against total receipts of $543.0 billion. It led the U.S. government and Congress in late 1989 to enact a law giving draconian powers to the IRS in investigating foreign companies operating in the United States, leading the examinations of transactions between foreign parents and their U.S. affiliates to become an important part of its enforcement duties and giving the IRS the power to make an arbitrary assessment of taxes if its agents conclude that a foreign owned company has not complied with a request for information.[19]

Import/Export Duty Considerations: The desire to reduce import/export duties is another consideration in the setting of transfer prices. Sylvain Plasschaert noted: "Underinvoicing imports in the host country obviously reduces the import duty bill. The saving thus obtainable may be sizeable in developing countries, in which import duties are quite high. One may add, however, that the duties on raw materials and on intermediates imported are typically much lower than those on final products."[20] It seems, however, that many companies no longer consider import/export duties as an important determinant of transfer pricing. On the one hand, governments are taking action to limit and contain the practice of underinvoicing imports. On the other hand, various countries are beginning to assess customs duties on equivalent market prices rather than on the invoice amount. In short, the manipulation of transfer prices to reduce import/export duties may appear to be irrelevant and useless.[21]

Exchange Rate Considerations: Exchange rate fluctuations may cause problems in the performance evaluation of divisions. To eliminate differences in profit evaluation due to exchange rate fluctuations, Duane Malstrom proposed a dollar-indexing formula used by Honeywell, where

NTP = new transfer price
OTP = old transfer price
CER = current exchange rate
PER = planned exchange rate.[22]

To illustrate the application of this formula, assume that a subsidiary in Country X sells goods to another subsidiary in Country Y. The two subsidiaries use a transfer price system based on U.S. dollars. The subsidiary in Country X produced 2,000 units to be sold to the subsidiary in Country Y for FC20,000 at a transfer price of $5 per unit. At the time of the sale, the planned exchange rate was $1 = FC8 (where FC is the currency of Country X). The financial performance for the subsidiary in Country X may be expressed as follows:

	$	Rate	FC
Sales	$10,000	$ 1 = FC8	FC80,000
Costs	2,500	$0.125 = FC1	FC20,000
Profit	$7,500		FC60,000
Percentage of Sales	75%		75%

Assume that as a result of a devaluation in the U.S. dollar, the exchange rate is $1 = FC4; the financial performance without any adjustment to the transfer price will be as follows:

	$	Rate	FC
Sales	$10,000	$ 1 = FC4	FC40,000
Costs	5,000	$0.25 = FC1	FC20,000
Profit	$ 5,000		FC20,000
Percentage of Sales	50%		50%

It appears that the profit performance is distorted and the performance evaluation is destroyed. To correct the situation the transfer price should be adjusted as follows:

$$ NTP = \$5 \times \frac{.25}{.125} = \$10 $$

Now, the profit performance after the devaluation may be expressed as follows:

	$	Rate	FC
Sales	$20,000	$ 1 = FC4	FC80,000
Costs	5,000	$0.25 = FC1	FC20,000
Profit	$15,000		FC60,000
Percentage of Sales	75%		75%

It appears that the adjustment of the transfer price has eliminated differences in profit evaluation due to exchange rate fluctuations. This dollar indexing as adopted by Honeywell's control systems has had the following benefits: ''By implementing this procedure Honeywell was able to eliminate distorted performance measurement of subsidiary locations, and allow the dollar transfer price of each product to accurately reflect its economic cost to the total corporation.''[23]

Cultural and National Considerations: A study by Jeffrey Arpan on non-U.S. transfer pricing systems found distinguishable national differences in the number of variables considered in transfer pricing determination, in the relative importance given these variables, and in preference to transfer pricing systems.[24] With respect to the relative importance of the variables in transfer pricing determination, the main findings are as follows: ''The degree of competition and differences in income tax rates emerge as the two most important variables, with custom duties, export subsidies and tax credits, exchange controls, inflation and changes in exchange rates receiving varying degrees of mentioned importance.''[25] With respect to the national preferences to transfer pricing systems, the main findings are as follows:

The French prefer non-market-oriented systems because they can thus minimize world tax payments. The English also prefer a cost orientation, but their goal is to achieve their target return on investment rates. The Italians use market-oriented systems to maximize corporate income in Italy, which is equivalent to minimizing their tax liability. Canadians also employ market-oriented systems, but essentially because of specific government regulations and a desire to maintain good relations with other governments. The Scandinavian firms view good relations with other governments as paramount, and consequently they are the biggest supporters and users of market-oriented systems. The Germans are the least concerned about transfer pricing, do not seem to prefer any given orientation, and do not exhibit any dominant pattern.[26]

Besides these national and cultural differences, governments tend to differ in their reactions to transfer pricing systems. Most of them try to exert influence on the transfer price indirectly through income taxes and import/export duties. If they feel that transfer prices are being manipulated to escape the income tax and customs duties constraints, some governments do not hesitate to dictate what is a fair transfer price. These interventions by governments, when transfer prices became the result of external pressures rather than internal considerations, were viewed by many multinational companies as a restraint on corporate goals.[27]

In their relations with multinationals, however, governments are beginning to view transfer pricing as one of many potentially negotiable elements, with the view that resources belong above all to the trading nations themselves. A case for this view of the role of government is made as follows:

Nations have varying powers to influence transfer prices exercised through income tax, customs and/or other government agencies, each agency operating under common direction consistent with agreed upon national goals. Fundamental to an effective transfer price bargaining position is acceptance of responsibility for (1) systematically monitoring these transactions where they affect national interests, and (2) acquiring sufficient accounting and economic expertise to be able to evaluate international companies transfer pricing positions.[28]

This role is accomplished in the United States through IRS Section 482. In Canada, the government established the Foreign Investment Review Agency to negotiate new international company investments. Most other countries have adopted some form of similar legislation.

Other Considerations: There are various other considerations that may motivate multinationals to overprice (overinvoice) or underprice (underinvoice) transfers between subsidiaries or between subsidiaries and the parent company. First, overpricing would yield benefits to the multinational corporations in the following cases:

1. The multinational corporation may attach an excessive value to assets-in-kind that it has contributed to the subsidiary. Such overpricing may not always be welcome in the developing countries. As noted by Plasschaert: "The complaint that the physical or intangible assets, thus transferred, are capitalized at an excessive price, is widespread in developing countries. Such overpricing also widens the base against which depreciation allowances can be charged for tax purposes."[29]

2. It may overprice the transfers to the subsidiaries to achieve a higher price for the final products in those situations in which there may be some form of price or wage freeze or control.

3. It may overprice to reduce the profits of the subsidiary and nullify claims for higher wages by local unions.

4. It may overprice to escape charges of antidumping practices.

5. It may overprice to repatriate profit and sometimes capital in those situations in which some constraints are being imposed on profit and capital repatriations or when some threat of expropriation without adequate compensation is perceived. By charging a high transfer price, the visible profits in the host country are low and funds are repatriated through payment of intercompany balances. But the local authorities are aware of such practices and may be on the lookout. An interesting observation is made by Fantl: "But even in lesser-developed countries, officials are not so naive as to let these subterfuges pass if they are too blatant. After all, many of these officials have graduated from prestigious American business schools. In many cases, for example, import tariffs are charged not on the listed transfer price but on the current market price for the product."[30]

Second, underpricing would yield benefits to the multinational company in the following cases:

1. The multinational may underprice to avoid antimonopoly indictments.

2. It may underprice to provide support to the subsidiary. As noted by Plasschaert: "This in-house favor is more likely when the subsidiary is still in an infant stage, and on its own, has not yet achieved the credit standing with the local financial community, needed to obtain working capital or other funds, without the guarantee of the parent company."[31] As an example, in a case examined by the U.S. tax court, in 1989 the IRS asserted that Yamaha's American affiliate, which imports and distributes motorcycles by Yamaha in Japan, understated its income and overstated the amount it paid to the parent company for motorcycles and related products, which resulted in an underpayment of taxes of $133 million from 1977 through 1989. Similar cases and the general opinion seems that on the average, foreign owned U.S. corporations pay substantially less tax to the U.S. government than the American firms with which they compete, giving them an unfair competitive edge.[32]

3. It may underprice as a way of achieving "predatory" pricing aimed at driving competitors out of the local market and at enlarging the subsidiary's market share.

4. Alex Milburn identified examples of other motivational factors that may be of equal or even greater importance than potential tax and custom duty savings as follows:

   • Transfer pricing policies may be structured to secure competitive advantages. . . .

   • There is the possibility of using transfer prices to minimize profits to be shared with foreign subsidiary minority interests. . . .

   • Transfer pricing variability might be used to try to limit foreign exchange losses and other risks of holding surplus assets in foreign countries. . . .

   • On the other hand, in some situations, management may feel that placing a low bias on transfers to or a high bias on transfers from a subsidiary may be the easiest and least expensive financing alternative, particularly if governments place controls on other means of moving funds.[33]

5. Another technique used for minimizing taxes is a quasi-legal fabrication reinvoicing, a paper shuffle that allows companies to rebook sales and profits in tax havens.

For example, one Fortune 500 corporation imports raw materials through an offshore dummy company, which buys shipments at the lowest possible price and resells the material to the parent firm at a high mark up. This dumps profits in the tax haven, while the U.S.-based company can boost its apparent cost to reduce taxes on the mainland. The profits can then be repatriated in the form of tax free "loans" from offshore entities to the U.S. parent corporation.[34]

International Tax Legislation on Transfer Pricing

Tax legislation may be needed to prohibit or control the use of most tax-avoidance schemes associated with transfer pricing. Some of these schemes include a potential shift of income to countries with lower tax rates, repatriation of profits in a transfer price rather than a dividend (which would be subject to withholding tax), reduction of customs, and sales in a low transfer pricing to and from foreign affiliates.[35] The issue is very important to any government. In effect, the incorrect pricing of goods or services exported from and imported to a given country would result in a material loss of tax revenue. Some of the legislation used in the industrialized world is presented next.

The Organization for Economic Cooperation and Development (OECD): In 1979 the OECD's Committee on Fiscal Affairs issued *Transfer Pricing and Multinational Enterprises* with the objective to set out, as far as possible, the considerations to be taken into account and to describe, when possible, generally agreed-upon practices in determining transfer prices for tax purposes. The OECD recommendations are the same as those prescribed under the Internal Revenue Code Section 488, namely, the comparable uncontrolled price method, the resale price method, the cost-plus method, and any other method found to be acceptable.

Canada: Tax legislation of transfer pricing in Canada is found in Subsections 69(1) and 69(3) of the Canadian Income Tax Act. They read as follows:

69(1) Except as expressly otherwise provided in this act

a) where a taxpayer has acquired anything from a person with whom he was not dealing at arm's length at an amount in excess to the fair market value thereof at the time he acquired it, he shall be deemed to have acquired it at the fair market value;

b) where a taxpayer has disposed of anything (i) to a person with whom he was not dealing at arm's length for no proceeds or for proceeds less than the fair market value at the time he so disposed of it, or (ii) to any person by way of gift inter vivos, he shall be deemed to have received proceeds of disposition therefore equal to that fair market value;

c) where a taxpayer has acquired property by way of gift, bequest or inheritance, he shall be deemed to have acquired the property at its fair market value at the time he acquired it.

69(2) Where a taxpayer carrying on business in Canada has not paid or agreed to pay, to a non-resident person with whom he was not dealing at arm's length as to price, rental, royalty, or other payment for, or for the use of or reproduction of any property, or as consideration for the carriage of goods or passengers or for other services, an amount greater than the amount (in this subsection referred to as "the reasonable amount") that would have been reasonable in the circumstances if the nonresident person and the taxpayer had been dealing at arm's length, the reasonable amount shall, for the purpose of computing the taxpayer's income from the business, be deemed to have been the amount that was paid or is payable therefore.

69(3) Where a nonresident person had paid, or agreed to pay, to a taxpayer carrying on business in Canada with whom he was not dealing at arm's length as price, rental, royalty or other payment for or for the use or reproduction of any property, or as consideration for the carriage of goods or passengers or for other services, an amount less than the amount (in this subsection referred to as "the reasonable amount") that would have been reasonable in the circumstances if the non-resident person and the taxpayer had been dealing at arm's length, the reasonable amount shall, for the purpose of computing the taxpayer's income from the business, be deemed to have been the amount that was paid or is payable therefore.

Subsection 69(1) was enacted to protect Canada against a loss of revenue resulting from income shifting at the domestic level, whereas Subsections 69(2) and 69(3) were enacted for the same purpose at the international level. Although Subsection 69(1) uses "fair market value" as the criteria to be used in nonarm's length transactions, Subsections 69(2) and 65(9) use "a reasonable in the circumstances" concept in setting nonarm's length prices. Naturally, questions arise as to what is meant by these two concepts. Are they similar or is there a distinction? Unfortunately, the act has no definitions or guidelines. Interpretation or a decision of the court remains the solution. The situation, as with IRS Section 482, is confusing and may lead to arbitrary, capricious, or unreasonable decisions. Witness the following remark by Roy Hog: "Although other cases unrelated to transfer pricing have tried to define fair market value, no concrete definition for income tax purposes has yet been developed. Judicial evaluation of the evidence presented was the overriding concern in these cases. Canadian management, therefore, will find little legislative or judicial help in finding guideposts in the pricing of non-arm's length transactions."[36]

It is easy to criticize the tax authorities; however, the transfer pricing review process must be complex, time consuming, and difficult. Revenue Canada has developed three review approaches to deal with the transfer pricing problem: the large file program, the industrywide evaluation approach, and simultaneous audit (joint audits). The *large file program* involves auditing the large Canadian companies on a national basis as opposed to a piecemeal approach by various district offices. The *industrywide evaluation* approach involves focusing on a major industry and thus guarantees consistency in the application of the tax provisions within the industry. The *simultaneous audit* involves a joint audit with the tax authorities of another country to audit multinational corporations operating in both countries.[37]

Other Industrialized Nations: Tax legislation of transfer pricing in Germany is found under Section 1 of the Aussenteuergesetz (1968 West German Tax Code, as amended by the 1980 Income Tax Act). It specifies that an arm's length price must be charged between related parties in an international transaction when available; if not, a cost-plus method is to be used.

Tax legislation of transfer pricing in the United Kingdom is found under Section 485 of the United Kingdom Income and Corporation Taxes Act of 1970. It specifies that when property is sold at less than fair market value or bought at more than fair market value, and one of the entities controls the other or both are under the control of a third entity, the Inland Revenue may use the arm's length price. No guidelines are provided for the determination of such price, however, hence joining IRS Section 482 and Canadian Sections 69(1), 69(2), and 69(3) in making transfer pricing more of an act than the practice of sound business judgment.

There is no doubt that most countries in the near future will become conscious of the need to monitor the transfer prices of multinational companies. Some may even view that it is in their national interest to do so. Various powers are available to countries for this task. As stated by Alex Milburn:

Nations have varying powers to influence transfer prices, exercised through income taxes, customs and/or other governmental agencies, each agency operating independently or all operating under common direction consistent with agreed upon national goals. Fundamental to an effective transfer price bargaining position is accepting responsibility for 1) systematically monitoring these transactions where they affect the national interests, and 2) acquiring sufficient accounting and economic expertise to be able to evaluate international companies' transfer pricing positions.[38]

The Accounting Profession: Of interest in the international transfer pricing problem is the accounting for related party transactions. It led to the adoption in the United States of the Statement of Financial Accounting Standard (SFAS) 57[39] or its international equivalent, the International Accounting Standard (IAS) 24.[40] The IAS 24 defines related parties as existing if one party has the ability to control the other party or exercise significant influence over the other party in making financial and operating decisions. Theory would dictate that in recording a nonarm's length transaction, an arm's length equivalent price should be used instead of the exchange price in order to measure the fair value of the resources exchanged.[41] However, neither the SFAS 57 nor the IAS 24 required a nonarm's length transaction to be disclosed in an amount different from the transaction price. The following disclosure is required by the SFAS 57:

• Financial statements shall include disclosures of material related party transactions, other than compensation arrangements, expense allowances and other similar items in the ordinary course of business. However, disclosure of transactions that are eliminated in the preparation of consolidated or combined financial statements is not required in those statements. The disclosures shall include:

   a. The nature of the relationship(s) involved.

   b. A description of the transactions, including transactions to which no amounts or nominal amounts were ascribed, for each of the periods for which income statements are presented, and such other information deemed necessary to an understanding of the effects of the transactions on the financial statements.

   c. The dollar amounts of transactions for each of the periods for which income statements are presented and the effects of any change in the method of establishing the terms from that used in the preceding period.

   d. Amounts due from or to related parties as of the date of each balance sheet presented and, if not otherwise apparent, the terms and manner of settlement.

• Transactions involving related parties cannot be presumed to be carried out on an arm's length basis, as the requisite conditions of competitive, free-market dealings may not exist. Representations about transactions with related parties, if made shall not imply that the related party transactions were consummated on terms equivalent to those that prevail in arm's length transactions unless such representations can be substantiated.

- If the reporting enterprise and one or more enterprises are under common ownership or management control and the existence of the control could result in operating results or financial position of the reporting enterprise significantly different from those that would have been obtained if the enterprises were autonomous, the nature of the control relationship shall be disclosed even though there are no transactions between the enterprises.[42]

Similarly, IAS 24 requires the following disclosure:

- Related party relationships where control exists should be disclosed irrespective of whether there have been transactions between related parties.
- If there have been transactions between related parties, the reporting enterprise should disclose the nature of the related party relationships as well as the types of transactions and the elements of the transactions necessary for an understanding of the financial statements.
- Items of a similar nature may be disclosed in aggregate except when separate disclosure is necessary for an understanding of the effects of related party transactions on the financial statements of the reporting enterprise.[43]

An explanatory paragraph 21 elaborates on the elements referred to in paragraph 26 as follows: "These elements would normally include: (a) an indication of the volume of the transactions either as an amount or as an appropriate proportion, (b) amounts or appropriate proportions of outstanding items, and (c) pricing policies."[44]

Although these disclosures may be useful to those interested in the related party transactions concerned with the pricing of goods and services between two or more related parties, they may be judged as insufficient from the point of view of the less developed countries weary of the unfairness of transfer pricing to them. It is not that the less developed countries can determine what are the fair prices. In fact, Mfandaidza Hove identified two real problems related to:

(1) determining arm's length prices where no comparable substitute exists (there can be wide variations, at any specific time or even a short period, in the prices of the products frequently traded—in similar quantities and on similar terms of sale—nationally and internationally by a number of enterprises); (2) difficulties in obtaining from firms the data necessary to reconstruct prices on the basis of actual costs.[45]

The less developed countries may require more disclosures that will allow them to control for the attempts by multinational corporations to use transfer pricing as mechanisms of minimizing taxes in those countries. Again, Hove proposed the following additional disclosures:

(a) Intercompany transactions with parent company:

   (i) goods purchased from parent company (description, quantity, raw material finished product, etc.);

   (ii) details of amounts paid for goods in (i) above—with documentary evidence, e.g., invoices, receipts, etc.;

   (iii) equipment and all other tangible assets purchased from the parent company (with full details including make, type, model, etc.);

   (iv) payments made for above assets, with documentary evidence;

   (v) details of all services provided by the parent company;

   (vi) particulars (including amounts) of all payments, other than interest, made to the parent company (amount of the loan, repayment terms and purpose for which the loan is made);

   (vii) details of loans made to the subsidiary by the parent company (amount of the loan, repayment terms and purpose for which the loan is made);

   (viii) repayments made to the parent company for the loan in (vii) above, broken down into (a) payments towards the capital sum and (b) payments for interest;

   (ix) dividends payable and paid to the parent company;

   (x) the subsidiary company (the reporting company) must disclose all the information as required by items (i)–(ix) above in cases where it is itself the seller of the foods, and/or services referred to.

(b) Intercompany transactions with other subsidiaries controlled by the parent company:

   (i) all details required in (i)–(x) above must be disclosed.

(c) Intercompany transactions with subsidiaries controlled by the reporting subsidiary:

   (i) details to be supplied as in (b) above.

(d) Intercompany transactions with companies associated with the parent company:

   (i) details to be supplied as in (b) above.

(e) Intercompany transactions with companies associated with the reporting subsidiary:

   (i) similarly, all details as required in (b) above should be supplied.

(f) Permissible transfer price:

   (i) only the "market price" shall be used for charging of goods and/or services transferred between enterprises with relationships outlined in general disclosure (i–v) above;

   (ii) confirmation that this price, in fact, has been used must be part of the disclosure of accounting policies used (II) (a)–(e) above.[46]

Similar calls for disclosure also came from concerned parties in the developing world given that management's international transfer pricing decisions can influence the decision process in the countries affected as well as impact the national interest. In the case of Canada, for example, Milburn called for the following specific disclosures:

(1) Identification of the parent company, and a description of the Canadian company's role within the international company group, including disclosure of dependencies as foreign affiliates for management, research and development, marketing services, etc. . . .

(2) Disclosures of dollar values assigned to export and import transfers, each classified by: (a) major types of products and services, and (b) major trading affiliates.

(3) A description of the transfer pricing bans used for each major product or service category as in (2), and any terms that differ significantly from similar arm's length sales.[47]

CONCLUSION

Both product pricing and transfer pricing internationally require the consideration of various factors and outcomes that can affect the total profit of the firm. The techniques needed for such strategy as well as their ramifications were presented in this chapter.

NOTES

1. Wright Patman, *The Robinson-Patman Act* (New York: Ronald Press, 1938), p. 3.

2. Ibid., p. 7.

3. Ahmed Belkaoui, *Cost Accounting: Theory and Practice* (Westport, Conn.: Quorum Books, 1990).

4. Sak Onkvisit and John J. Shaw, *International Marketing: Analysis and Strategy* (Columbus, Ohio: Merrill, 1989), pp. 677–678.

5. J. Dean, "Decentralization and Intracompany Pricing," *Harvard Business Review*, July-August 1955, pp. 65–74; David H. Li, "Interdivisional Transfer Planning," *Management Accounting*, June 1965, pp. 51–54; Timothy P. Haidinger, "Negotiate for Profits," *Management Accounting*, December 1970, pp. 25–31; and H. James Shaub, "Transfer Pricing in a Decentralized Organization," *Management Accounting*, April 1978, pp. 33–36, 42.

6. R. K. Mautz, *Financial Reporting by Diversified Companies* (New York: Financial Executives Research Foundation, 1968), p. 36.

7. R. Cyert and J. March, *A Behavioral Theory of the Firm* (Englewood Cliffs, N.J.: Prentice-Hall, 1963), p. 276.

8. Nicholas Dopuch and D. F. Drake, "Accounting Implications of a Rathomatically Programming Approach to Transfer Price Problem," *Journal of Accounting Research*, Spring 1964, pp. 10–21.

9. National Association of Accountants, "Accounting for Intracompany Transfers," *Research Report No. 30* (New York, 1954), pp. 31–36.

10. Martin Shubik, "Incentives, Decentralized Control: The Assignment of Joint Costs and Internal Pricing," in *Management Controls: New Directions in Basic Research,* ed. C. P. Bonini, R. K. Jaedicke, and H. M. Wagner (New York: McGraw-Hill, 1964), pp. 221–222.

11. Price Waterhouse, *Transfer Pricing Practices of American Industry* (New York, 1984).

12. Ibid.

13. R. Tang, "Environmental Variables of Multinational Transfer Pricing: A U.K. Perspective," *Journal of Business Finance and Accounting,* Summer 1982, p. 182.

14. Irwin Fantl, "Transfer Pricing—Tread Carefully," *The CPA Journal,* December 1972, p. 44.

15. U.S. Internal Revenue Code (1954), Section 482.

16. Ibid., Section 482–1 (e)(2)(ii).

17. Michael P. Casey, "International Transfer Pricing," *Management Accounting,* October 1985, p. 33.

18. Ibid., p. 34.

19. Robert Pear, "IRS Investigating Foreign Companies Over Units in U.S.," *New York Times,* February 18, 1990, pp. 1, 17.

20. Sylvain R. F. Plasschaert, "The Multiple Motivations for Transfer Pricing Modulations in Multinational Enterprises and Governmental Counter-Measures: An Attempt at Clarification," *Management International Review* 21, no. 1 (1981): 52.

21. Jeffrey S. Arpan, *International Intracorporate Pricing: Non-American Systems and Views* (London: Praeger, 1971).

22. Duane Malstrom, "Accommodating Exchange Rate Fluctuations in Intercompany Pricing and Invoicing," *Management Accounting* 59 (September 1977): 24–28.

23. Ibid., p. 28.

24. Jeffrey S. Arpan, "International Intracorporate Pricing: Non-American Systems and Views," *Journal of International Business Studies* 3 (Spring 1972): 1–8.

25. Ibid., p. 9.

26. Arpan, *International Intracorporate Pricing,* p. 105.

27. James Green and Michael G. Duerr, *Intercompany Transactions in the Multinational Firm* (New York: National Industrial Conference Board, 1970).

28. Alex J. Milburn, "International Transfer Transactions: What Price?" *Canadian Chartered Accountant Magazine,* December 1976, p. 105.

29. Plasschaert, "The Multiple Motivations for Transfer Pricing Modulations," p. 54.

30. Fantl, "Transfer Pricing," p. 44.

31. Plasschaert, "The Multiple Motivations for Transfer Pricing Modulations," p. 55.

32. Pear, "IRS Investigating Foreign Companies Over Units in U.S.," p. 17.

33. Milburn, "International Transfer Transactions," p. 25.

34. Jonathan Beaty and Richard Hornik, "A Torrent of Dirty Dollars," *Time,* December 18, 1989, pp. 53–54.

35. Pricing subsidiaries as an alternative means of financing overseas operations and the use of transfer pricing to thwart exchange controls and to circumvent profit or price controls in the host country are some nontax issues.

36. Roy D. Hog, "A Canadian Tax Overview of Transfer Pricing," *CA Magazine,* December 1983, p. 59.

37. Ibid., p. 60.

38. Milburn, "International Transfer Transactions," p. 26.

39. Financial Accounting Standards Board, "Related Party Disclosures," *Statement of Financial Accounting Standards No. 57* (Stamford, Conn., 1982).

40. International Accounting Standards Committee, "Related Party Disclosures," *International Accounting Standards No. 24* (London, 1984).

41. S. Chong and G. Dean, "Related Party Transactions: A Preliminary Evaluation of SFAS 57 and IAS 24 Using Four Case Studies," *ABACUS* 1 (1985): 84–100.

42. Financial Accounting Standards Board, "Related Party Disclosures," parags. 2, 3, and 4.

43. International Accounting Standards Board, "Related Party Disclosures," parags. 25, 26, and 27.

44. Ibid., parags. 21.

45. Mfandaidza Hove, "The Inappropriateness of International Accounting Standards in Less Developed Countries: The Case of International Accounting Standards Number 24, Related Party Disclosures, Concerning Transfer Prices," *The International Journal of Accounting Education and Research* 24, no. 2 (1989): 170.

46. Ibid., pp. 175–176.

47. Milburn, "International Transfer Transactions," p. 26.

REFERENCES

Arpan, Jeffrey S. *International Intracorporate Pricing: Non-American Systems and Views*. London: Praeger, 1971.

———. "International Intracorporate Pricing: Non-American Systems and Views." *Journal of International Business Studies* 3 (Spring 1972): pp. 1–18.

Beaty, Jonathan, and Richard Hornik. "A Torrent of Dirty Dollars." *Time*, December 18, 1989, pp. 53–54.

Belkaoui, Ahmed. *Cost Accounting: Theory and Practice*. Westport, Conn.: Quorum Books, 1990.

Casey, Michael P. "International Transfer Pricing." *Management Accounting*, October 1985, pp. 16–34.

Chong, S., and G. Dean. "Related Party Transactions: A Preliminary Evaluation of SFAS 57 and IAS 24 Using Four Case Studies." *ABACUS* 1 (1985): 84–100.

Cyert, R., and J. March. *A Behavioral Theory of the Firm*. Englewood Cliffs, N.J.: Prentice-Hall, 1963.

Dean, J. "Decentralization and Intracompany Pricing." *Harvard Business Review*, July-August 1955, pp. 65–74.

Dopuch, Nicholas, and D. F. Drake. "Accounting Implications of a Rathomatically Programming Approach to Transfer Price Problem." *Journal of Accounting Research*, Spring 1964, pp. 10–21.

Fantl, Irwin. "Transfer Pricing—Tread Carefully." *The CPA Journal*, December 1972, pp. 42–46.

Financial Accounting Standards Board. "Related Party Disclosures." *Statement of Financial Accounting Standards No. 57*. Stamford, Conn., 1982.

Green, James, and Michael G. Duerr. *Intercompany Transactions in the Multinational Firm*. New York: National Industrial Conference Board, 1970.

Haidinger, Timothy P. "Negotiate for Profits." *Management Accounting*, December 1970, pp. 25–31.

Hog, Roy D. "A Canadian Tax Overview of Transfer Pricing." *CA Magazine*, December 1983.

Hove, Mfandaidza. "The Inappropriateness of International Accounting Standards in Less Developed Countries: The Case of International Accounting Standards Number 24, Related Party Disclosures, Concerning Transfer Prices." *The International Journal of Accounting Education and Research* 24, no. 2 (1989).

International Accounting Standards Committee. "Related Party Disclosures." *International Accounting Standards No. 24*. London, 1984.

Li, David H. "Interdivisional Transfer Planning." *Management Accounting*, June 1965, pp. 51–54.

Malstrom, Duane. "Accommodating Exchange Rate Fluctuations in Intercompany Pricing and Invoicing." *Management Accounting* 59 (September 1977): 24–28.

Mautz, R. K. *Financial Reporting by Diversified Companies*. New York: Financial Executives Research Foundation, 1968.

Milburn, Alex J. "International Transfer Transactions: What Price?" *Canadian Chartered Accountant Magazine*, December 1976.

National Association of Accountants. "Accounting for Intracompany Transfers." *Research Report No. 30*. New York, 1954, pp. 31–36.

Onkvisit, Sak, and John J. Shaw. *International Marketing: Analysis and Strategy*. Columbus, Ohio: Merrill, 1989.

Patman, Wright. *The Robinson-Patman Act*. New York: Ronald Press, 1938.

Pear, Robert. "IRS Investigating Foreign Companies Over Units in U.S." *New York Times*, February 18, 1990, pp. 1, 17.

Plasschaert, Sylvain R. F. "The Multiple Motivations for Transfer Pricing Modulations in Multinational Enterprises and Governmental Counter-Measures: An Attempt at Clarification." *Management International Review* 21, no. 1 (1981): 49–63.

Price Waterhouse. *Transfer Pricing Practices of American Industry*. New York, 1984.

Shaub, H. James. "Transfer Pricing in a Decentralized Organization." *Management Accounting*, April 1978, pp. 33–36, 42.

Shubik, Martin. "Incentives, Decentralized Control: The Assignment of Joint Costs and Internal Pricing." In *Management Controls: New Directions in Basic Research*. Edited by C. P. Bonini, R. K. Jaedicke, and H. M. Wagner. New York: McGraw-Hill, 1964, pp. 205–225.

Tang, R. "Environmental Variables of Multinational Transfer Pricing: A U.K. Perspective." *Journal of Business Finance and Accounting*, Summer 1982.

10

Analysis of the Lease-or-Buy Decision

Leasing has recently become an important international source of financing many types of assets. The lessee acquires the use of an asset while the title is retained by the lessor. More specifically, a lease is a contract between an owner (the lessor) and another party (the lessee) that grants the lessee the right to use the lessor's property under certain conditions and for a specified period. Because of the contractual nature of lease obligations, a lease should be considered a financing device and an alternative to debt financing. Both the lease rental payments and the payments of principal and interest on debt are fixed obligations. Any default in the payment of either obligation can create serious problems for a firm.

The decision to lease an asset is generally evaluated by comparing it with the borrowing decision necessary for an outright purchase of the same asset. Different valuation models have been proposed, and any choice can be challenged because of the controversial issues surrounding a given model and its corresponding variables and parameters. The main purpose of this chapter is to explain leasing arrangements and the main issues in financial leasing and to provide a methodology for international analysis.

The lease as a new form of financing undergoes constant change, as shown by the number and variations of the sources of leasing arrangements. Financial institutions involved in leasing differ mainly in their degree of specialization and include independent leasing companies, service leasing companies, lease brokers, commercial brokers, and insurance companies.

TYPES OF LEASING ARRANGEMENTS

Although it is possible to describe major forms of lease arrangements, the options, terms, and conditions may vary from contract to contract, giving a firm great flexibility in the adaptation of leasing as a financing method.

Operating versus Financial Leases

The first distinction to be made in leasing is between operating and financial leases. Under both contracts, the lessee agrees to make periodic rental payments. An *operating lease* is a short-term contract that is cancelable, given proper notice at the option of the lessee, whereby the lessor gives the lessee the use of property in exchange for rental payments and at the same time retains the usual ownership risks (such as obsolescence) and rewards (such as a gain from appreciation in value at the end of the lease period). To compensate the lessor for assuming the ownership risks, the periodic rental payments of an operating lease will include a return on investment plus most ownership costs, such as maintenance, taxes, depreciation, obsolescence, casualty losses, and so forth. Examples of operating leases include car rentals, apartment rentals, telephone service, and space rental in shopping centers.

A *financial lease* is a comparatively long-term contract that is noncancelable by the lessor, who assumes little or no ownership costs. As a result, the periodic rental payments include only a return on investment, and the lessee may be required to pay most of the ownership costs. At the termination of the lease, options may exist allowing the lessee to acquire the asset at either a nominal cost or no cost at all. The financial lease allows the lessor to recover the investment and even realize a profit through the lessee's continuous rental payments over the period specified by the contract. The financial lease gives the lessee continuous use of the asset at a certain cost and, consequently, is a means of financing the use (and not the ownership) of the asset. In other words, the difference between the operating and financial lease lies mainly in the cancellation and financing options. As opposed to an operating lease, a financial lease is noncancelable, and it can be perceived as a financing instrument.

Sale and Leaseback, Direct Leasing, and Leverage Leases

Another important distinction in lease financing is made between the sale and leaseback and direct lease arrangements. The difference lies in the nature of the prior ownership of the asset to be leased. Under the *sale and leaseback* arrangement, a firm sells an asset it owns to another party, which in turn leases it back to the previous owner. Under this popular arrangement, a company in need of liquidity receives cash from the sale of the asset while retaining the economic use of the asset during the lease period.

Under *direct leasing,* the lessee acquires the use of an asset it did not previously own. The lessee can enter into the leasing arrangement with a manufacturer, independent leasing company, or financial instruction.

With the advent of direct leasing through commercial banks in 1963, a new lease arrangement appeared called a *leverage lease*. This is a tripartite arrangement whereby the lessor finances a portion of the acquisition of the asset (50 to 80 percent of the purchase price) from a lender (commercial bank), securing the loan by a mortgage of the leased property as well as the assignment of the lease and lease payments. The leverage lease is a popular instrument for special-purpose leasing companies and partnerships of individuals in high tax brackets because of the tax benefits provided by the accelerated depreciation charges, the investment tax credit, and the interest on debt and because of the favorable return on the equity participation by the lessor. From the point of view of the lessee, the leverage lease is similar to any other lease and, consequently, does not affect the method valuation.[1]

Leverage leasing involves at least four parties: a lessee, a manufacturer (or distributor), a lessor, and a lender. Arrangements are complex, and the parties enter into the agreement primarily for tax and financial cost savings rather than convenience. The lessee is able to obtain financial leasing from the lessor at a cost lower than the usual cost of capital; the lessor, being of a high income tax bracket, gains an investment tax credit (or capital cost allowance) benefit resulting in reduced taxes. The lessor passes on some of this benefit to the lessee through reduced lease costs.

Direct leasing, sale and leaseback, and leverage leasing are illustrated in Exhibit 10.1.

Maintenance, Nonmaintenance, and Net Leases

The assignment of responsibility for the maintenance of the asset during the life of a lease takes three forms: the maintenance lease, nonmaintenance lease, and net lease.

A *maintenance lease* assigns responsibility for the maintenance of a leased asset's good working order to the lessor. The lessor is required to incur the maintenance and repair expenses and the local and state taxes and to provide insurance for the leased asset. The maintenance lease is preferable when the lessor is better equipped than the lessee to provide low-cost repair in terms of technology and skills. It is used mostly in rentals of automobiles, trucks, and specialized equipment, like computers, requiring a highly qualified maintenance staff.

A *nonmaintenance lease* assigns the responsibility for the maintenance of a leased asset to the lessee. The lessee is required to pay for all maintenance and repair costs and the local and state taxes and to provide insurance. The nonmaintenance lease occurs principally in long-term leasing of land and buildings.

A *net lease* assigns total responsibility for an asset's maintenance to the lessee to the point that the lessee may be required to absorb all losses incurred by the

Exhibit 10.1
Leases According to Parties Involved

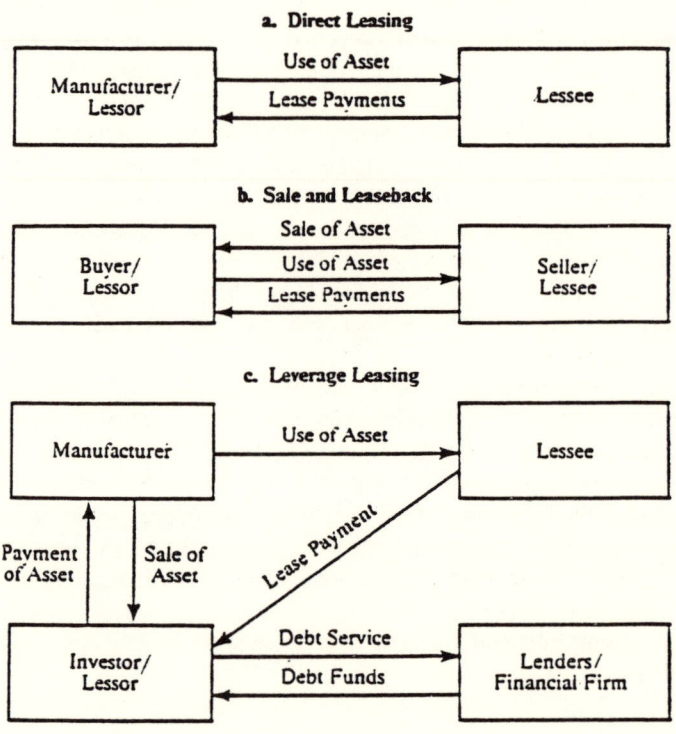

sale of the asset at the end of the life of the lease. This is typical in fleet leasing of vehicles. In car leasing the net lease is sometimes referred to as an *open-end lease*: In return for a slightly lower monthly lease fee, the lessee agrees to make up the price differential if the leased car sells for less than the prearranged price when the lease expires because of excess mileage, poor maintenance, or any other reason.

ADVANTAGES OF LEASING

When a multinational firm wishes to have the use and services of an asset, it either can purchase the asset or lease it. The decision to purchase the asset entails first borrowing the funds and then buying the asset. Thus when evaluating the advantages of the leasing alternative, a firm should keep in mind the fact that the other alternative is to borrow and buy, rather than just buy. The lease-or-buy decision rests on the comparison between two methods of financing, both requiring a fixed obligation redeemable over a future period. The leasing alternative, then, should be evaluated by comparing its advantages and effects on the lessee's cash flow with those of the borrowing alternative. Often-cited advantages of leasing as opposed to borrowing include (1) shifting the risks of ownership, (2) the avoidance of restrictions associated with debt, (3) the effect on cash and borrowing capacity, and (4) tax advantages.

Shifting the Risks of Ownership

A firm that purchases an asset is subject to the risk of obsolescence due to innovation in the field. Generally, in the decision to lease or buy an asset subject to a high rate of obsolescence, the leasing alternative will appear more appropriate. Through leasing rather than buying the asset, the lessee can shift the risk of obsolescence and of ownership to the lessor.

This argument in favor of leasing relies heavily on the assumption that the lessor is not aware of the rate of obsolescence and innovation in the field. In most cases, however, the lessor is very knowledgeable and is in a better position to anticipate the rate of obsolescence than the lessee. The lessor, well aware of the risks of ownership, will attempt to recover the investment plus interest in the lease over the lease period and probably will include an implicit charge for obsolescence in the computation of the rental payments. Only when the lessor inaccurately estimates the rate of obsolescence does the lessee benefit from shifting the risks of ownership. If the asset becomes obsolete more rapidly than the lessor anticipated, the leasing alternative will be beneficial to the lessee. The lessor can keep the rental payments low by spreading the risk of obsolescence over many lease contracts. The diversification in this case will benefit both the lessor and the lessee.

Avoidance of Restrictions Associated with Debt

Leasing is assumed to offer fewer restrictions than debt and, consequently, to provide more flexibility. Most loan agreements and bond indentures include protective covenant restrictions, but similar limitations are not as common in leasing. One usual restriction accompanying leasing is in the use of the leased property. For example, the use of the leased equipment may be limited in terms of the number of hours per day. Changes and adjustments in the leased equipment may also be prohibited unless authorized by the lessor.

The advantage of fewer restrictions with leasing than with debt financing will probably disappear in the near future. Most lenders impose restrictions on the amount to be leased for firms financed heavily by debt. Because leasing is becoming more and more accepted as a form of financing, protective covenants will probably be drafted for both leasing and bond indentures.

Effect on Cash and Borrowing Capacity

It is often said that leasing allows a firm to conserve cash and raise more funds than debt financing. This is based on the following claims—some supportable and some unsupportable—made on behalf of leasing.

People often argue that leasing allows the optional use of cash leading to an improvement in a firm's total earning power. Thus, it is maintained, the capital intended for the purchase of fixed assets with low turnover is tied up for the acquisition of current assets with high turnover. Retailers most often are advised to rent their premises and allocate their capital to Inventory and Accounts Receivable. Although seemingly attractive, this claim on behalf of leasing is the result of confusion about the relationship between the investment and financing decisions. It assumes that the financing method is a determinant of the mix of assets. A firm actually decides first on the optimal mix of assets necessary for its line of business and then decides on the proper way of financing this mix by comparing the costs of buying and leasing. The firm can decide either to borrow or lease. In either case it decides to use the optimal mix of assets effectively and efficiently.

People also argue that leasing permits a firm not only to avoid buying assets but also to finance up to 100 percent of the cost of the asset. What is the impact on a firm's borrowing capacity? Does leasing provide more funds? The usual assumption is that leasing has no effect on a firm's borrowing power and a positive effect on its borrowing capacity. However, this line of reasoning is misleading. Given the fixed obligatory nature of the lease, it should be considered equivalent to an implicit loan of 100 percent of the funds needed. The borrowing capacity is definitely reduced, and the borrowing power must be compared with debt financing. The erroneous assumption that leasing provides more funds results from the conventional accounting treatment, whereby lease obligations are not shown by liabilities on the balance sheet. This situation has changed, and accounting treatments now tend to favor the capitalization of long-term leases.

Leasing permits the financing of capital on a piecemeal basis. To be practical, long-term debt financing must usually be arranged on a much larger scale than lease financing, which can be adjusted to each individual unit of property acquired. This can be a valid reason for using lease financing to make occasional asset acquisitions spaced over a period of time. This justification loses its validity, however, when the total amount of capital additions over a given period is large enough to justify a debt issue. Long-term debt financing can be adapted to the timing of expenditures either through the use of interim bank borrowings with subsequent refunding or by a direct placement of securities with institutional investors, providing for a series of takedown.[2]

Tax Advantages

A common argument in the lease-or-buy controversy is whether leasing offers tax advantages over ownership. Under present tax laws, rental payments are considered an operating expense and can be deducted from taxable income. This gives rise to two basic differences in the tax effects of leasing as compared with ownership.

First, leasing makes it possible, in effect, to write off a depreciable portion of property over the basic term of a lease, which is generally shorter than the period that would be permitted for depreciation. The result is not a tax savings but a shift in the timing of deductions and tax payments similar to the effects of accelerated depreciation. To the extent that tax payments are deferred, the company benefits by having the use of these funds for the additional period.

Second, leasing makes it possible, in effect, to write off land values against taxable income, which is not allowed for depreciation purposes. The effect can be very significant when land represents a substantial portion of the total investment, as in urban department store properties. Although leasing provides a way of recovering part of the investment in land during the basic period of the lease, it also deprives the company of 100 percent of this value at the end of the period—which still leaves a net loss of 48 percent. Furthermore, if past trends in land value are any indication of the future trends, the loss could be considerably greater.[3]

Another cost implicitly packaged in the terms of any leasing contract is corrected with the federal income tax deduction. One of the frequently cited advantages of equipment leasing is that a leasing contract permits the lessee to enjoy a more advantageous stream of income tax expense deductions than would be possible with outright ownership of the equipment, whereby only depreciation and interest could be deducted. In fact, there may be some advantage if the lease payments are scheduled so that they are higher in the earlier years of the lease than the sum of depreciation and interest and, conversely, lower in later years. Under these conditions, the present value of the tax deductions received under the lease plan is greater than the present value of the tax deductions under outright ownership. This advantage can be achieved in another way under financial leases. The agreement can be made for a relatively short initial term such as five years. During this time the lessor recovers the entire cost of the equipment; if the lessee purchased the equipment directly, it would have to be depreciated over a longer time span such as seven to ten years.[4]

In the United States the Economic Recovery Tax Act of 1981 allows companies to transfer the tax benefits of tax credits and of the Accelerated Cost Recovery System (ACRS) on new plants and equipment bought between January 1 and August 13, 1981, through what is called *safe-harbor leasing*. Such transactions are safe as long as the Internal Revenue Service regulations are followed precisely. This is possible in two cases:

First, under a reciprocal lease-sublease, the seller of the tax benefits (the lessor-sublessee) acquires new equipment for its own use and, within three months of purchase, leases it to the buyer of the tax credits (the lessee-sublessor). The seller transfers tax credits to the buyer via the lease, and the buyer simultaneously subleases the property back to the seller (the user) without those credits. The rentals payable by the buyer exceed the rentals received by the buyer. This differential is effectively the purchase price of the tax credits transferred.

Second, under a sale leaseback, the seller of the tax benefits (the seller and lessee of the property) acquires new equipment for its own use and, within three months of purchase, sells it to the buyer of the tax benefits (the buyer and lessor of the property). This enables the seller to transfer to the buyer the tax benefits related to the equipment. The consideration is composed of a cash down payment of at least 10 percent of the original cost of the property and a note for the remainder. The buyer then leases the property back to the seller for a lease term that is equal to the term of the note. If the rentals under the lease are equal to the payments on the note (principal and interest), the buyer's initial investment (the down payment) is the purchase price of the tax benefits. The seller continues to be the user of the property. The seller may retain title to the property or reacquire title at the end of the lease term for a nominal amount, such as $1.[5]

The intent of the legislation is that tax leases will allow firms that do not owe taxes or are unable to realize certain tax benefits to realize those benefits by making them transferable. Instead of receiving the benefits directly as a reduction of income taxes payable, firms not owing taxes can realize them by selling the right to those benefits to other firms that can use them to reduce taxes payable.

Shortly after the passage of the act, Ford Motor Company announced that it was selling to International Business Machines Corporation (IBM) its investment tax and depreciation deductions on "under $1 billion" worth of machinery, equipment, and tools acquired so far in 1981. Similarly, Bethlehem Steel Corp. and R. R. Donnelley & Sons Co. entered into a safe-harbor lease transaction that involves the exchange of tax credits. Donnelley will buy steel manufacturing equipment from Bethlehem and lease it back to the steelmaker.

A NORMATIVE MODEL FOR LEASE EVALUATION

Any model for lease evaluation is determined on a cash flow basis. The treatment of the variables in the model differ, depending on whether it is the lessee's or the lessor's model.

Lessor's Analysis

The lessor attempts to determine a rental payment amount that will insure that the present value of rental payments plus the present value of the salvage value of the asset equals or exceeds the original cost of the asset. The discount rate the lessor chooses will be adjusted for the recovery of both the cost of capital of the lessor and other ownership costs before taxes. The lessee may have the option of paying the rental payments at the beginning or the end of each year. Both cases will be examined using the following sample problem.

Assume that a firm has decided to lease an asset under the following conditions:

Purchase price of the asset (A_o)	=	$30,000
Expected salvage value of the asset (S)	=	$10,000
Before tax of return (K_M)	=	8%

Salvage value discount rate (K_τ)	=	20%
Lease period (n)	=	5 years

To compute the rental payment, proceed as follows: The present value of the salvage value $(S_{\pi X})$ is:

$$S_{\pi X} = \frac{S}{(1 + K_\tau)^\xi} = \frac{\$10,000}{(1 + 0.20)^5} = \$4,018$$

The rental (R_κ) if paid in advance is:

$$A_0 - S_{\pi X} = R_1 + \sum_{\kappa=2}^{5} \frac{R_\kappa}{(1 + K_M)^{\kappa-1}} = R_1 + \sum_{\kappa=2}^{5} \frac{R_\kappa}{(1 + 0.08)^{\kappa-1}}$$

$$\$30,000 - \$4,018 = R_\kappa (1 + 3.31213)$$
$$R_\kappa = \$6,025$$

The rental (R_κ) if paid at the end of period is:

$$A_0 - S_{\pi X} = \sum_{\kappa=1}^{\xi} \frac{R_\kappa}{(1 + K_M)^\kappa}$$

$$\$30,000 - \$4,018 = \sum_{\kappa=1}^{5} \frac{R_\kappa}{(1 + 0.08)^\kappa} = R_\kappa(3.99271)$$

$$R_\kappa = \$6,507$$

Lessee's Analysis

The lessee's approach concentrates on how the asset is to be acquired, leaving to more conventional capital budgeting techniques the prior decision on whether the asset is to be acquired at all. Thus the question the lessee examines is whether to borrow and buy or lease. The answer is found by comparing the respective costs of both alternatives. The summary measure used for the comparison can be either the net present value advantage of leasing (NAL) or the pretax interest rate on the lease $(X\iota)$. The NAL measure is expressed as follows:

$$NAL = A_0 - \underset{[1]}{\sum_{\kappa=1}^{\xi} \frac{R_\kappa}{(1 + X_1)^\kappa}} + \underset{[2]}{\sum_{\kappa=1}^{\xi} \frac{TR_\kappa}{(1 + X_2)^\kappa}} - \underset{[3]}{\sum_{\kappa=1}^{\xi} \frac{TD_\kappa}{(1 + X_3)^\kappa}}$$

$$\underset{[5]}{- \sum_{\kappa=1}^{\xi} \frac{TI_\kappa}{(1 + X_4)^\kappa}} + \underset{[6]}{\sum_{\kappa=1}^{\xi} \frac{O_\kappa (1 - T)}{(1 + X_5)^\kappa}} - \underset{[7]}{\frac{V_\xi}{(1 + K_\tau)^\kappa}}$$

The variables included in the NAL equation are defined as follows:

A_0 = purchase price of the asset

R_κ = lease payment in period j

D_κ = depreciation charge in period j

V_ξ = expected after tax salvage value of the asset = $S_\iota - (S_\kappa - B_\kappa) T_\eta$

S_ι = salvage value in period j

B_κ = book value in period j

X_ι = discount rates to apply to the various cash flow streams of the equation

T_η = tax rate applicable to gains and losses on the disposal of fixed assets

T = corporate income tax rate

n = number of years covered by the lease agreement

I_κ = interest component of the loan payment

K_ρ = salvage value discount rate

O_κ = incremental operating costs of ownership in period t

The interpretation of the NAL equation is influenced by the treatment of the key variables in the lease evaluation decision. The seven terms in the NAL equation can be interpreted as follows:

1. The purchase price of the asset is an unavoidable cost of purchasing.

2. The present value of the rental payments is a cost of leasing.

3. The present value of the tax shield provided by the rental payments is a benefit of leasing and, consequently, an opportunity cost of purchasing.

4. The present value of the tax shield provided by the depreciation expense is a benefit of purchasing.

5. The present value of the tax shield provided by the interest expense on a "loan equivalent" to a lease is another benefit of purchasing.

6. The present value of the after tax operating cost is a burden of ownership.

7. The present value of the after tax residual value is a benefit of ownership.

Summing the seven terms, the basic equation provides the net present value advantage of leasing. Setting NAL equal to zero and solving for X_ι provides the pretax interest rate on the lease. The NAL equation can also be explained as follows: The present value of the borrow-and-buy alternative is

$$A_0 - \sum_{\kappa=1}^{\xi} \frac{TD_\kappa}{(1 + X_3)^\kappa} - \sum_{\kappa=1}^{\xi} \frac{TI_\kappa}{(1 + X_4)^\kappa}$$
$$+ \sum_{\kappa=1}^{\xi} \left[\frac{O_\kappa (1 - T)}{(1 = X_5)^\kappa} \right] - \frac{V_\xi}{(1 + K_\tau)_\kappa} \tag{1}$$

The present value of leasing is

$$\sum_{\kappa=1}^{\xi} \frac{R_\kappa}{(1 + X_1)^\kappa} - \sum_{\kappa=1}^{\xi} \frac{TR_\kappa}{(1 + X_2)^\kappa}$$

NAL = present value of borrowing and buying − present value of leasing

Two problems in the applicability of the NAL equation lie in the choice of the appropriate discount rates to be used and the computation of the loan equivalent to the lease.

The discount rates X_1, X_2, X_3, X_4, and X_5 are those applied by the market to evaluate the streams of distribution of R_κ, TD_κ, TI_κ, and O_κ $(1 - T)$. Possible alternatives are a single discount rate or an appropriate rate for each stream. We first use the after tax cost of debt as a single discount rate for all streams; later in the chapter the other alternatives proposed in the literature are discussed. Thus the after tax cost of debt will be used for cash flow stream except V_ξ, which will be discounted at its own rate ($K_\tau = 20$ percent) due to the uncertainty associated with this "estimated" value.

The loan equivalent decision also has generated a debate in the literature. This chapter proposes a first alternative and later presents the other proposed alternatives. For the first alternative, it is assumed that $P_0 = A_0$, and

$$P_0 = \sum_{\kappa=1}^{\xi} \frac{L_\kappa}{(1 + r)^\kappa}$$

where

P_0 = present value of the loan equivalent
L_κ = loan payment at the end of each period j
r = pretax interest rate on term loans "comparable" to the lease

To illustrate the lessee's analysis, the same problem presented in the lessor's analysis will be used. The data required are as follows:

A_0 = $30,000
S = $10,000
R_κ = $6,025 (at the beginning of each period)
R_κ = $6,507 (at the end of each period)
D_κ = straight-line depreciation at period j = $\dfrac{A_0 - S}{n}$ = $4,000
O_κ = $2,000
B = 0
T_n = 10%
V_ξ = S − [(S − B) T_n] = $9,000
r = 6%
T = 50%
n = 5 years

$K_r = 20\%$

The lessee's analysis proceeds as follows: 1. For the loan payment computation, it has been assumed in this analysis that $P_0 = A_0$, and

$$P_0 = \sum_{\kappa=1}^{\xi} \frac{L_\kappa}{(1 + r)_\kappa}$$

Given a 6 percent pretax interest rate on loans, the amount of the annual loan payment at the end of each year is found by solving the following equation for L_κ:

$$\$30,000 = \sum_{\kappa=1}^{5} \frac{L_\kappa}{(1 + 0.06)_\kappa}$$

$$L_\kappa = \$7,122$$

When the rental payments are made in advance, the lease evaluation analysis proceeds by the computation of the NAL as follows:

$$
\begin{aligned}
NAL = \$30,000 &- \left[\$6,025 + \sum_{\kappa=1}^{4} \frac{\$6,025}{(1 + 0.03)^\kappa} \right] + \sum_{\kappa=1}^{5} \frac{(\$6,025)(0.5)}{(1 + 0.03)^\kappa} \\
&- \sum_{\kappa=1}^{5} \frac{(\$4,000)(0.5)}{(1 + 0.03)^\kappa} - \left[\frac{\$800(0.5)}{(1 + 0.03)^1} + \frac{\$1,480(0.5)}{(1 + 0.03)^2} \right. \\
&+ \frac{\$1,142(0.5)}{(1 + 0.03)^3} + \frac{\$783(0.5)}{(1 + 0.03)^4} + \left. \frac{\$403(0.5)}{(1 + 0.03)^5} \right] \\
&+ \sum_{\kappa=1}^{5} \left[\frac{\$2,000(1 - 0.5)}{(1 + 0.03)^\kappa} \right] - \frac{\$9,000}{(1 + 0.20)^5} \\
= \$30,000 &- (\$6,025 + \$22,396) + \$13,796 - \$9,159 - \$2,130 + \$4,580 \\
&- \$3,617 = \$5,048
\end{aligned}
$$

The lease evaluation analysis when the rental payments are made at the end of the period is as follows:

$$
\begin{aligned}
NAL = \$30,000 &- \sum_{\kappa=1}^{5} \frac{\$6,507}{(1 + 0.03)^\kappa} + \sum_{\kappa=1}^{5} \frac{\$6,507(0.5)}{(1 + 0.03)^\kappa} - \sum_{\kappa=1}^{5} \frac{\$4,000(0.5)}{(1 + 0.03)^\kappa} \\
&- \left[\frac{\$800(0.5)}{(1 + 0.03)^1} + \frac{\$1,480(0.5)}{(1 + 0.03)^2} + \frac{\$1,142(0.5)}{(1 + 0.03)^3} \right. \\
&+ \frac{\$783(0.5)}{(1 + 0.03)^4} + \left. \frac{\$403(0.5)}{(1 + 0.03)^5} \right] \\
&+ \sum_{\kappa=1}^{5} \left[\frac{\$2,000(1 - 0.5)}{(1 + 0.03)^\kappa} \right] - \frac{\$9,000}{(1 + 0.20)^5} \\
= \$30,000 &- \$29,800 + \$14,900 - \$9,159 - \$2,130 + \$4,580 - \\
\$3,617 &= \$4,774
\end{aligned}
$$

These computations show the lease alternative to be preferable to the purchase alternative. Several points should be further emphasized:

1. Changing the depreciation method from straight-line to accelerated depreciation may change the outcome.

2. The timing of the rental payments has an impact on the NAL.

3. The analysis assumes that the acquisition price of the asset is equal to the principal of the loan.

4. All of the cash flow streams except for the salvage value are discounted at the after tax cost of debt.

5. It is assumed that the investment decision has been deemed acceptable. Only the financing decision remains to be evaluated in terms of a choice between borrowing and leasing.

ALTERNATIVE CALCULATIONS

The Johnson and Lewellen Approach

R. W. Johnson and W. G. Lewellen examined (1) whether the financing and investment decisions should be mixed in appraising lease possibilities and (2) which discount rate should be used.[6]

Johnson and Lewellen posed the decision problem as a lease-or-buy rather than a lease-or-borrow decision, since a lease contract is simply an arrangement for the long-term acquisition of service, which does not differ in financing terms from the alternative acquisition-of-service arrangement called *purchase*. Hence the inclusion of a charge for interest as a "cost" of owning is viewed as a deficiency of current models for lease evaluation, and the concept of a loan equivalent is not necessary in the lease evaluation model.

The issue of the appropriate rate to use in discounting the cash flows relevant to the decision has been investigated by Johnson and Lewellen. They emphasized the following ideas:

1. The after tax cash flows with predictability, matching that associated with the firm's debt service obligations, should be capitalized at the firm's after tax borrowing rate (after tax cost of debt). This will include the obligations incurred under the lease contract, such as lease payments and their respective tax savings.

2. The after tax cash flows with uncertainty, like the general risks faced by the firm in its line of business, should be discounted at the firm's cost of capital. This will include the depreciation tax shield, the after tax operating costs, and the salvage value.

The Johnson and Lewellen model now can be presented. It states:

$$NPV = NPV(P) - NPV(L) = \sum_{\kappa=1}^{\xi} \left[\frac{D_\kappa T - O_\kappa(1 - T)}{(1 + K)^\kappa} \right] + \frac{V_\xi}{(1 + K)^\kappa} - A_0$$
$$+ \sum_{\kappa=1}^{\xi} \frac{R_\kappa(1 - T)}{[1 + r(1 - T)]^\kappa}$$

where

NPV   = change in the firm's net present value
NPV (P) = the net present value of borrowing and buying
NPV (L) = the net present value of leasing
K   = cost of capital at 12 percent

A positive value of NPV would imply that purchasing the asset is economically superior to leasing it. This would occur if the net salvage value exceeded after tax operating costs or if the purchase price less depreciation tax savings were less than the burden of lease payments.

Using the data in the previous illustration, the Johnson and Lewellen model proceeds as follows: If the rental payments are made at the beginning of the period,

$$NPV = \sum_{\kappa=1}^{5} \left[\frac{\$2,000 - \$1,000}{(1 + 0.12)^\kappa} \right] + \frac{\$9,000}{(1 + 0.12)^5} - \$30,000$$
$$+ \left[\$6,025 + \sum_{\kappa=1}^{4} \frac{\$6,025}{1.03^\kappa} \right] - \sum_{\kappa=1}^{5} \left[\frac{\$6,025(1 - 0.5)}{(1 + 0.03)^\kappa} \right]$$
$$= \$(6,664)$$

Thus leasing is preferred.
If the rental payments are made at the end of the period,

$$NPV = \sum_{\kappa=1}^{5} \left[\frac{\$2,000 - \$1,000}{(1 + 0.12)^\kappa} \right] + \frac{\$9,000}{(1 + 0.12)^5} - \$30,000$$
$$+ \sum_{\kappa=1}^{4} \left[\frac{\$6,507}{1.03^\kappa} \right] - \sum_{\kappa=1}^{5} \left[\frac{\$6,507(1 - 0.5)}{(1 + 0.03)^\kappa} \right] = \$(6,388)$$

Leasing is preferred in this case as well.

As a result of discounting the costs of financing at $r(1 - T)$ and the ownership cash flows at K, the Johnson and Lewellen approach in this case creates a bias in favor of leasing. R. S. Bower contested the choice:

Johnson and Lewellen's selection of K as the discount rate is understandable but unappealing. It is understandable because K is the rate used in discounting depreciation shelters in conventional capital budgeting, where the shelter is part of the cash flow calculation. The selection of K is unappealing, though, because it involves discounting some of the tax shelter given up in leasing at a high rate K, and discounting all of the tax shelter that comes with leasing at a low rate, r (1−T). It is difficult to avoid the conclusion that a higher discount rate for the shelter element of lease cost does a great deal more to bias the analysis in favor of leasing than it does to recognize any real difference in risk.[7]

The Roenfeldt and Osteryoung Approach

The approach by R. L. Roenfeldt and J. S. Osteryoung expanded on the Johnson and Lewellen approach by categorically separating the investment decision from the financing decision.[8] The methodology used consisted of (1) determining the desirability of the investment decision and, (2) given that the investment decision was deemed desirable, evaluating the financing decision by comparing the after tax cost of borrowing (r_β) with the after tax cost of leasing (r_μ).

Using the data from the illustration in the previous section, the Roenfeldt and Osteryoung approach proceeds as follows.

Step 1. The Investment Decision: The investment decision is made on the basis of a net present value or internal rate-of-return approach following traditional capital budgeting techniques. (See chapter 11.) The computation of a net present value or internal rate of return involves estimating the annual sales generated by the asset and computing the resulting net cash flows, as follows:

	0	1	2	3
		Year		
1. Sales (assumed)		$20,000	$20,000	$20,000
2. Depreciation		4,000	4,000	4,000
3. Cash operating costs		2,000	2,000	2,000
4. Taxable income (line 1 − line 2 − line 3)		14,000	14,000	14,000
5. Tax liability (4 × T)		7,000	7,000	7,000
6. Net cash flow (line 1 − line 2 − line 3)		11,000	11,000	11,000
7. Salvage value (V_ξ)				
8. Discount factor (K = 12)				
9. Discount factor (K_τ = 20)				
10. Present value of cash flow				
11. Present value of V_ξ				
12. Total present value (line 10 + line 11)				

	4	5
1. Sales (assumed)	$20,000	$20,000
2. Depreciation	4,000	4,000
3. Cash operating costs	2,000	2,000
4. Taxable income (line 1 − line 2 − line 3)	14,000	14,000
5. Tax liability (4 × T)	7,000	7,000
6. Net cash flow (line 1 − line 2 − line 3)	11,000	11,000

	5
7. Salvage value (V_ξ)	9,000
8. Discount factor (K = 12)	3,605
9. Discount factor (K_τ = 20)	0.402
10. Present value of cash flow	39,655
11. Present value of V_ξ	3,618
12. Total present value (line 10 + line 11)	43,273

Thus the net present value is equal to $13,273, or $43,273 − $30,000, and the investment is deemed desirable.

Step 2: The Financing Decision: The financing decision—to borrow or to lease—is made on the basis of a criterion of least cost by comparing the after tax cost of borrowing (r_β) to the after tax cost of leasing (r_μ).

To compute r_β, the rate that equates the after tax interest payments and amortization of the principal to the loan amount, the following formula is used:

$$A_0 = \sum_{\kappa=1}^{\xi} \frac{L_\kappa - i\, I_\kappa T}{(1 + r_\beta)^\kappa}$$

or

$$\$30,000 = \sum_{\kappa=1}^{5} \frac{\$7,122 - [0.5\,(I_\kappa)]}{(1 + r_\beta)^\kappa}$$

The numerator (the net costs of borrowing) is computed as follows:

Year	Loan Payment	Interest	Interest Tax Shield ($I_\kappa T$)	Net Cost of Borrowing
1	$7,122	$1,800	900.0	$6,222.0
2	7,122	1,480	740.0	6,382.0
3	7,122	1,142	571.0	6,551.0
4	7,122	783	391.5	6,730.5
5	7,122	403	201.5	6,920.5

Solving for r_β yields

$$r_\beta = 3\%$$

To compute $r\mu$, the rate that equates the adjusted rental payments to the cost of the asset (A_0), Roenfeldt and Osteryoung made the following changes:

1. The rental payments are reduced by the amount of any operating costs assumed by the lessor.
2. The depreciation tax shield and after tax salvage value are added to the cost of leasing.

3. Certainty equivalents are introduced into the operating and residual cash flows to adjust for risk.

The following formula is then used:

$$V_0 = \left\{ \sum_{k=1}^{\xi} \frac{[(L_\kappa - \alpha_\kappa O_\kappa)(1 - T)] + D_\kappa T}{(1 + r_\mu)^\xi} \right\} + \left\{ \frac{\alpha_\xi S_\xi - (\alpha_\xi S_\xi - B) T_\eta}{(1 + r_\mu)^\xi} \right\}$$

where

α_κ = certainty equivalent for the operating costs
α_ξ = certainty equivalent for the salvage value

Assuming $\alpha_\kappa = 0.6$ and $\alpha_\xi = 0.99$, the cost of leasing (r_μ) can be computed as follows: If the rental payments are made at the end of the period,

$$\$30,000 = \left\{ \sum_{\kappa=1}^{5} \frac{[\$6,507 - 0.6(\$2,000)](1 - 0.5) + [(\$4,000)(0.5)]}{(1 + r_\mu)^\xi} \right\}$$
$$+ \left\{ \frac{0.99(\$10,000) - [0.99(\$10,000) - 0](0.10)}{(1 + r_\mu)^\xi} \right\} \tag{1}$$
$$= \sum_{\kappa=1}^{5} \left[\frac{\$4,653.5}{(1 + r_\mu)^\xi} \right] + \left[\frac{\$8,910}{(1 + r_\mu)^\xi} \right]$$

Then $r_\mu = 2$ percent, and leasing is preferable to borrowing.
  If the rental payments are made in advance,

$$\$30,000 = \left\{ \sum_{\kappa=1}^{4} \frac{[\$6,025 - 0.6(\$2,000)](1 - 0.5) + [(\$4,000)(0.5)]}{(1 + r_\mu)^\xi} \right\}$$
$$+ \left[\frac{\$8,910}{(1 + r_\mu)^\xi} \right] \tag{2}$$

Then $r_\mu = 2.1$ percent, and leasing is still preferable to borrowing.

Issues in Lease Financing

Bower summarized the following points of agreement and disagreement in the differing approaches to the lease-or-buy decision. All the models require inputs that include the purchase price of the asset to be leased (A_0), lease payments at the end or at the beginning of the period (R_κ), a depreciation charge relevant for tax payments at the end of the period (D_κ), a cash operating cost expected to occur in the period if the asset is purchased but not if it is leased (O_κ), an expected after tax salvage value of the asset at the end of the last period covered by the lease agreement (V_ξ), a pretax interest rate on the loan equivalent to the lease (r), an after tax cost of capital for the corporation (k), a corporate income tax rate (T), and the number of periods covered by the lease agreement (n).

The points of disagreement relating to the lease-or-buy analysis include the following:

1. The choice of a summary measure, either the pretax interest rate on a lease (i) or the net advantage to a lease (NAL)
2. The inclusion or exclusion of some of the terms previously presented in the normative model
3. The computation of the loan equivalent
4. The choice of a discount rate for each of the cash flows included in the normative model

The Bower Approach: A Decision Format

Bower has developed a decision format to reconcile the disagreements among the various approaches to the lease-or-buy analysis and still permit those interested to take advantage of the model's broad agreement on other points.[9] The decision format examines the decision implications associated with different tax shelter discount rates.

The decision format uses the cost of capital (K) to calculate benefits that involve the purchase price, operating savings, and salvage value; it uses the appropriate interest rate (r) to calculate the present cost of the lease payments. The tax shelter effect is then calculated for rates of discount (X) from zero through 14 percent.

The cost of purchasing (COP) depends on the purchase price, depreciation tax shelter, cash operating cost avoided by leasing, and salvage value:

$$COP = A_0 - \sum_{\kappa=0}^{\xi} \left[\frac{TD_\kappa}{(1 + X)^\kappa} \right] + \sum_{\kappa=0}^{\xi} \left[\frac{O_\kappa (1 - T)}{(1 + K)^\kappa} \right] - \frac{V_\xi}{(1 + K)^\xi}$$

The cost of leasing (COL) depends on the lease payment, lease tax shelter, and the interest tax shelter lost by leasing:

$$COL = \sum_{\kappa=0}^{\xi} \left[\frac{R_\kappa}{(1 + r)^\kappa} \right] - \sum_{\kappa=0}^{\xi} \left[\frac{TR_\kappa}{(1 + X)^\kappa} \right] + \sum_{\kappa=0}^{\xi} \left[\frac{TI_\kappa}{(1 + X)^\kappa} \right]$$

An illustrative example of Bower's decision format will be given using the data presented in the example in the section "A Normative Model for Lease Evaluation." There is, however, one major change: The lease payment (R_κ), as calculated in the lessor's analysis, will no longer be used. The equivalent loan is computed by Bower as follows:

$$\text{Loan equivalent } (P_0) = \sum_{\kappa=1}^{\xi} \frac{P}{(1 + r)^\kappa}$$

where

R_κ (lease payment) = loan payment (L_κ)
r = pretax interest rate on term loans "comparable" to the lease

Although most of the data supplied in the original example applies here, assume that as an alternative to purchasing, the asset can be leased for five years for a payment of $7,962 per annum.

In this case, the loan equivalent no longer equals the purchase price of the asset; instead, the following holds true:

$$\text{Loan equivalent } (P_0) = \sum_{\kappa=1}^{\xi} \frac{\$7,962}{(1 + 0.06)^\kappa} = \$33,538$$

The loan equivalent is:

Year	Loan Payment	Loan Balance (Year Start)	Interest (6%)	Principal Repayment	Loan Balance (Year-End)
1	$7,962	$33,538	$2,012	$5,950	$27,588
2	7,962	27,588	1,655	6,307	21,281
3	7,962	21,281	1,277	6,685	14,596
4	7,962	14,596	876	7,086	7,510
5	7,962	7,510	452	7,511	0

The decision format is presented in Exhibits 10.2 and 10.3. The columns at the right in Exhibit 10.2 show that when the tax shelter is discounted at $r(1 - T)$ = 10.0 percent, the net advantage of purchasing is $49. At all discount rates above 9.65 percent, the lease has a net disadvantage. Therefore, if a decision maker analyzing a graph such as Exhibit 10.3 believes that the proper tax shelter discount rate lies well below the intersection point, the decision to lease rather than purchase would provide the greater financial benefit to the company.

In developing this decision format, Bower has devised a composite approach to the lease-or-buy decision that enables the executive to make a judgment on the principal disagreement among academicians and on how the proper tax shelter discount rate, $r(1 - T)$, may affect the ultimate cost of a decision.

CONCLUSION

A multinational firm may enter into a leasing arrangement for many reasons. Some of the primary motivations follow:

Exhibit 10.2
Decision Format Table

Year t	Purchase Price A_t	Lease Payment $R_t = L_t$	Tax Shelter Lease Payment TR_t	Tax Shelter Depreciation TD_t	Tax Shelter Loan Interest TI_t	After-Tax Operating Saving $O_t(1-t)$	After-Tax Salvage V_t
0	30,000						
1		7,962	3,981	2,000	1,006	1,000	
2		7,962	3,981	2,000	828	1,000	
3		7,962	3,981	2,000	638	1,000	
4		7,962	3,981	2,000	438	1,000	
5		7,962	3,981	2,000	226	1,000	9,000

Present Value at

$k = 0.12$	30,000					3.605	5.107
$r = 0.06$		33.538					

						Cost of Purchasing	Cost of Leasing
0			19.905	10.000	3.136	18.498	16.769
0.02			18.764	9,427	2.993	19.071	17.767
0.04			17.223	8.904	2.868	19.594	19.183
0.06			17.769	8.425	2.737	20.073	19.506
0.08			15.895	7.985	2.624	20.513	20.267
0.10			15.091	7.582	2.518	20.916	20.965
0.12			14.351	7.210	2.419	21.288	21.606
0.14			13.667	6.866	2.327	21.632	22.198

Exhibit 10.3
Decision Format Graph

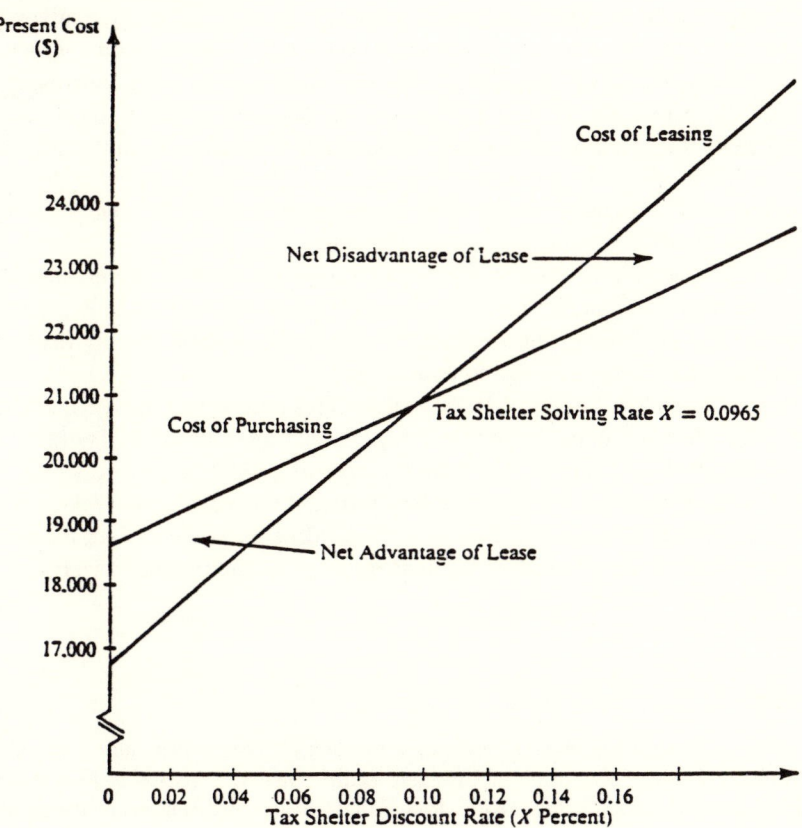

1. Leasing enables a firm to take advantage of tax shelters.

2. A leasing arrangement conserves working capital.

3. There are cash budgeting benefits because leasing permits accurate predictions of cash needs.

4. Leasing allows a company to retain a degree of flexibility lost by debt financing (that is, bond indenture sometimes imposes restrictions on future financing).

5. A leasing arrangement provides convenience.

6. Leasing can provide an economical means of obtaining excellent servicing and maintenance of equipment if a maintenance lease is included.

7. An operating lease provides more flexibility than ownership if the asset becomes unprofitable; it avoids part or all the risk of obsolescence; and it can provide for modern equipment from year to year.

Most of the significant methods of analyzing lease-or-buy alternatives use the same basic formula for calculation, but there is considerable disagreement in the calculation methods. The disagreement lies with both relevant alternatives and the choice of the best summary measure of comparison. The relevant alternatives include the outstanding principal of the loan equivalent, loan payments at the end of the period the interest component of the loan payment, the principal component, the present value of the lease claim, and the discount rates to be applied to cash flows in each category, which are intended to reflect opportunity cost. Summary measures are either the increment in net present value of owners' wealth or the after tax interest rate on the lease.

The disagreement is more significant in the treatment of the terms, including lease payments and the tax shelter acquired or given up if the lease is accepted. This is most obvious in the decision to include or exclude the tax deduction associated with interest on the equivalent loan.

Bower's decision format of lease analysis is the most appropriate method to use today. It is a composite of the factors agreed upon by other theorists, and it enables decision makers to choose the cost of capital and interest rate they feel is most appropriate during the relevant period for making their lease-or-buy decision. Bower's decision format also enables decision makers to see the effects of other costs and rates and make their decision in light of the uncertainty of these factors.

NOTES

1. For a discussion of leverage leasing, see Robert C. Wiar, "Economic Implications of Multiple Rates of Return in the Leverage Lease Context," *Journal of Finance,* December 1973, pp. 1, 275–286; and E. Richard Packham, "An Analysis of the Risks of Leverage Leasing," *Journal of Commercial Bank Lending,* March 1975, pp. 2–29.

2. D. R. Gant, "Illusion in Lease Financing," *Harvard Business Review,* March–April 1959, p. 129.

3. Ibid., p. 126.

4. R. F. Vancil, "Lease or Borrow: New Method of Analysis," *Harvard Business Review,* September–October 1961, p. 127.

5. Financial Accounting Standards Board, *Accounting for the Sale or Purchase of Tax Benefits through Tax Leases,* Exposure draft (Stamford, Conn., November 30, 1981), p. 11.

6. R. W. Johnson and W. G. Lewellen, "Analysis of the Lease or Buy Decision," *Journal of Finance,* September 1972, pp. 815–823.

7. R. S. Bower, "Issues in Lease Financing," *Financial Management,* Winter 1973, p. 29.

8. R. L. Roenfeldt and J. S. Osteryoung, "Analysis of Financial Leases," *Financial Management,* Spring 1973, pp. 74–87.

9. Bower, "Issues in Lease Financing," p. 27.

REFERENCES

Beechy, T. H. "The Cost of Leasing: Comment and Correction." *Accounting Review*, October 1970, pp. 769–773.

———. "Quasi-Debt Analysis of Financial Leases." *Accounting Review*, April 1969, pp. 375–381.

Billiam, Phillip L. "Lease versus Purchase: A Practical Problem." *Cost and Management*, September–October 1974, pp. 32–36.

Bower, R. S. "Issues in Lease Financing." *Financial Management*, Winter 1973.

Bower, R. S., F. C. Herringer, and J. P. Williamson. "Lease Evaluation." *Accounting Review*, April 1966, pp. 257–265.

Burns, Jane O., and Kathleen Bindon. "Evaluating Lease with LP." *Management Accounting*, February 1980, pp. 48–53.

Doenges, E. C. "The Cost of Leasing." *Engineering Economist*, Winter 1971, pp. 31–44.

Duty, Glen L. "A Leasing Guide to Taxes." *Management Accounting*, August 1980, pp. 45–51.

Ferrara, William L., James B. Thies, and Mark W. Dirsmith. "The Lease-Purchase Decision." *Management Accounting*, May 1980, pp. 57–59.

Financial Accounting Standards Board. *Accounting for the Sale or Purchase of Tax Benefits through Tax Leases*. Exposure draft. Stamford, Conn., November 30, 1981.

Findlay, M. Chapman, III. "Financial Lease Evaluation: Survey and Synthesis." Mimeograph. Abstracted in *Proceedings of the 1973 Annual Meeting of the Eastern Finance Association*. Edited by Donald E. Fisher. Storrs, Conn.: Eastern Finance Association, April 12–14, 1973, p. 136.

———. "A Sensitivity Analysis of IRR Leasing Model." *Engineering Economist*, Summer 1975, pp. 231–242.

Frank, Julian R., and Stewart D. Hodges. "Valuation of Financial Lease Contracts: A Note." *Journal of Finance*, May 1978, pp. 657–669.

Gant, D. R. "Illusion in Lease Financing." *Harvard Business Review*, March–April 1959.

Johnson, R. W., and W. G. Lewellen. "Analysis of the Lease or Buy Decision." *Journal of Finance*, September 1972, pp. 815–823.

Levy, Haim, and Marshall Sarnat. "Leasing, Borrowing, and Financial Risk." *Financial Management*, Winter 1979, pp. 47–54.

Loretucci, Joseph A. "Financial Leasing: What's the Best Replacement Cycle?" *Management Accounting*, August 1979, pp. 45–48.

Millar, James A. "Hospital Equipment Leasing: The Breakeven Discount Rate." *Management Accounting*, July 1979, pp. 21–26.

Miller, M. H., and C. W. Upton. "Leasing, Buying, and the Cost of Capital Services." *Journal of Finance*, July 1976, pp. 761–786.

Mitchell, G. B. "After-Tax Cost of Leasing." *Accounting Review*, April 1970, pp. 308–314.

Mokkelbost, Per B. "The Value of Leasing." Paper presented at the 1976 meeting of the Canadian Association of Administrative Sciences, Université Laval, Quebec City, Quebec, May 31–June 2, 1976.

Myers, S. C., D. A. Dill, and A. J. Bautista. "Valuation of Financial Lease Contracts." *Journal of Finance*, June 1976, pp. 799–819.

Packham, E. Richard. "An Analysis of the Risks of Leverage Leasing." *Journal of Commercial Bank Lending*, March 1975, pp. 2–29.

Roenfeldt, R. L., and J. S. Osteryoung. "Analysis of Financial Leases." *Financial Management*, Spring 1973, pp. 74–87.

School, Lawrence D. "The Lease-or-Buy and Asset Acquisition Decision." *Journal of Finance*, September 1974, pp. 1, 203–211, 214.

Vancil, R. F. "Lease or Borrow: New Method of Analysis." *Harvard Business Review*, September–October 1961, pp. 122–136.

Wiar, Robert C. "Economic Implications of Multiple Rates of Return in the Leverage Lease Context." *Journal of Finance*, December 1973, pp. 1, 275–286.

Wyman, H. E. "Financial Lease Evaluation under Conditions of Uncertainty." *Accounting Review*, July 1973, pp. 489–493.

11

Advanced Capital Budgeting

The capital budgeting decision requires different approaches in cases involving (a) capital rationing, (b) uncertainty associated with cash flows, (c) an inflationary environment, and (d) investment in new technology. This chapter elaborates on the techniques used in capital budgeting literature to deal with each of these issues.

CAPITAL RATIONING

Capital rationing exists when a firm has limited funds, which precludes the acceptance of potentially profitable projects. Among the causes cited for capital rationing are (1) limits imposed on new borrowing, (2) a debt limit imposed by an outside agreement (for example, bond covenants), (3) limits on capital spending imposed on divisional management, and (4) management's desire to maintain a given dividend policy or a specific earnings-per-share or price-earnings ratio.[1]

Conventional methods of evaluation with capital rationing consist of (1) ranking the projects under consideration from highest to lowest for whichever evaluation model is used, that is, Internal Rate of Return (IRR), NPV, or the profitability index (PI); and (2) selecting projects starting at the top of the ranking until funds are exhausted. Although these conventional methods based on either the IRR or the NPV techniques are simple, discontinuities or size disparities between projects prevent the choice of optimal projects. For example, a 20 percent return on $1,000 is considered better than a 15 percent return on $2,000, according to the conventional capital rationing method.

To correct the limitations of the conventional capital rationing methods, mathematical programming can be used to select the optimal combination of projects. In 1955 James H. Lorie and Leonard J. Savage were the first to suggest math-

ematical programming—in the form of a heuristic programming approach—to
deal with capital rationing.[2] This attempt was followed by a more comprehensive
treatment of the problem by H. Martin Weingartner, whose basic model follows:[3]

Capital Rationing Example

Investment Proposal	Present Value of Outlay (Period I)	Present Value of Outlay (Period 2)	NPV
1	$10	$ 5	$20
2	20	10	30
3	30	10	40
4	40	30	50

Maximize

$$\sum_{j=1}^{m}$$

subject to

$$\sum_{j=1}^{m} C_{ij} \leq C_t \text{ for } t = 1,\ldots,n$$
$$0 \leq X_j \leq 1$$

where

X_j is an integer.

b_j = net present value of investment proposal j.
X_j = 0 if the project is accepted, and 1 if the project is rejected.
C_{ij} = net cash needed for proposal j in period t.
C_t = total budget for period t

Because of the use of the last two constraints, this mathematical programming
model is known as integer programming.

To illustrate the integer programming approach to capital budgeting, let us
use the data shown in the above table. The present values of the two budget
constraints are $90 in period 1 and $30 in period 2. The model will look like
the following:
Maximize

$$20x_1 + 30x_2 + 40x_3 + 50x_4$$

subject to

$$10x_1 + 20x_2 + 30x_3 + 40x_4 \leq 90$$
$$5x_1 + 10x_2 + 10x_3 + 30x_4 \leq 30$$
$$0 \leq X_j \leq 1 \text{ for } j = 1,2,3, \text{ and } 4$$

X_j is an integer.

CAPITAL BUDGETING UNDER UNCERTAINTY

Nature of Risk

Because the cash flows of a project often may be estimated on the basis of incomplete information, the capital budgeting evaluation must be performed in a climate of uncertainty. Although *uncertainty* and *risk* are sometimes used synonymously, they are different in the strict mathematical sense. *Risk* refers to the possible outcomes of a project to which probabilities can be assigned, whereas *uncertainty* refers to outcomes to which it is difficult to assign probabilities. Thus the real interest lies with risk, because it is measurable.

Most decision makers are risk averse and perceive risk in different ways:

1. The *dollar-price risk* is the risk associated with a decline in the number of dollars used to acquire a financial asset.
2. The *purchasing power risk* is the risk associated with a decline in the purchasing power of the monetary unit.
3. The *interest rate risk* is the risk associated with changes in the interest rate, which affect market values of many types of securities.
4. The *business risk* is the risk associated with the operational cash flows of a firm.
5. The *financial risk* is the risk associated with financial leverage.
6. The *systematic risk* or *market risk* is the risk associated with the common stocks of a particular industry.
7. The *unsystematic risk* is the risk associated with a particular company.

Because the perception of risk by decision makers affects their decisions, it should be taken into account in the decision-making process. Capital budgeting under uncertainty should incorporate risk in the evaluation process.

Risk-Adjusted Discount Rate Method

One of the techniques for incorporating risk in the evaluation process is the risk-adjusted discount rate, which consists of manipulating the discount rate applied to the cash flows to reflect the amount of risk inherent in a project. The higher the risk associated with a project, the higher the discount rate applied to the cash flows. If a given project is perceived to be twice as risky as most acceptable projects to the firm and the cost of capital is 12 percent, the correct risk-adjusted discount rate is 24 percent.

In spite of its simplicity, the risk-adjusted discount rate method is subject to the following limitations:

1. The determination of the exact risk-adjusted discount rate is subjective and, therefore, subject to error.
2. The method adjusts the discount rate rather than the future cash flows, which are subject to variability and risk.

Certainty-Equivalent Method

Another technique for incorporating risk in the evaluation process is the certainty-equivalent method, which involves adjusting the future cash flows so that a project can be evaluated on a riskless basis. The adjustment is formulated as follows:

$$\text{NPV} = \sum_{t=1}^{n} \left[\frac{\alpha_t \, \text{CF}_t}{(1 + R_f)} \right] - I_o$$

where

$$\begin{aligned}
\text{NPV} &= \text{Net present value} \\
\alpha_t &= \text{risk coefficient applied to the cash flow of period t (CF}_t). \\
I_o &= \text{Initial cost of the project.} \\
R_f &= \text{risk-free rate.}
\end{aligned}$$

As this formula shows, the method proceeds by multiplying the future cash flows by certainty equivalents to obtain a riskless cash flow. Note also that the discount rate used is R_f, which is the risk-free rate of interest.

To illustrate the certainty-equivalent method, assume an investment with the following characteristics:

$$\begin{aligned}
I_o &= \text{initial cost} = \$30,000 \\
\text{CF}_1 &= \text{cash flow, year 1} = \$10,000 \\
\text{CF}_2 &= \text{cash flow, year 2} = \$20,000 \\
\text{CF}_3 &= \text{cash flow, year 3} = \$30,000 \\
\alpha_1 &= \text{certainty equivalent, year 1} = 0.9 \\
\alpha_2 &= \text{certainty equivalent, year 2} = 0.8 \\
\alpha_3 &= \text{certainty equivalent, year 3} = 0.6
\end{aligned}$$

The NPV of the investment using a risk-free discount rate of 6 percent is computed as follows:

Period	Cash Flow (CF_t)	Risk Coefficient (α_t)	Certainty Equivalent	Risk-free Rate (R_F)	Present Value
1	$10,000	0.9	$ 9,000	0.943	$ 8,487
2	20,000	0.8	16,000	0.890	14,240
3	30,000	0.6	18,000	0.840	15,120
Present value of cash flows					$37,847
Initial investment					30,000
Net present value					$ 7,847

Since the NPV is positive, the investment should be considered acceptable. The main advantage of the certainty-equivalent method is that it allows the assignment of a different risk factor to each cash flow, given that risk can concentrate in one or more periods.

The certainty-equivalent method and the risk-adjusted discount rate method are comparable methods of evaluating risk. To produce similar ranking, the following equation must hold:

$$\frac{\alpha_t \, CF_t}{(1 + R_F)} = \frac{CF_t}{(1 + R_A)^t}$$

where

α_t = risk coefficient used in the certainty-equivalent method
R_F = risk-free discount rate
R_A = risk-adjusted discount rate used in the risk-adjusted discount rate method.
CF_t = future cash flow

Solving for α_t yields

$$\alpha_t = \frac{(1 + R_F)^t}{(1 + R_A)_t}$$

Given that R_A and R_F are constant and $R_A > R_F$, then α_t decreases over time, which means that risk increases over time. To illustrate, assume that in the previous example $R_A = 15$ percent. Then,

$$\alpha^1 = \frac{(1 + R_F)^1}{(1 + R_1)^1} = \frac{(1 + 0.06)^1}{(1 + 0.15)^1} = 0.921$$

$$\alpha_2 = \frac{(1 + R_F)^2}{(1 + R_A)^2} = \frac{(1 + 0.06)^2}{(1 + 0.15)^2} = 0.848$$

$$\alpha_2 = \frac{(1 + R_F)^3}{(1 + R_A)^3} = \frac{(1 + 0.06)^3}{(1 + 0.15)^3} = 0.783$$

In many cases this assumption of increasing risk may not be realistic.

Probability Distribution

The probability distribution approach to the evaluation of risk assigns probabilities to each cash flow outcome. Various measures of risk then can be computed, giving information about the dispersion or tightness of the probability distribution. *Standard deviation* is a conventional measure of dispersion. For a single period, the standard deviation is computed as follows:

$$\delta = \sum_{i=1}^{n} [X_{it} - E_t (X)]_2 \, P(X_i)_t$$

where

δ_t = standard deviation of period t's cash flows
X_{it} = cash flow for the ith outcome in period t
$E_t(X)$ = expected value of cash flows in period t
$P(X_i)_t$ = probability of occurrence of cash flow X_i in period $_t$.

The expected cash flow $E_t (X)$ is computed as follows:

$$E_t (X) = \Sigma \, X_{it} \, P (X_i)_t$$

All things being equal, the higher the standard deviation, the greater the risk associated with the expected value.

Another measure of relative dispersion is the *coefficient of variation* (CV), a measure that compares the expected value and risk of a probability distribution. The coefficient of variation is computed as follows:

$$CV = \frac{\delta}{E(X)}$$

All things being equal, the smaller the coefficient of variation, the better the project. To illustrate these risk concepts, assume that projects A and B have the following discrete probability distributions of expected cash flows in each of the next three years:

Project A		Project B	
Probability	Cash Flow	Probability	Cash Flow
0.2	$1,000	0.3	$1,500
0.5	2,000	0.3	1,000
0.2	3,000	0.2	3,500
0.1	4,000	0.2	3,750

The expected value of cash flows of both projects can be computed as follows:

$$E(A) = 0.2(\$1,000) + 0.5(\$2,000) + 0.2(\$3,000) + 0.1(\$4,000) = \$2,200$$
$$E(B) = 0.3(\$1,500) + 0.3(\$1,000) + 0.2(\$3,000) + 0.2(\$3,750) = \$2,200$$

On the basis of the expected values as a measure of central tendency in the distribution, projects A and B are equivalent. To determine which project is riskier, the standard deviations for both projects can be computed as follows:

$$\delta(A) = [0.2(\$1,000 - \$2,200)^2 + 0.5(\$2,000 - \$2,200)^2 + 0.2(\$3,000 - \$2,200)^2 + 0.1(\$4,000 - \$2,200)^2]^{1/2} = \$871.77$$
$$\delta(B) = [0.3(\$1,500 - \$2,200)^2 + 0.3(1,000 - \$2,200)^2 + 0.2(\$3,500 - \$2,200)^2 + 0.2(\$3,750 - \$2,200)^{1/2} = \$1,182.15$$

Thus project B has a significantly higher standard deviation, indicating a greater dispersion of possible cash flows.

The standard deviation is an absolute measure of risk. For comparison, the projects also should be evaluated on the basis of their coefficient of variation, which measures the relative dispersion within the distribution. The coefficient of variation for both projects can be computed now:

$$CV(A) = \frac{\delta_A}{E(A)} \times 100 = \frac{\$871.77}{\$2,200} = 39.6\%$$

$$CV(B) = \frac{\delta_B}{E(B)} \times 100 = \frac{\$1,182.15}{\$2,200} = 53.7\%$$

The coefficient of variation for project B is significantly higher than for project A, which indicates again that project B presents a greater degree of risk.

The coefficient of variation is an especially useful measure when the comparison between projects leads to the acceptance of a given project based on a comparison between means or when the comparison leads to the acceptance of a different project based on a comparison between standard deviations.

Multiperiod Projects

The computation of the measures of risk becomes more complicated when several periods are involved. Some assumptions must be made regarding the relationships between the period cash flows, namely, whether the cash flows are independent or dependent.

To illustrate, return to project A and assume (1) that the applicable discount rate (R) is 10 percent and (2) that the project calls for a $5,000 investment.

Independent of the nature of the relationship between cash flows in the three periods, the NPV of project A can be computed as follows:

$$NPV = \sum_{i=1}^{3} \frac{(\$2,200)}{(1 + ?).10)^i} - \$5,000 = \$471$$

Independent Cash Flows: If we assume serial independence of the cash flows between the periods, the standard deviation of the entire project is

$$\delta = \sqrt{\sum_{i=1}^{n} \frac{\delta_t^2}{(1 + r)^{2t}}}$$

where

δ_t = standard deviation of the probability distribution of the cash flows in period t

Hence the standard deviation of project A, assuming serial independence, is

$$\delta_A = \sqrt{\frac{(\$871)^2}{(1 + 0.10)^2} + \frac{(\$871)^2}{(1 + 0.10)^4} + \frac{(\$871)^2}{(1 + 0.10)^6}} = \$354.04$$

Dependent Cash Flows: In general, the cash flows of a given period are expected to influence the cash flows of subsequent periods. In the case of perfect correlation, the standard deviation of the entire project is

$$\delta = \sum_{i=1}^{n} \frac{\delta_t}{(1 + r)^t}$$

Therefore, the standard deviation of project A, assuming perfect correlation between interperiod cash flows, is

$$\delta = \sum_{i=1}^{3} \frac{\$871}{(1 + 0.10)^i} = \$2,166.17$$

Note that the standard deviation under the assumption of independence is $358.04, whereas under the assumption of perfect dependency it is considerably higher ($2,166.17). If the cash flows are perfectly correlated, there is more risk inherent in the project than if the cash flows are independent.

Mixed Correlation: A project may include some independent and some dependent cash flows. Frederick Hillier proposed a model to deal with a mixed situation.

$$\delta = \sum_{t=0}^{T} \frac{\delta_{Yt}^2}{(1 + r)^{2t}} + \sum_{j=1} \left[\sum_{j=1} \frac{\delta_{Zjt}}{(1 + r)^t} \right]^2$$

where

Y_t = the independent component of the net cash flow in period t
Z_{jt} = the jth perfectly correlated component of the net cash flow in period t[4]

To illustrate the computation of the standard deviation of a project with mixed correlation, Hillier assumed the following project data for a new product addition:

Year	Source	Expected Value of Net Cash Flows (in Thousands)	Standard Deviation
0	Initial investment	$(600)	$ 50
1	Production cash outflow	(250)	20
2	Production cash outflow	(200)	10
3	Production cash outflow	(200)	10
4	Production outflow—salvage value	(100)	$10 \sqrt{10}$
1	Marketing	300	50
2	Marketing	600	100
3	Marketing	500	100
4	Marketing	400	100
5	Marketing	300	100

Hillier also assumed that all outflows were independent and that all marketing flows were perfectly correlated. If 10 percent is used as the risk-free rate, the expected value of the NPV for the proposal is

$$NPV = \sum_{t=1} \left[\frac{X}{(1 + 0.10)^t} \right] - C_o$$

or

$$NPV = \frac{\$300 - \$250}{(1.10)^5} + \frac{\$600 - \$200}{(1.10)^2} + \frac{\$500 - \$200}{(1.10)^3}$$
$$+ \frac{\$400 - \$200}{(1.10)^4} + \frac{\$300 - \$100}{(1.10)^5} - \$600 = \$262$$

The standard deviation is

$$\delta = \sqrt{50^2 + \frac{20^2}{(1.10)^2} + \ldots + \frac{(10\sqrt{10})^2}{(1.10)^{10}} + \left[\frac{50}{(1.10)} + \ldots + \frac{100^2}{(1.10)^5} \right]^2} = \$339$$

Moderate Correlation: In most cases, cash flows cannot be easily classified as either independent or perfectly correlated, and a decision tree approach can be used. In a capital budgeting context, this approach involves the multiplication of the conditional probabilities of correlated periods to obtain the joint probabilities that will specify the probabilities of multiple events. Exhibit 11.1 illus-

Exhibit 11.1
Decision Tree Approach to Capital Budgeting

Period 1		Period 2				Total	Expected Value of
Net Cash Flows A_1	Initial Probability $p(1)$	Net Cash Flows A_2	Conditional Probability $p(2/1)$	Number of Cases	Joint Probability[a] p_j	Net Cash Flows[b] A_j	Total Net Cash Flows
		$20	0.3	1	0.18	$50	$ 9.00
$30	0.6	30	0.4	2	0.24	60	14.40
		40	0.3	3	0.18	70	12.60
		30	0.2	4	0.08	70	5.60
40	0.4	40	0.5	5	0.2	80	16.00
		50	0.3	6	0.12	90	10.80
Mean Value							$68.40

[a] $p_j = p(1) \times p(2/1)$.
[b] $A_j = A_1 + A_2$.

trates the decision tree approach to compute the joint probabilities and the expected value of a project.

Simulation: The preceding methods of dealing with uncertainty apply only when two probability distributions are considered. In most capital budgeting situations, more than two variables are significant, and more than two variables are subject to uncertainty. The simulation technique takes into account the interacting variables and their corresponding probability distributions. David B. Hertz proposed a simulation model to obtain the dispersion about the expected rate of return for an investment proposal. He established nine separate probability distributions to determine the probability distribution of the average rate of return for the entire project. The following nine variables were considered for market analysis:

1. Market size
2. Selling price
3. Market growth rate
4. Share of market

For investment cost analysis:

5. Investment required
6. Residual value of investment

For operating and fixed costs:

7. Operating costs
8. Fixed costs
9. Useful life of facilities.[5]

The computer simulates trial values of each of the nine variables and then computes the return on investment based on the simulated values obtained. These trials are repeated often enough to obtain a frequency distribution for the return on investment. This approach can also be used to determine the NPV or the IRR of a project.

CAPITAL BUDGETING UNDER INFLATION

Beginning with seminal work by Irving Fisher, economists have shown fairly conclusively that market rates of interest include an adjustment of expected inflation rate—the nonexistent "homogeneous expectation." This consensus forecast, therefore, is built into the discount rate used in capital budgeting. When rates of inflation were relatively low (e.g., 2 to 3 percent), this did not lead to serious distortions in the IRR or NPV models, because any error in the rate estimation was immaterial in most cases. With the higher rates of inflation we are now experiencing, it is desirable to consider explicitly the rate of inflation in developing cash flow forecasts. The correct analysis can be done in either of two ways: (1) using a money discount rate to discount money cash flows or (2) using a real discount rate to discount real cash flows.

Before illustrating either approach, let us explore the differences between money cash flows and real cash flows and between real discount rate and money discount rate. *Money cash flows* are cash flows measured in dollars from various periods having different purchasing power. *Real cash flows* are cash flows measured in dollars having the same purchasing power. The real cash flow for a given year $_t$ expressed in terms of dollars of year^0 (the base year) is equal to the money cash flow for that year $_t$ multiplied by the following ratio:

$$\frac{\text{Price level index in year}_0}{\text{Price level index in year}_t}$$

For example, if an investment promised a money return of \$100 for three years and the price index for years zero through three is 100.0, 110.0, 121.0, and 133.1, respectively, the real cash flows are as follows:

Year 1: \$100 × 100/110   = 90.90
Year 2: \$100 × 100/121   = 82.64
Year 3: \$100 × 100/133.1 = 75.13

The money discount rate r can also be computed. Assuming that f is the annual rate of inflation, i is the real discount rate, and the decision maker is in the zero bracket, then

$$r = (1 + f)(1 + i) - 1$$

or

$$r = i + f + if$$

For example, if the real return before taxes is 3 percent and the rate of inflation is 10 percent, the nominal discount rate is

$$0.03 + 0.10 + 0.003 = 0.133$$

To illustrate the correct analysis under inflation, assume the same data as in the previous example. The correct analysis can be either of two procedures as follows:

The first analysis discounts the money cash flows using a money discount rate. The present value of the investment will be computed as follows:

Period	Money Cash Flow	Nominal Present Value Factor at 13.3%	Present Value
1	100	0.8826	88.26
2	100	0.7792	77.92
3	100	0.6874	68.74
			234.92

The second analysis discounts the real cash flows using a real discount rate. The present value of the investment will give the same present value as follows:

Period	Real Cash Flow	Real Present Value at 3%	Present Value
1	90.90	0.9709	88.254
2	82.64	0.9426	77.896
3	75.13	0.9151	68.751
			234.901

Assuming a marginal tax rate t on nominal income, the nominal discount rate will be computed as follows:

$$1 + (1 - t)r = (1 + f) + 1 + i(1 - t)$$

or

$$r = i + if + f/(1 - t)$$

Assuming the tax rate to be 30 percent, the nominal rate is then computed as follows:

$$r = 0.03 + (0.03 \times 0.10) + 0.10/(1 - 0.30) = 0.1758$$

In other words, a nominal rate of 17.58 is needed for an investor in a 30 percent tax bracket and facing an inflation rate of 10 percent to earn a real discount rate of 3 percent.

Investment in New Technology

The use of conventional capital budgeting techniques to evaluate proposed investments in new technology is generally met with skepticism since "the willingness of managers to view the future through the reversed telescope of discounted cash flow analysis is seriously shortchanging the futures of corporations."[6] In the words of one senior IBM executive on the subject of the use of discounted cash flow methods (DCF): "Let's be more practical, DCF is not the only gospel. Many managers have become too absorbed with DCF to the extent that practical strategic directional considerations have been overlooked. DCF analysis tends to look at discrete investment opportunities, which are perhaps myopic when compared to the urgency of implementing integrated systems to vast productivity improvements."[7] What is needed is a theory and methods to measure better the benefits of automation to justify the high costs associated with industrial automation.[8] One step is to avoid some of the flows associated with discounted cash flows when used to justify investments in new technology. R. S. Kaplan and A. A. Atkinson suggested that those flows occur when managers

1. Require payback over arbitrary short time periods

2. Use excessively high discount rates

3. Adjust inappropriately for risk

4. Compare new investments with unrealistic status quo alternatives

5. Emphasize incremental rather than global opportunities

6. Fail to recognize all the costs of the new investment

7. Ignore important benefits from the new investment[9]

CONCLUSION

Conventional capital budgeting techniques based on the discounted cash flow methods need to be adjusted to deal with complex managerial problems. Examples of these problems treated in this chapter include (a) capital rationing, (b) capital budgeting under uncertainty, (c) capital budgeting under inflation, and (d) investments in new technology.

NOTES

1. James M. Fremgen, "Capital Budgeting Practices: A Survey," *Management Accounting*, May 1973, pp. 23–24.

2. James H. Lorie and Leonard J. Savage, "Three Problems in Rationing Capital," *Journal of Business*, October 1955, pp. 229–239.

3. H. Martin Weingartner, *Mathematical Programming and the Analysis of Capital Budgeting Problems* (Englewood Cliffs, N.J.: Prentice-Hall, 1963).

4. Frederick Hillier, "The Deviation of Probabilistic Information for the Evaluation of Risky Investments," *Management Science*, April 1963, pp. 443–457.

5. David B. Hertz, "Risk Analysis in Capital Investment," *Harvard Business Review*, January–February 1964, pp. 95–106; and David B. Hertz, "Investment Policies That Pay Off," *Harvard Business Review*, January–February 1968, pp. 96–108.

6. Robert H. Hayes and Daniel A. Garvin, "Managing as if Tomorrow Mattered," *Harvard Business Review*, May–June 1982, p. 72.

7. J. P. Van Blois, "Economic Models: The Future of Robotic Justification," Technical Paper M583–318 (Dearborn, Mich.: Society of Manufacturing Engineers, 1983), p. 3.

8. Sandra B. Dornan, "Justifying New Technologies," *Production*, July 1987, p. 50.

9. R. S. Kaplan and A. A. Atkinson, *Advanced Management Accounting* (Englewood Cliffs, N.J.: Prentice-Hall, 1982), p. 475.

REFERENCES

Dornan, Sandra B. "Justifying New Technologies." *Production*, July 1987, p. 50.

Fremgen, James M. "Capital Budgeting Practices: A Survey." *Management Accounting*, May 1973, pp. 23–24.

Hayes, Robert H., and Daniel A. Garvin. "Managing as if Tomorrow Mattered." *Harvard Business Review*, May–June 1982, p. 72.

Hertz, David B. "Investment Policies That Pay Off." *Harvard Business Review*, January–February 1968, pp. 96–108.

———. "Risk Analysis in Capital Investment." *Harvard Business Review*, January–February 1964, pp. 95–106.

Hillier, Frederick. "The Deviation of Probabilistic Information for the Evaluation of Risky Investments." *Management Science*, April 1963, pp. 443–457.

Kaplan, R. S., and A. A. Atkinson. *Advanced Management Accounting*. Englewood Cliffs, N.J.: Prentice-Hall, 1982.

Lorie, James H., and Leonard J. Savage. "Three Problems in Rationing Capital." *Journal of Business*, October 1955, pp. 229–239.

Van Blois, J. P. "Economic Models: The Future of Robotic Justification." Technical Paper M583–318. Dearborn, Mich.: Society of Manufacturing Engineers, 1983, p. 3.

Weingartner, H. Martin. *Mathematical Programming and the Analysis of Capital Budgeting Problems*. Englewood Cliffs, N.J.: Prentice-Hall, 1963.

Index

About the Author

AHMED BELKAOUI is Professor of Accounting at the University of Illinois at Chicago. His thirteen previous books with Quorum include *Judgment in International Accounting* (1990), *The Coming Crisis in Accounting* (1989), and *Behavioral Accounting* (1989).